SPEECHES
THAT CHANGED
THE WORLD

Quercus

Contents

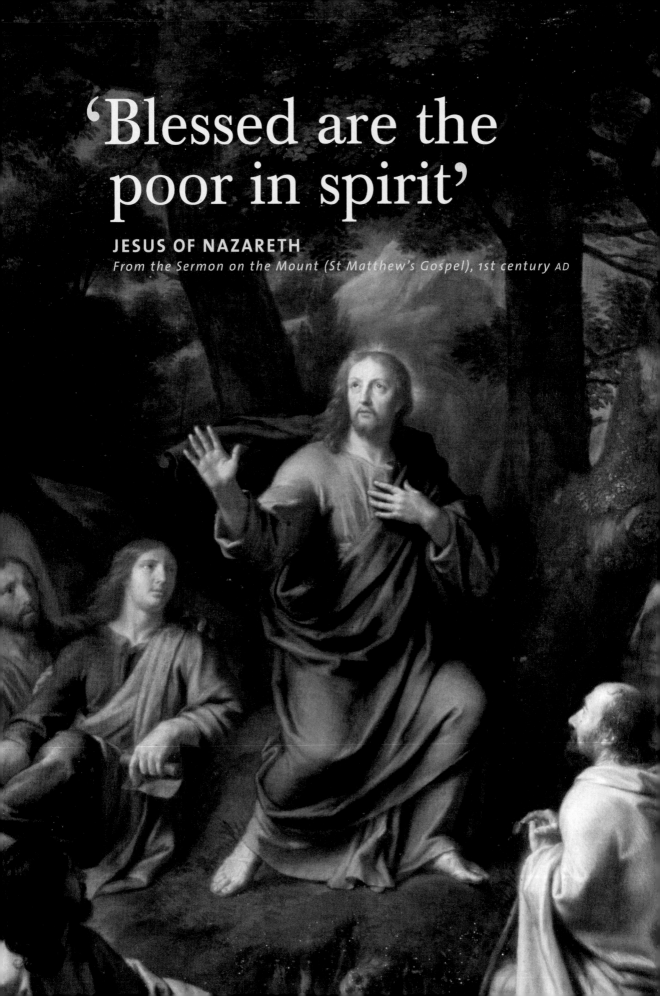

'Blessed are the poor in spirit'

JESUS OF NAZARETH

From the Sermon on the Mount (St Matthew's Gospel), 1st century AD

FOR MANY PEOPLE, THE SAYINGS OF JESUS as presented in the Sermon on the Mount constitute the essence of Christian teaching. Beyond the Christian faith itself, they have informed basic ethical principles about how human beings should treat one another, and certain passages – including the verses known as the 'Beatitudes' (Blessings) and the Lord's Prayer – have often become ingrained at childhood. Some Christian thinkers and biblical scholars view the sermon as a collection of discrete sayings gathered by early Christian writers, rather than a speech delivered on a particular occasion.

In historical terms, Jesus was born in Roman-ruled Palestine, under a puppet Jewish regime, at the end of the 1st century BC or early in the 1st century AD. He grew up in Nazareth and became an itinerant preacher in North Palestine for three years, during which time he gathered many followers who were attracted by his interpretation of Jewish law and the miracles ascribed to him. His criticism of Jewish religious leaders and warnings of the imminence of God's rule replacing human rule provoked opposition from the Jewish and Roman establishments, leading to his death by crucifixion.

The four Gospels (meaning 'Good News') of the New Testament recount Jesus' life and teachings, and are credited to four of his disciples: Matthew (which contains the Sermon on the Mount), Mark, Luke and John. They portray Jesus as living a life without material security or family support, often mixing with the poor and society's outcasts, and constantly teaching that he would be rejected by the authorities, persecuted, suffer and die in order to fulfil God's purpose. The Gospel writers vary in details, but all claim that Jesus rose from the dead and appeared to them on the same day, in fulfilment of Jesus' claim to be the Messiah, the 'Son of God'.

JESUS OF NAZARETH

Born c.4 BC or a little later in Bethlehem, Judaea (Palestine).

The Gospels record episodes from his adult life of preaching, healing, performing miracles, and challenging Jewish religious and political authority, as well as his travels through Galilee and beyond the Jewish world in Tyre and Sidon. On visiting Jerusalem some time between AD 26 and AD 30, where he was feted, he was condemned to death for blasphemy, and a sentence of crucifixion was imposed by the Roman prefect Pontius Pilate.

Died c. AD 26–30 in Palestine. In Christian belief, Jesus' death was followed by his resurrection.

The historical Jesus has been variously viewed among non-Christians as a moral reformer, political revolutionary, Palestinian peasant, and charismatic rabbi. To Christians he might be all these things, but above all he was a prophet with a unique relationship with God, evidenced at his divine birth, whose death and resurrection delivered salvation to mankind.

The Christian movement quickly spread throughout the Mediterranean and was savagely suppressed in the 1st century AD by the Roman emperors Claudius and Nero. By the end of the century Jewish authorities in Palestine had adopted policies aimed at sharply differentiating Christians from Jews. But a world religion had been born, one that would underpin the development of Western society and culture.

MATTHEW 5, VERSES 3–11 ('The Beatitudes')

Blessed are the poor in spirit: for theirs is the kingdom of heaven.

Blessed are they that mourn: for they shall be comforted.

Blessed are the meek: for they shall inherit the earth.

Blessed are they which do hunger and thirst after righteousness:
for they shall be filled.

Blessed are the merciful: for they shall obtain mercy.

Blessed are the pure in heart: for they shall see God.

Blessed are the peacemakers: for they shall be called the
children of God.

Blessed are they which are persecuted for righteousness' sake:
for theirs is the kingdom of heaven.

Blessed are ye, when men shall revile you, and persecute you,
and shall say all manner of evil against you falsely,
for my sake.

MATTHEW 6, VERSES 9–13 ('The Lord's Prayer')

After this manner therefore pray ye:
Our Father which art in heaven, Hallowed be thy name.

Thy kingdom come, Thy will be done in earth, as it is in heaven.

Give us this day our daily bread.

And forgive us our debts, as we forgive our debtors.

And lead us not into temptation, but deliver us from evil:
For thine is the kingdom, and the power, and the glory, for ever.
Amen.

'Turn then your face towards the Sacred Mosque'

THE PROPHET MOHAMMED
From the Surah al-Baqarah (Qu'ran), 7th century AD

FOR MUSLIMS, THE QU'RAN (or Koran) contains the words of Allah (God) as revealed to the Prophet Mohammed early in the 7th century AD. They were written down in a canonical version some years after Mohammed's death, producing an Arabic text that has since not varied. The Qu'ran, together with the *hadith* (the life and teachings of Mohammed), form the twin pillars of Islam. As such, they have been hugely influential in structuring Muslim societies and the lives of individual believers, from the unification of the Arab tribes in the 7th century to the present day.

Among the revelations is God's instruction concerning the *qiblah*, the direction in which Mohammed and his followers should pray, and which accounts for the practice of Muslims facing towards Mecca when at prayer. The Qu'ran is divided into *surahs* (verse-sections), and this passage occurs in the Surah al-Baqarah ('The Cow'), Verse 2 (144–50).

The historical background to the passage relates to the year 622, when Mohammed and his followers fled the hostility of the unconverted Meccans to establish themselves in the northern city of Medina, a relocation known to Muslims as the *hegira* (or *hijra*). Medina also contained other religious groups – Jews, Nazarenes and Christians – who all offered their prayers towards Jerusalem, a city central to their beliefs. There were also worshippers in Medina who would turn towards the Ka'aba (literally 'cube'), an ancient religious shrine and site of pilgrimage in Mecca. Mohammed at first offered his prayers towards Jerusalem; but he felt drawn towards offering his prayers towards the Ka'aba, the house that his ancestors

THE PROPHET MOHAMMED

Born in 570, in Mecca, western Arabia. Orphaned at a young age, Mohammed was brought up by his grandfather and uncle.

At 25 he married a wealthy widow, Khadijah, and became a merchant in her business. In 610 Mohammed reported a vision of the Angel Gabriel who transmitted to him the first of many divine revelations, which he began to disseminate, attracting followers as well as opponents. In 619, the 'year of sorrows', his wife and uncle died, and his revelations reached their most intense phase. He escaped persecution, going north to Medina in 622 and establishing a loyal following there; subsequent years saw violent clashes with the Meccan nonbelievers. In 629 he undertook the first *Haj* (pilgrimage) to Mecca, but after a truce with Mecca broke down he led his forces to capture the city in 630.

Died 632 in Medina. Around 650, the third caliph, Uthman, ordered the creation of an authoritative Qu'ran.

and the prophets Abraham and Ishmael had rebuilt many centuries before, but which now housed idols. He was troubled by this impulse until Allah directed him to do so. The Ka'aba is now at the centre of Mecca's mosque complex.

As the verses suggest, Islam is not an entirely separate belief system from the Judeo-Christian tradition. It embraces much from those faiths, and Mohammed referred to himself as the 'seal of the prophets', the last of a long line including Moses and Jesus. Abraham represented a supreme example of godly humility because he had submitted to the will of God in offering to sacrifice his son to Him. And 'Islam' itself means 'submission to the will of God'.

INDEED WE SEE THE TURNING OF YOUR FACE TO HEAVEN, so We shall surely turn you to a *qiblah* [prayer direction] which you shall like; turn then your face towards the Sacred Mosque, and wherever you are, turn your face towards it, and those who have been given the Book [Scriptures, i.e. Jews and Christians] most surely know that it is the truth from their Lord; and Allah is not at all heedless of what they do.

'The truth is from your Lord, therefore you should not be of the doubters'

And even if you bring to those who have been given the Book every sign they would not follow your *qiblah*, nor can you be a follower of their *qiblah*, neither are they the followers of each other's *qiblah*, and if you follow their desires after the knowledge that has come to you, then you shall most surely be among the unjust.

Those whom We have given the Book recognize him as they recognize their sons, and a party of them most surely conceal the truth while they know (it).

The truth is from your Lord, therefore you should not be of the doubters.

And every one has a direction to which he should turn, therefore hasten to (do) good works; wherever you are, Allah will bring you all together; surely Allah has power over all things.

'And from whatsoever place you come forth, turn your face towards the Sacred Mosque'

And from whatsoever place you come forth, turn your face towards the Sacred Mosque; and surely it is the very truth from your Lord, and Allah is not at all heedless of what you do.

And from whatsoever place you come forth, turn your face towards the Sacred Mosque; and wherever you are turn your faces towards it, so that people shall have no accusation against you, except such of them as are unjust; so do not fear them, and fear Me, that I may complete My favour on you and that you may walk on the right course.

'I have the heart and stomach of a king'

QUEEN ELIZABETH I

Speech to encourage the English militia at Tilbury, 8 August 1588

B Y POPULAR TRADITION, the reign of Elizabeth I is regarded as a golden age of English history. To a large extent, this is attributable to the flourishing of culture and the beginnings of a maritime empire that took place during the reign. But the queen contributed to her myth by, among other things, her defiance of the mighty Spanish Empire, and in particular for the rousing speech she is recorded as giving when Spain threatened invasion.

By 1588, Anglo-Spanish hostility had reached a peak. Elizabeth's 30-year-old reign had cemented Henry VIII's break from Rome, and the Church of England had moved increasingly towards Protestant practices. In 1570, Pope Pius V excommunicated Elizabeth, an act that technically delegitimized her as queen in the eyes of Catholics. Fear of Spanish-backed Catholic schemes to topple Elizabeth became intense, and in the 1580s plots, real and imagined, were revealed. In 1583, the Spanish Ambassador left England for good.

Particularly irksome to Spain was the fact that Elizabeth's regime had offered economic and then outright military support to the Dutch rebels fighting for independence in what was then the Spanish Netherlands. And in the Caribbean and Atlantic, English privateers – government-backed pirates – were harrying ships conveying treasure from the Spanish colonies back to the motherland. In 1587 a fleet commanded by Sir Francis Drake famously 'singed the king of Spain's beard' when it destroyed more than 24 of Philip II's ships in the port of Cadiz. That was the last straw for Philip, and by early 1588 the English authorities learned that he was planning a huge armada of vessels to invade England.

QUEEN ELIZABETH I

Born 7 September 1533 in Greenwich, England, the daughter of Henry VIII and his second wife, Anne Boleyn.

Succeeded to the throne in 1558, following the reigns of her younger Protestant half-brother Edward VI (1549–53) and elder Catholic half-sister Mary I (1553–58). Elizabeth's reign saw the entrenchment of the Church of England, increasing strictures on Catholics, and assistance to Dutch rebels and French Huguenots. The birth of professional playhouses saw the rise of Shakespeare, and sea-going adventurers established the American colony of Virginia, named after the 'Virgin Queen'. In 1587, she reluctantly authorized the execution of her relative Mary Queen of Scots, for complicity in plots, and in 1588 she gave a rousing speech to troops defending England against the Spanish Armada. Having never married or borne children, she was the last Tudor monarch, the throne passing to Mary Queen of Scots' Protestant son, James.

Died 24 March 1603 at Richmond Palace, England.

England was rendered particularly vulnerable in continental politics by the fact that in France's long-running religious wars, the Catholic faction currently had the upper hand. At the end of May, over 130 Spanish ships and as many as 18,000 men, commanded by the Duke of Medina Sidonia, set sail from Spain to rendezvous with land forces under the Duke of Parma near Calais. On 28–9 July, the English commander, Lord Howard of Effingham, ordered English fireships to attack the Spanish fleet off the French coast, resulting in the so-called 'Battle of Gravelines'. Much of the armada then dispersed towards the North Sea, eventually rounding Scotland; but it encountered gales and shipwrecks off Ireland, and few ships or men made it back to Spain. Peace with Spain was several years off, but never again would Spain be able to threaten England with such a show of force.

On 8 August, though, the English could not know that the danger of invasion was diminishing. On that day, Elizabeth travelled to the hastily assembled militia at Tilbury, on the Thames Estuary, where she gave her memorable speech to inspire them in defence of their homeland and their monarch.

MY LOVING PEOPLE,

We have been persuaded by some that are careful of our safety, to take heed how we commit ourselves to armed multitudes, for fear of treachery; but I assure you I do not desire to live to distrust my faithful and loving people. Let tyrants fear, I have always so behaved myself that, under God, I have placed my chiefest strength and safeguard in the loyal hearts and good-will of my subjects; and therefore I am come amongst you, as you see, at this time, not for my recreation and disport, but being resolved, in the midst and heat of the battle, to live and die amongst you all; to lay down for my God, and for my kingdom, and my people, my honour and my blood, even in the dust.

'I myself will take up arms, I myself will be your general, judge, and rewarder of every one of your virtues in the field'

I know I have the body but of a weak and feeble woman; but I have the heart and stomach of a king, and of a king of England too, and think foul scorn that Parma or Spain, or any prince of Europe, should dare to invade the borders of my realm; to which rather than any dishonour shall grow by me, I myself will take up arms, I myself will be your general, judge, and rewarder of every one of your virtues in the field. I know already, for your forwardness you have deserved rewards and crowns; and We do assure you in the word of a prince, they shall be duly paid you. In the mean time, my lieutenant general shall be in my stead, that whom never prince commanded a more noble or worthy subject; not doubting but by your obedience to my general, by your concord in the camp, and your valour in the field, we shall shortly have a famous victory over those enemies of my God, of my kingdom, and of my people.

'I go from a corruptible to an incorruptible crown'

KING CHARLES I
Speech on the scaffold, 30 January 1649

ON 30 JANUARY 1649, CHARLES I – King of England, Scotland and Ireland – having been found guilty of 'high treason and other high crimes', ascended the scaffold outside the Banqueting House in Whitehall, London, to face the executioner's axe. This act of regicide, which much of Europe regarded with horror, concluded a reign that had torn the kingdom apart in civil war since 1642. His death would also mean a temporary end to that 'kingdom', for Britain then entered the uncharted waters of 11 years of government without a monarch.

KING CHARLES I

Born 19 November 1600 in Fife, Scotland, the son of James VI and I (of Scotland and England respectively).

He acceded to the throne in 1625, and married Princess Henrietta Maria of France the same year. Quarrels with Parliaments – over finance, over his advisers, over church practices – provoked him to rule without calling Parliament between 1629 and 1640. In 1642, civil war erupted, with Parliament's supporters pitted against the king's. After renewed outbreak of war, 1647–8, army commanders and the Rump Parliament of radical Independent MPs procured a trial of Charles for high treason.

Executed 30 January 1649, in London.

Charles I's reign encountered problems from the start. His marriage to a French Catholic princess, Henrietta Maria, was unpopular with the more rigorously Protestant of his subjects, and he was soon at odds with a largely Puritan Parliament over money. Charles adhered to a belief in the Divine Right of Kings – that they answered to God for their actions, not to their subjects. He regarded Parliament as using its leverage over royal finance to coerce him into granting it greater influence over his policies and the make-up of his government. A struggle developed in which each side considered that the other was encroaching on its rights and freedoms. To add to the combustible mix, Charles's High Church Protestantism, especially as it developed under Archbishop Laud, aroused considerable opposition from those who wanted a simpler church.

In 1629 Charles dissolved Parliament and ruled without it for 11 years, attempting to raise money by other means. Conflict in Scotland in 1637 (when Charles attempted to impose bishops on the presbyterian church), and later in the North of England and Ireland, forced him to recall Parliament. Tensions came to a head in 1642. Fleeing the largely pro-Parliamentary London, the king raised his standard at Nottingham on 22 August. The complex civil war, sometimes called the War of the Three Kingdoms (for it played out in Scotland and Ireland too), had begun. Their causes remain much debated.

Although Charles was brave, sincere, deeply religious, a loyal husband and father, and a great patron of the arts, he was also reserved, inflexible, politically deceitful, overconfident and a poor strategist. By 1647, his Royalist supporters were overwhelmed and he was in captivity. It appeared as though negotiations with Parliament might proceed, but divisions within Parliament and between Parliament and the army complicated the situation. In the event, Charles escaped and conflict broke out again, until defeat of his Scottish backers at the Battle of Preston in 1648 ended his hopes of victory. To Oliver Cromwell, who, with Sir Thomas Fairfax, had directed Parliament's New Model Army, Charles was 'the grand author of our troubles', who could now not be trusted to negotiate in good faith. In December 1648, the army purged Parliament of its conciliatory majority, leaving a more radical rump of Independents, who agreed to put the king on trial.

It was an entirely novel scenario. Charles refused to accept the legal basis of either the court or the case against him, and therefore refused to defend himself against the charges. But the verdict was not in doubt. Ten days after the trial began, the names of 60 signatories (including Cromwell) appeared on the king's death warrant, and the following day the sentence was carried out. It is said that Charles wore two shirts, so that he should not be seen to tremble in the cold, lest anyone should think he was afraid.

His valedictory speech was entirely typical of his character and convictions. It was brave and resolute, but also betrayed little sense of the impact of his actions. He affirmed that it was a king's obligation to ensure the security of his subjects' 'life and goods' through maintaining the laws of the land, but repeated that 'a subject and a sovereign are clean different things', and subjects should not aspire to have a role in governing. Paradoxically, he presented himself – a king – as a 'martyr of the people'; in his eyes, he was paying the price for resisting a form of martial law. Strange though those words may seem, there was a prophetic element in them, as power was passing swiftly from Parliament to Cromwell and the army.

I SHALL BE VERY LITTLE HEARD OF ANYBODY HERE . . . Indeed, I could hold my peace very well, if I did not think that holding my peace would make some men think that I did submit to the guilt, as well as to the punishment: but I think it is my duty to God first, and to my country, for to clear myself both as an honest man, and a good King and a good Christian.

I shall begin first with my innocency. In troth I think it not very needful for me to insist upon this, for all the world knows that I never did begin a war with the two Houses of Parliament, and I call God to witness, to whom I must shortly make an account, that I never did intend for to incroach upon their privileges, they began upon me, it is the militia they began upon, they confess that the militia was mine, but they thought it fit for to have it from me.

God forbid that I should be so ill a Christian, as not to say that God's judgements are just upon me: many times he does pay justice by an unjust sentence, that is ordinary: I will only say this, that an unjust sentence that I suffered to take effect, is punished now by an unjust sentence upon me, that is, so far I have said, to show you that I am an innocent man.

Now for to show you that I am a good Christian: I hope there is a good man that will bear me witness, that I have forgiven all the world, and even those in particular that have been the chief causers of my death: who they are, God knows, I do not desire to know, I pray God forgive them.

But this is not all, my charity must go farther, I wish that they may repent, for indeed they have committed a great sin in that particular: I pray God with St Stephen, that this be not laid to their charge, nay, not only so, but that they may take the right way to the peace of the kingdom, for my charity commands me not only to forgive particular men, but my charity commands me to endeavour to the last gasp the peace of the kingdom …

. . . For the people: and truly I desire their liberty and freedom as much as any body whomsoever, but I must tell you, that their liberty and their freedom consists in having of government; those laws, by which their life and their goods may be most their own.

'I have a good cause, and a gracious God on my side'

It is not for having share in government (Sir) that is nothing pertaining to them; a subject and a sovereign are clean different things, and therefore until they do that, I mean, that you do put the people in that liberty as I say, certainly they will never enjoy themselves. Sirs, it was for this that now I am come here: if I would have given way to an arbitrary way, for to have all laws changed according to the power of the sword, I needed not to have come here, and therefore I tell you (and I pray God it be not laid to your charge) that I am the martyr of the people.

In troth Sirs, I shall not hold you much longer, for I will only say thus to you, that in truth I could have desired some little time longer, because I would have put then that I have said in a little more order, and a little better digested than I have done, and therefore I hope you will excuse me.

I have delivered my conscience, I pray God that you do take those courses that are best for the good of the kingdom, and your own salvations.

. . . In troth Sirs, my conscience in religion I think is very well known to all the world, and therefore I declare before you all, that I die a Christian, according to the profession of the Church of England, as I found it left me by my father, and this honest man I think will witness it.

. . . I have a good cause, and a gracious God on my side . . . I go from a corruptible to an incorruptible crown; where no disturbance can be, no disturbance in the world.

'In the name
of God, go!'

OLIVER CROMWELL
Speech dismissing the Rump Parliament, 20 April 1653

N 1653, BRITAIN WAS FOUR YEARS into its experiment with a military-republican government, following the years of civil war in the 1640s and the trial and execution of the Stuart king, Charles I. Since the later 1640s, the pivotal figure in the country's politics had been Oliver Cromwell. An East Anglian gentleman-farmer and Puritan convert, Cromwell emerged as the Parliamentary cause's military leader of distinction. His skill had proved decisive in defeating the Royalists, and his political arm-twisting helped ensure the 'cruel necessity' (as he put it) of executing Charles I in January 1649.

Despite the king's death, the new 'commonwealth' remained vulnerable. In 1649 Cromwell led his troops to victory over pro-Stuart Catholics in Ireland, but not without earning an enduring reputation for unnecessary ferocity. In 1650, he defeated Scottish rebels. Most significantly, he vanquished the combined Scottish-English Royalists supporting Prince Charles's attempt to claim his father's throne, at the Battle of Worcester in 1651.

In the absence of traditional hierarchies of church and state, it now fell to Cromwell to impose order but also to balance the interests of a fragmenting country. The position of Parliament remained difficult. Ostensibly, the civil wars had been fought to protect the rights of Parliament. But Parliament itself was beset by disagreements, and the emergence of the New Model Army as the most powerful entity in the land complicated matters. Already, in December 1649, soldiers under Colonel Pride had purged the Long Parliament (sitting since 1640) of members not deemed radical enough, leaving a Rump Parliament of about 60 members more conducive to the army's agenda. But tensions remained, and in 1653 Cromwell's patience gave way in spectacular style.

On 20 April, Cromwell attended Westminster Hall as members of the Rump Parliament commenced a third reading of bill about rights for particular categories of electors, contravening an agreement with the army that this would not happen. His patience snapped, as he harangued the 'factious' members as 'a pack of mercenary wretches' and 'sordid prostitutes', who, in his view, had grown 'intolerably odious to the whole nation'. Summoning soldiers to remove the mace (the 'shining bauble') from the

OLIVER CROMWELL

Born 25 April 1599 in Huntingdon, England.

Cromwell became a Member of Parliament in 1628 and on the outbreak of civil war he emerged as a highly competent cavalry commander. He was largely responsible for the victory at Marston Moor (1644). With Sir Thomas Fairfax, he reorganized Parliamentary forces into the New Model Army and won the important Battle of Naseby (1645). He was one of the first signatories of Charles I's death warrant in 1649, and by now the most powerful figure in the country. He spent much of 1649–51 suppressing rebellion in Ireland, Scotland and at the Battle of Worcester (1651). The next seven years of his 'commonwealth' regime saw war at sea with the Dutch and Spanish, reforms to improve Irish and Scottish political representation (though parliaments were intermittent), the readmittance of Jews to England, and attempts at religious toleration. In 1657 he refused the crown, preferring his title 'Lord Protector of England, Scotland and Ireland'.

Died 3 September 1658 in London. In 1661 his body was exhumed after the restoration of Charles II, and strung up.

chamber – the symbol of Parliament's authority – Cromwell concluded his lambasting by order-ing the MPs: 'In the name of God, go!' It was a phrase that would echo down the ages. It was used again, devastatingly, against Prime Minister Neville Chamberlain in May 1940 just before his resignation.

A new Parliament, the so-called Barebones Parliament of 140 appointees, was called but soon dismissed. Cromwell's chief instrument of authority became his council of state, and later he accepted the title of 'lord protector', a quasi-royal status. The Cromwellian years remained paradoxical, for although the methods of governing were experimental and often authoritarian, the reforms and goals were sometimes relatively liberal, for example in readmitting Jews into the country and striving for religious toleration. But the centre could not hold in the absence of its figurehead. When Cromwell died in 1657, his designated successor – his son Richard – failed to exert authority. In 1660 it was another military commander, General Monk, who engineered the return of the monarchy in the shape of Charles II.

IT IS HIGH TIME FOR ME to put an end to your sitting in this place, which you have dishonoured by your contempt of all virtue, and defiled by your practice of every vice; ye are a factious crew, and enemies to all good government; ye are a pack of mercenary wretches, and would like Esau sell your country for a mess of potage, and like Judas betray your God for a few pieces of money; is there a single virtue now remaining amongst you? Is there one vice you do not possess? Ye have no more religion than my horse; gold is your God; which of you have not barter'd your conscience for bribes? Is there a man amongst you that has the least

'Make haste! Ye venal slaves be gone!'

care for the good of the Commonwealth? Ye sordid prostitutes have you not defil'd this sacred place, and turn'd the Lord's temple into a den of thieves, by your immoral principles and wicked practices? Ye are grown intolerably odious to the whole nation; you were deputed here by the people to get grievances redress'd, are yourselves become the greatest grievance. Your country therefore calls upon me to cleanse this Augean stable,* by putting a final period to your iniquitous proceedings in this House; and which by God's help, and the strength he has given me, I am now come to do; I command ye therefore, upon the peril of your lives, to depart immediately out of this place; go, get you out! Make haste! Ye venal slaves be gone! Go! Take away that shining bauble there, and lock up the doors. In the name of God, go!

*In Greek mythology, cleaning out the stables of King Augeas of Elis was Hercules' sixth labour.

'A passionate attachment of one nation for another produces a variety of evils'

GEORGE WASHINGTON
Presidential farewell address, 17 September 1796

AS THE FIRST PRESIDENT OF THE UNITED STATES, and the commander of the Continental Army that won its independence, George Washington holds a unique place in American history. He served two terms as president, and could have stood for re-election, for at that time there was no restriction on how long a president could serve. But he chose not to, and on 17 September 1796 he delivered his carefully thought-out farewell address, which was printed for the public to read two days later. It became a landmark document of US principles, widely popularized, and for many years afterwards it received an annual airing in Congress.

The speech contained two main thrusts. First, as the head of state of a young nation created in the heat of revolution, Washington stressed the need for unity among the states, parties and citizens that comprised the Union. He stressed the values, religion and culture that were common to all. (He was not, of course, addressing African American slaves or Native American 'Indians' – he was rather speaking to those of European extraction, the citizenry.) In Washington's view, for the United States to survive and prosper, the word 'United' had to be sacrosanct, over and above any other internal debate or disagreement. It was a message to both political parties, the Federalists and Thomas Jefferson's Republicans.

A large part of the speech was devoted to foreign affairs. In Washington's view, it was essential for the United States to remain aloof from systems of alliances and to avoid favouring one foreign country over another. He was speaking at a time when Europe was being convulsed by the French Revolution's aftermath and Napoleon was sweeping through Italy. Closer to home, the United States remained sandwiched between British Canada and the territories still under Franco-Spanish sway. On the one hand, and despite the American Revolution, many in the United States felt culturally British and were inclined to support Britain, and this view was predominant among the Federalists. However, others – particularly among the Republicans – felt drawn to French republican ideals, and of course France had aided the American independence struggle. Instead, Washington proposed a kind of principled neutrality. It would become a tenet of American foreign policy up until the 20th century.

From his own long experience, Washington had good reasons for the advice he gave. He saw early action in the French and Indian War (1754–63), the bloodiest American war of the 18th century. That

GEORGE WASHINGTON

Born 22 February 1732 in Bridges Creek, Virginia.

Joined the Virginia militia, and by 1755 was commanding it in the French and Indian War. Returned to manage his recently inherited estates at Mount Vernon, 1759–75, where he married and became a leading figure in colonial politics, taking up the complaints of landowners against the British authorities. He represented Virginia in the Continental Congresses in 1774–5, and on the outbreak of the Revolutionary War became commander of the new Continental Army. Initial success at Boston was followed by defeat at the Battle of Long Island; he took the British by surprise at Trenton and Princeton, but then lost Philadelphia. His victory at Yorktown, in 1781, led to British surrender and American independence. After some years at Mount Vernon, he chaired the Philadelphia convention that produced the American Constitution, and at the end of April 1789 he was elected as the first US president by unanimous vote of the Electoral College. He served for two terms, and retired to Mount Vernon.

Died 14 December 1799 in Virginia.

war was the North American aspect of a wider conflict – the Seven Years War – in which the British finally overcame the French in the struggle for supremacy in colonial North America. Indeed, some historians have called that war the first 'world' war. Washington served in it with bravery, revealing his natural military talents.

He was able to spend his time rather more peacefully in the 1760s and early 1770s, attending to wealthy estates he'd inherited around Mount Vernon and becoming politically active in the Virginia House of Burgesses. He became a Virginia representative at the Continental Congresses held in 1774 and 1775 to express colonists' dissatisfaction at British policies. When dissatisfaction turned into war, Washington was the natural candidate to lead the hastily put together Continental Army.

What Americans call the 'Revolutionary War', and what the British call the 'American War of Independence', was in many respects a form of civil war, pitting pro-independence colonists against loyalist colonists. But it too became internationalized, once France intervened in 1778 on the side of the revolutionaries. Washington's eventual triumph over the British General Cornwallis at Yorktown, Virginia, in 1781, came at the end of a hard-fought struggle, in which the Continental Army had at one point appeared shattered. Indeed, in winter 1777–8 but for Washington's qualities as leader, the revolutionary cause might have been lost.

It is no wonder that, as president, and with more than his fair share of soldiering behind him, Washington sought to use his office to emphasize the causes of American unity and American avoidance of entanglement in Europe's squabbles.

FRIENDS AND FELLOW-CITIZENS: the period for a new election of a citizen, to administer the executive government of the United States, being not far distant, and the time actually arrived when your thoughts must be employed in designating the person who is to be clothed with that important trust, it appears to me proper, especially as it may conduce to a more distinct expression of the public voice, that I should now apprise you of the resolution I have formed, to decline being considered among the number of those out of whom a choice is to be made . . .

. . . I have the consolation to believe that, while choice and prudence invite me to quit the political scene, patriotism does not forbid it.

. . . A solicitude for your welfare which cannot end but with my life, and the apprehension of danger, natural to that solicitude, urge me, on an occasion like the present, to offer to your solemn contemplation, and to recommend to your frequent review, some sentiments which are the result of much reflection, of no inconsiderable observation, and which appear to me all-important to the permanency of your felicity as a people.

Interwoven as is the love of liberty with every ligament of your hearts, no recommendation of mine is necessary to fortify or confirm the attachment.

The unity of government, which constitutes you one people, is also now dear to you. It is justly so; for it is a main pillar in the edifice of your real independence, the support of your tranquillity at home, your peace abroad; of your safety; of your prosperity; of that very liberty, which you so highly prize . . . Citizens, by birth or choice, of a common country, that country has a right to concentrate your affections. The name of American, which belongs to you, in your national capacity, must always exalt the just pride of patriotism, more than any appellation derived from local discriminations. With slight shades of difference, you have the same religion, manners, habits and political principles. You have in a common cause fought and triumphed together; the independence and liberty you possess are the work of joint counsels, and joint efforts, of common dangers, sufferings and successes.

'Your Union ought to be considered as a main prop of your liberty'

But these considerations, however powerfully they address themselves to your sensibility, are greatly outweighed by those, which apply more immediately to your interest. Here every portion of our country finds the most commanding motives for carefully guarding and preserving the Union of the whole . . . [Y]our Union ought to be considered as a main prop of your liberty, and that the love of the one ought to endear to you the preservation of the other.

. . . Observe good faith and justice towards all nations; cultivate peace and harmony with all. Religion and morality enjoin this conduct; and can it be, that good policy does not equally enjoin it? It will be worthy of a free, enlightened, and, at no distant period, a great nation, to give to mankind the magnanimous and too novel example of a people always guided by an exalted justice and benevolence. Who can doubt, that, in the course of time and things, the fruits of such a plan would richly repay any temporary advantages, which might be lost by a steady adherence to it? Can it be, that Providence has not connected the permanent felicity of a nation with its virtue? The experiment, at least, is recommended by every sentiment which ennobles human nature. Alas! Is it rendered impossible by its vices?

. . . A passionate attachment of one nation for another produces a variety of evils. Sympathy for the favourite nation, facilitating the illusion of an imaginary common interest, in cases where no real common interest exists, and infusing into one the enmities of the other, betrays the former into a participation in the quarrels and wars of the latter, without adequate inducement or justification. It leads also to concessions to the favourite nation of privileges denied to others, which is apt doubly to injure the nation making the concessions; by unnecessarily parting with what ought to have been retained; and by exciting jealousy, ill-will, and a disposition to retaliate, in the parties from whom equal privileges are withheld. And it gives to ambitious, corrupted or deluded citizens (who devote themselves to the favourite nation) facility to betray or sacrifice the interests of their own country, without odium, sometimes even with popularity; gilding, with the appearances of a virtuous sense of obligation, a commendable deference for public opinion, or a laudable zeal for public good, the base or foolish compliances of ambition, corruption, or infatuation . . . .

'Foreign influence is one of the most baneful foes'

. . . Against the insidious wiles of foreign influence (I conjure you to believe me, fellow-citizens,) the jealousy of a free people ought to be constantly awake; since history and experience prove, that foreign influence is one of the most baneful foes of republican government. But that jealousy, to be useful, must be impartial; else it becomes the instrument of the very influence to be avoided, instead of a defence against it. Excessive partiality for one foreign nation, and excessive dislike of another, cause those whom they actuate to see danger only on one side, and serve to veil and even second the arts of influence on the other. Real patriots, who may resist the intrigues of the favourite, are liable to become suspected and odious; while its tools and dupes usurp the applause and confidence of the people, to surrender their interests . . .

The great rule of conduct for us, in regard to foreign nations, is, in extending our commercial relations, to have with them as little political connection as possible. So far as we have already formed engagements, let them be fulfilled with perfect good faith. Here let us stop.

Europe has a set of primary interests, which to us have none, or a very remote relation. Hence she must be engaged in frequent controversies, the causes of which are essentially foreign to our concerns. Hence, therefore, it must be unwise in us to implicate ourselves, by artificial ties, in the ordinary vicissitudes of her politics, or the ordinary combinations and collisions of her friendships or enmities.

Our detached and distant situation invites and enables us to pursue a different course. If we remain one people, under an efficient government, the period is not far off, when we may defy material injury from external annoyance; when we may take such an attitude as will cause the neutrality, we may at any time resolve upon, to be scrupulously respected; when belligerent nations, under the impossibility of making acquisitions upon us, will not lightly hazard the giving us provocation; when we may choose peace or war, as our interest, guided by justice, shall counsel.

'It is our true policy to steer clear of permanent alliances'

Why forego the advantages of so peculiar a situation? Why quit our own to stand upon foreign ground? Why, by interweaving our destiny with that of any part of Europe, entangle our peace and prosperity in the toils of European ambition, rivalship, interest, humour or caprice?

It is our true policy to steer clear of permanent alliances with any portion of the foreign world; so far, I mean, as we are now at liberty to do it; for let me not be understood as capable of patronizing infidelity to existing engagements. I hold the maxim no less applicable to public than to private affairs, that honesty is always the best policy . . . Taking care always to keep ourselves, by suitable establishments, on a respectable defensive posture, we may safely trust to temporary alliances for extraordinary emergencies.

. . . Though, in reviewing the incidents of my administration, I am unconscious of intentional error, I am nevertheless too sensible of my defects not to think it probable that I may have committed many errors. Whatever they may be, I fervently beseech the Almighty to avert or mitigate the evils to which they may tend. I shall also carry with me the hope, that my country will never cease to view them with indulgence; and that, after forty-five years of my life dedicated to its service with an upright zeal, the faults of incompetent abilities will be consigned to oblivion, as myself must soon be to the mansions of rest.

Relying on its kindness in this as in other things, and actuated by that fervent love towards it, which is so natural to a man, who views it in the native soil of himself and his progenitors for several generations; I anticipate with pleasing expectation that retreat, in which I promise myself to realize, without alloy, the sweet enjoyment of partaking, in the midst of my fellow-citizens, the benign influence of good laws under a free government, the ever favourite object of my heart, and the happy reward, as I trust, of our mutual cares, labours and dangers.

'We are all Republicans,
we are all Federalists'

THOMAS JEFFERSON
Presidential inaugural address, 4 March 1801

THE VIRGINIAN-BORN THOMAS JEFFERSON was no natural public speaker. But that was one of the few talents that this republican genius, who drafted the Declaration of Independence in 1776, did not possess. Neither did his disinclination for oratory damage his political career, for in 1801 he was chosen as the United States' third president. For this occasion he did deliver a memorable address, brimming with his own kind of intellectual sparkle, generosity of spirit, humility and idealism about America's path. It was a bravura beginning for his two-term presidency.

Jefferson interwove his strongly held beliefs about liberty, equality and America's future with promises to serve the whole nation, not just his natural supporters. In the past, he had established something of a reputation as a partisan figure. He spent the years 1784–9 in Paris on diplomatic service, mostly as the United States' Minister to France. There, he was able to observe at first hand the events leading to the French Revolution, which he welcomed. His French sojourn influenced his ideas on equality and democracy, and encouraged his Francophilia and republican idealism. When President Washington recalled him to become his secretary of state, Jefferson soon became leader of one of the emerging political groupings, the Republicans, who stressed individual liberty, decentralization, and who tended to be pro-French. It was, though, a minority position within the government; most of his colleagues supported the Federalist position, which stressed the Union, and which tended to be pro-British in international affairs. Jefferson resigned and he temporarily withdrew from political life in 1794.

In 1801, Jefferson gave his inaugural speech against a background of political wrangling at home and bloody turmoil abroad, as Europe underwent the chaos of the Napoleonic Wars. He sought to unify, mollify and invigorate. He contrasted the golden opportunities presented by America's 'rising nation, spread over a wide and fruitful land' with the 'exterminating havoc of one quarter of the globe', and expressed his desire that the United States should maintain its neutrality – as the country's first president, Washington, had argued. He expressed his trust in the ability of citizens to govern themselves – that it could produce the 'strongest government on earth' – and mocked those who might imagine there existed 'angels in the forms of kings to govern'. He affirmed that protecting the rights of minorities was an obligation on the part of the majority. Importantly, in stressing the rights of the US states that

THOMAS JEFFERSON

Born 13 April 1743 into a well-established Virginia family. At William and Mary College, Williamsburg, he revealed the natural scholarship that he displayed all through life.

He became involved in Virginia politics, attending the second Continental Congress in 1776 and drafting the Declaration of Independence. He was a diplomat in France (1784–9) and then US secretary of state until 1794. He became vice-president to John Adams in 1796, and then served as president from 1801 to 1809, during which time the country was considerably enlarged through the 'Louisiana Purchase' of French-held territory. In later years he founded the University of Virginia and designed his Virginian house of Monticello, both long-cherished projects. Jefferson wrote his own epitaph for his gravestone: 'Here was buried Thomas Jefferson, author of the Declaration of American Independence, of the statute of Virginia for religious freedom, and father of the University of Virginia.'

Died 4 July 1826.

made up the Union, as well as the role of the federal government in protecting the Union as a whole at home and abroad, he sought to bring both sides of the political debate together. In this way he could claim, in the speech's most famous phrase, 'We are all Republicans, we are all Federalists.'

Friends and fellow-citizens: Called upon to undertake the duties of the first executive office of our country, I avail myself of the presence of that portion of my fellow-citizens which is here assembled to express my grateful thanks for the favour with which they have been pleased to look toward me, to declare a sincere consciousness that the task is above my talents, and that I approach it with those anxious and awful presentiments which the greatness of the charge and the weakness of my powers so justly inspire. A rising nation, spread over a wide and fruitful land, traversing all the seas with the rich productions of their industry, engaged in commerce with nations who feel power and forget right, advancing rapidly to destinies beyond the reach of mortal eye – when I contemplate these transcendent objects, and see the honour, the happiness and the hopes of this beloved country committed to the issue, and the auspices of this day, I shrink from the contemplation, and humble myself before the magnitude of the undertaking. Utterly, indeed, should I despair did not the presence of many whom I here see remind me that in the other high authorities provided by our Constitution I shall find resources of wisdom, of virtue and of zeal on which to rely under all difficulties. To you, then, gentlemen, who are charged with the sovereign functions of legislation, and to those associated with you, I look with encouragement for that guidance and support which may enable us to steer with safety the vessel in which we are all embarked amidst the conflicting elements of a troubled world.

During the contest of opinion through which we have passed the animation of discussions and of exertions has sometimes worn an aspect which might impose on strangers unused to think freely and to speak and to write what they think; but this being now decided by the voice of the nation, announced according to the rules of the Constitution, all will, of course, arrange themselves under the will of the law, and unite in common efforts for the common good. All, too, will bear in mind this sacred principle, that though the will of the majority is in all cases to prevail, that will to be rightful must be reasonable; that the minority possess their equal rights, which equal law must protect, and to violate would be oppression. Let us, then, fellow-citizens, unite with one heart and one mind. Let us restore to social intercourse that harmony and affection without which liberty and even life itself are but dreary things.

And let us reflect that, having banished from our land that religious intolerance under which mankind so long bled and suffered, we have yet gained little if we countenance a political intolerance as despotic, as wicked, and capable of as bitter and bloody persecutions. During the throes and convulsions of the ancient world, during the agonizing spasms of infuriated man, seeking through blood and slaughter his long-lost liberty, it was not wonderful that the agitation of the billows should reach even this distant and peaceful shore; that this should be more felt and feared by some and less by others, and should divide opinions as to measures of safety. But every difference of opinion is not a difference of principle. We have called by different names brethren of the same principle. We are all Republicans, we are all Federalists. If there be any among us who would wish to dissolve this Union or to change its republican form, let them stand undisturbed as monuments of the safety

'Let us, then, with courage and confidence pursue our own Federal and Republican principles'

with which error of opinion may be tolerated where reason is left free to combat it. I know, indeed, that some honest men fear that a republican government cannot be strong, that this government is not strong enough; but would the honest patriot, in the full tide of successful experiment, abandon a government which has so far kept us free and firm on the theoretic and visionary fear that this government, the world's best hope, may by possibility want energy to preserve itself? I trust not. I believe this, on the contrary, the strongest government on earth. I believe it the only one where every man, at the call of the law, would fly to the standard of the law, and would meet invasions of the public order as his own personal concern. Sometimes it is said that man can not be trusted with the government of himself. Can he, then, be trusted with the government of others? Or have we found angels in the forms of kings to govern him? Let history answer this question.

Let us, then, with courage and confidence pursue our own Federal and Republican principles, our attachment to union and representative government. Kindly separated by nature and a wide ocean from the exterminating havoc of one quarter of the globe; too high-minded to endure the degradations of the others; possessing a chosen country, with room enough for our descendants to the thousandth and thousandth generation; entertaining a due sense of our equal right to the use of our own faculties, to the acquisitions of our own industry, to honour and confidence from our fellow-citizens, resulting not from birth, but from our actions and their sense of them; enlightened by a benign religion, professed, indeed, and practised in various forms, yet all of them inculcating honesty, truth, temperance, gratitude and the love of man; acknowledging and adoring an overruling Providence, which by all its dispensations proves that it delights in the happiness of man here and his greater happiness hereafter – with all these blessings, what more is necessary to make us a happy and a prosperous people? Still one thing more, fellow-citizens – a wise and frugal government, which shall restrain men from injuring one another, shall leave them otherwise free to regulate their own pursuits of industry and improvement, and shall not take from the mouth of labour the bread it has earned. This is the sum of good government, and this is necessary to close the circle of our felicities.

'Equal and exact justice to all men, of whatever state or persuasion, religious or political'

About to enter, fellow-citizens, on the exercise of duties which comprehend everything dear and valuable to you, it is proper you should understand what I deem the essential principles of our government, and consequently those which ought to shape its administration. I will compress them within the narrowest compass they will bear, stating the general principle, but not all its limitations. Equal and exact justice to all men, of whatever state or persuasion, religious or political; peace, commerce, and honest friendship with all nations, entangling alliances with none; the support of the state governments in all their rights, as the most competent administrations for our domestic concerns and the surest bulwarks against anti-republican tendencies; the preservation of the general government in its whole constitutional vigour, as the sheet anchor of our peace at home and safety abroad; a jealous care of the right of election by the people – a mild and safe corrective of abuses which are lopped by the sword of revolution where peaceable remedies are unprovided; absolute acquiescence in the decisions of the majority, the vital principle of republics, from which is no appeal but to force, the vital principle and immediate parent of despotism; a well-disciplined militia, our best reliance in peace and for the first moments of war, till regulars may relieve them; the supremacy of the civil over the military authority; economy in the public expense, that labour may be lightly burthened; the honest payment of our debts and sacred preservation of the public faith; encouragement of agriculture, and of commerce as its handmaid; the diffusion of information and arraignment of all abuses at the bar of the public reason; freedom of religion; freedom of the press and freedom of person under the protection of the habeas corpus, and trial by juries impartially selected. These principles form the bright constellation which has gone before us and guided our steps through an age of revolution and reformation. The wisdom of our sages and blood of our heroes have been devoted to their attainment. They should be the creed of our political faith, the text of civic instruction, the touchstone by which to try the services of those we trust; and should we wander from them in moments of error or of alarm, let us hasten to retrace our steps and to regain the road which alone leads to peace, liberty and safety.

> 'When right, I shall often be thought wrong by those whose positions will not command a view of the whole ground'

I repair, then, fellow-citizens, to the post you have assigned me. With experience enough in subordinate offices to have seen the difficulties of this the greatest of all, I have learnt to expect that it will rarely fall to the lot of imperfect man to retire from this station with the reputation and the favour which bring him into it. Without pretensions to that high confidence you reposed in our first and greatest revolutionary character, whose pre-eminent services had entitled him to the first place in his country's love and destined for him the fairest page in the volume of faithful history, I ask so much confidence only as may give firmness and effect to the legal administration of your affairs. I shall often go wrong through defect of judgement. When right, I shall often be thought wrong by those whose positions will not command a view of the whole ground. I ask your indulgence for my own errors, which will never be intentional, and your support against the errors of others, who may condemn what they would not if seen in all its parts. The approbation implied by your suffrage is a great consolation to me for the past, and my future solicitude will be to retain the good opinion of those who have bestowed it in advance, to conciliate that of others by doing them all the good in my power, and to be instrumental to the happiness and freedom of all.

Relying, then, on the patronage of your good will, I advance with obedience to the work, ready to retire from it whenever you become sensible how much better choice it is in your power to make. And may that Infinite Power which rules the destinies of the universe lead our councils to what is best, and give them a favourable issue for your peace and prosperity.

'Soldiers of my
Old Guard: I bid
you farewell'

NAPOLEON BONAPARTE
*Farewell speech to the Imperial
Guard, 20 April 1814*

ON 20 APRIL 1814, NAPOLEON BONAPARTE, the French scourge of Europe, bade farewell to officers from his most loyal troops, the Old (or Imperial) Guard. He had finally succumbed to pressure to abdicate as France's ruler, as the European empire he had built up through military conquest over 20 years unravelled. The catalyst for his defeat was the ill-advised invasion of Russia in 1812. Despite victory at the Battle of Borodino (6 September) and the burning of Moscow, Napoleon's once-mighty *Grande Armée* was decimated by disease and the ravages of the Russian winter on its return. As former French allies sensed weakness and switched sides, and as the opposing European Alliance forced Paris to surrender, Napoleon stood down to save France from further disaster.

Considering the depredations through which he had put his soldiers, not just in Russia but through years of warfare, and the extent of his personal ambition, it is hard to imagine that his rather self-regarding words could have found willing ears. But Napoleon was, above all, a professional soldier, and he never lost the loyalty of a hard core of those who served under him. Indeed, just one year after his abdication, having escaped exile on his island 'principality' of Elba, he was able to rely on the loyalty of soldiers to turn against their government paymasters and restore him to power – though his encore would last just 100 days.

The man who had led France to military glory was actually born in Corsica. In 1779 he began military school in France, where he earned the nickname 'the little corporal' because of his short stature. In 1785 he was commissioned as a 2nd lieutenant in artillery, and in 1793 he gained national recognition and promotion to the rank of general after defeating the British at Toulon. He came to the defence of the Revolutionary government in Paris through a show of force in 1794 – the so-called 'whiff of grapeshot'.

NAPOLEON BONAPARTE

Born 15 August 1769 in Corsica, of Italian descent. He became an army officer in 1785, beginning a brilliant military career, perhaps the most dazzling since Alexander the Great.

In 1796 he married Josephine de Beauharnais, but they had no children; he later divorced her to marry Marie Louise, daughter of the Austrian emperor. He became First Consul in 1799 and Emperor of the French five years later. By repeated victories over European coalitions, he extended French rule (and his own dynastic ambitions) throughout much of Europe, making France a continental superpower, albeit at a cost of thousands of French lives. He also revolutionized military organization and training. He abdicated twice, first in 1814 after Paris fell to his enemies and again in 1815, after surrendering himself to the British in the aftermath of Waterloo. He continues to be regarded as a French national hero, with a tomb in Les Invalides in Paris. Napoleon's lasting legacy is the system of civil law (*Code Napoléon*) and the many institutions bearing his name that exist in France today.

Died in exile on St Helena, 5 May 1821.

Under the new French regime, the five-member *Directoire*, Napoleon now got to flex his military muscles. In a series of victories in 1796–8, France gained control of much of Italy. But Rear-Admiral Nelson's destruction of the French fleet at the Battle of the Nile in 1798 confounded Napoleon's ambitions in Egypt.

With his star high, Napoleon effected a coup against the *Directoire*, becoming France's 'First Consul' – in effect, military dictator. By the start of the 1800s, Napoleon had subordinated Holland, Spain, the Austrian Netherlands, most of Italy, and neutralized Prussia and Russia. And by 1804, Napoleon was 'Emperor' of France, and his military forces were gathering at Boulogne to invade Britain. Maritime supremacy saved Britain, but Napoleon instead turned the might of his land forces against Austria, achieving his greatest victory (over a combined Austrian and Russian force) at Austerlitz in 1806. The years 1807–8 represented the apex of Napoleon's power. As unrivalled master of continental Europe, he now resorted to economic warfare against the recalcitrant British. He imposed the Continental System, forbidding his vassal states from buying British goods.

However, in 1808 the military commander who would be Napoleon's nemesis was already making his mark. By 1813, the Duke of Wellington had forced the French out of Portugal and Spain, and had crossed the Pyrenees, putting pressure on Napoleon from the south, just as the reinvigorated Allies were invading France from the east. At the same time, the Napoleonic system, under which three of the Napoleon's brothers, and his son, sat on European thrones, was breaking up.

Napoleon's story was not quite over yet. On 1 March 1815, having landed in France from Elba and received the army's support, he marched on Paris, which welcomed him. The frantic Allies, discussing how to organize post-Napoleonic Europe at the Congress of Vienna, hurriedly debated what to do. They put their trust in Wellington. At the Battle of Waterloo (18 June), Napoleon and his commanders made some uncharacteristically poor tactical decisions. When the Prussians under Blücher reinforced Wellington, even Napoleon's Old Guard fled under relentless fire. This time, words of encouragement from their emperor were not enough.

SOLDIERS OF MY OLD GUARD: I bid you farewell. For twenty years I have constantly accompanied you on the road to honour and glory. In these latter times, as in the days of our prosperity, you have invariably been models of courage and fidelity. With men such as you our cause could not be lost; but the war would have been interminable; it would have been civil war, and that would have entailed deeper misfortunes on France.

I have sacrificed all of my interests to those of the country.

I go, but you, my friends, will continue to serve France. Her happiness was my only thought. It will still be the object of my wishes. Do not regret my fate; if I have consented to survive, it is to serve your glory. I intend to write the history of the great achievements we have performed together. Adieu, my friends. Would I could press you all to my heart.

'Government of the people, by the people, for the people'

ABRAHAM LINCOLN
The Gettysburg Address, 19 November 1863

FOR PRESIDENT ABRAHAM LINCOLN, and for the policies and principles that he stood for, the year 1863 was momentous. It began when his Emancipation Proclamations of the previous year came into effect, on 1 January. These declared freedom for slaves in all territories controlled by his Confederate opponents who were fighting to secede from the United States. Eleven months later, on 19 November, Lincoln gave an address dedicating a war cemetery for his fallen soldiers. In between, and the pretext for his November speech, came the Pennsylvania battle that altered the course of the war and the future of United States: Gettysburg.

By mid-1863, the American Civil War was over two years old, but the main fighting had begun only in the spring of 1862. The outnumbered and outresourced Confederate forces had benefited from the superior leadership of the likes of generals Robert E. Lee and Thomas 'Stonewall' Jackson. They had managed to turn back Union invasions of Virginia and take the battle into Kentucky and Maryland, slave-owning states which had not seceded. Although the Battle of Antietam, in Maryland (17 September 1862), had temporarily stopped Lee's northern advance, by June 1863 his forces were invading Pennyslvania. In fields outside the town of Gettysburg, on 1–3 July, the Confederate army clashed with General George Meade's Army of the Potomac. The casualties – as many as 51,000 – were divided almost equally between the two sides, but Meade's forces prevailed and Lee was forced to begin his retreat back to Virginia.

The next day, the Confederate war effort in the southwest received a fatal blow, as the fortress of Vicksburg on the Mississippi fell to the Union's own military genius, Ulysses S. Grant, giving control of the mighty river to the Union side. Although the Civil War would play out for a further two years, after Gettysburg and Vicksburg the Southern rebels were on the back foot. And Gettysburg played a significant role in convincing foreign nations, notably Britain (to which the Confederacy was looking for material and diplomatic support), that Southern secession had little realistic chance of ultimate success. On 9 April 1865, Lee surrendered his army, and in June the last Confederate fighters made peace.

In the aftermath of Gettysburg, local residents prompted the state authorities to help purchase part of the

ABRAHAM LINCOLN

Born 12 February 1809 in rural Kentucky, his family later moved to Indiana.

He was largely self-taught. Moved to Illinois in 1831, where he became a (unsuccessful) storekeeper, postmaster, surveyor, and learned law, which he practised. Served as member of the Illinois House of Representatives (as a Whig), 1834–42. He was elected to Congress in 1854, and became a leading light of the new anti-slavery Republican Party. When elected US president in 1860, seven Southern states seceded to create the Confederacy, and the attack by Confederate forces on Fort Sumter (1861) began the American Civil War. Lincoln imposed a blockade against the South and proved ruthless in removing inefficient Union generals. The emancipation of slaves became part of the Union strategy, as reflected in Lincoln's Emancipation Proclamations, enacted in 1863. His Gettysburg Address (1863) summarized Union war aims. He won re-election on a landslide vote in 1864.

Assassinated by the actor John Wilkes Booth on 14 April 1865, while attending a theatre performance. In December 1865, the 13th Amendment to the Constitution abolished slavery in the United States.

battlefield as a final resting place for the Union dead, whose bodies lay scattered in various unmarked graves. While work on gathering the remains of the fallen continued, President Lincoln himself arrived at the site on 19 November 1863 to 'dedicate a portion of that field as a final resting place for those who here gave their lives', soldiers whom the world would 'never forget'. In an address lasting little more than two minutes, Lincoln defined the war as a test of whether a nation 'conceived in liberty and dedicated to the proposition that all men are created equal' could survive. The struggle now was for 'a new birth of freedom', for the survival of 'government of the people, by the people, for the people'. In a deft way, Lincoln honoured the dead but also demonstrated the extent to which the war was now not just about preserving the Union, but also about individual rights, which meant inevitably about the emancipation of slaves.

Lincoln thought that people would 'little note nor long remember what we say here'. But the Gettysburg Address lasted very much longer that did Lincoln himself, who fell prey to a Confederate sympathizer's bullet in 1865. The speech achieved immortality as a succinct encapsulation of American sacrifice in the cause of freedom.

FOUR SCORE AND SEVEN YEARS AGO our fathers brought forth on this continent a new nation, conceived in liberty and dedicated to the proposition that all men are created equal. Now we are engaged in a great civil war, testing whether that nation or any nation so conceived and so dedicated can long endure. We are met on a great battlefield of that war. We have come to dedicate a portion of that field as a final resting place for those who here gave their lives that that nation might live. It is

> 'From these honoured dead we take increased devotion to that cause'

altogether fitting and proper that we should do this. But in a larger sense, we cannot dedicate, we cannot consecrate, we cannot hallow this ground. The brave men, living and dead who struggled here have consecrated it far above our poor power to add or detract. The world will little note nor long remember what we say here, but it can never forget what they did here. It is for us the living rather to be dedicated here to the unfinished work which they who fought here have thus far so nobly advanced. It is rather for us to be here dedicated to the great task remaining before us – that from these honoured dead we take increased devotion to that cause for which they gave the last full measure of devotion – that we here highly resolve that these dead shall not have died in vain, that this nation under God shall have a new birth of freedom, and that government of the people, by the people, for the people shall not perish from the earth.

'Are women persons?'

SUSAN B. ANTHONY

Touring lecture 'Is It a Crime for a Citizen of the United States to Vote?', February–June 1873

THE MIDDLE OF THE 19TH CENTURY was a period when the United States' rifts led to civil war and where causes and ideals found expression in vigorous popular movements. Within this climate, a number of women achieved high profiles, often well beyond their actual capacity to determine events. Massachusetts-born Susan Brownell Anthony was one such, and in 1872 her deliberate provocation in casting an 'illegal' vote created a landmark moment in the campaign for female suffrage.

The serious-minded Anthony grew up in a Quaker tradition, became a school-teacher and, through encounters with Abolitionists and temperance advocates, threw herself into campaigns against slavery and alcohol. But she became frustrated at the obstacles to effective female participation, which came to a head in 1852 when she was denied an opportunity to speak at a temperance meeting. Her typical response was to create, with the like-minded campaigner Elizabeth Cady Stanton, the Woman's New York State Temperance Society.

Anthony and Stanton would go on to campaign together throughout their careers. They and their supporters realized that getting their views across on national and local issues involved, first and foremost, advancing women's civil, political and economic rights. These issues would dominate their lives.

In 1868, Congress passed the much-debated 14th Amendment to the Constitution. One of the three 'Reconstruction Amendments', it was designed to bolster newly emancipated African American men's voting rights. But there was ambiguity in its construction. One of its clauses appeared to undermine women's rights as US 'citizens', while another clause, depending on interpretation, could be held as confirming a woman's right to vote. The next year, the 15th Amendment asserted that 'The right of citizens of the United States to vote shall not be denied or abridged by the United States or by any State on account of race, color, or previous condition of servitude', but gender was not mentioned. An unfortunate effect of the amendments was to drive a wedge between campaigners for female suffrage and their male colleagues in the Abolitionist movement.

In 1872, Anthony decided to make a stand and test out the interpretation of the amendments in New York State. Some western states were making moves towards women's enfranchisement, but the East Coast remained intransigent.

SUSAN B. ANTHONY

Born in Massachusetts, 15 February 1820. Well educated, she taught for a living until returning to the family farm near Rochester, New York, in 1851.

Thereafter she devoted herself to the causes of temperance, emancipation (New York agent for the American Anti-Slavery Association from 1856), and above all women's rights. She became the owner of the weekly *Revolution*, 1869–70. With Elizabeth Cady Stanton, led the relatively radical National Women's Suffrage Association from 1869. She registered and cast an 'illegal' vote in the federal election, 1872: her subsequent indictment, speech in defence and trial became landmark events in the campaign for women's suffrage. Continued campaigning across the country as individual US states considered women's voting rights. She became president of the recently merged umbrella group, the National American Woman Suffrage Association, from 1892 to 1900.

Died in Rochester, New York, 13 March 1906.

Having managed (with some other women) to register in Rochester, she cast a vote in the federal election of 5 November. Just over three weeks later, she was arrested for illegally voting, and in January 1873 she was indicted for her offence. Her lawyer arranged bail, contrary to her wishes, but this allowed her to launch herself on an intensive local speaking tour, where she gave an impassioned speech entitled 'Is It a Crime for a Citizen of the United States to Vote?' In it, she argued the unconstitutionality of 'the disenfranchisement of one entire half of the people' and abhorred the 'hateful oligarchy of [the male] sex'.

Her trial in June 1873 inevitably found her guilty, and a fine was imposed (it remained unpaid). But Anthony gained a platform for her views, and the trial itself pushed the issue of the female franchise up the national agenda. She continued campaigning into her seventies. Although she did not live to see full female enfranchisement, which came when all states ratified the 19th Amendment to the Constitution in 1920, her pre-eminent role in the struggle has long been acknowledged.

FRIENDS AND FELLOW-CITIZENS: I stand before you tonight, under indictment for the alleged crime of having voted at the last presidential election, without having a lawful right to vote. It shall be my work this evening to prove to you that in thus voting, I not only committed no crime, but, instead, simply exercised my citizen's right, guaranteed to me and all United States citizens by the National Constitution, beyond the power of any state to deny.

Our democratic-republican government is based on the idea of the natural right of every individual member thereof to a voice and a vote in making and executing the laws. We assert the province of government to be to secure the people in the enjoyment of their unalienable rights. We throw to the winds the old dogma that governments can give rights.

. . . Nor can you find a word in any of the grand documents left us by the [founding] fathers that assumes for government the power to create or to confer rights. The Declaration of Independence, the United States Constitution, the constitutions of the several states and the organic laws of the territories, all alike propose to protect the people in the exercise of their God-given rights. Not one of them pretends to bestow rights.

'All men are created equal, and endowed by their Creator with certain unalienable rights. Among these are life, liberty and the pursuit of happiness. That to secure these, governments are instituted among men, deriving their just powers from the consent of the governed.'

Here is no shadow of government authority over rights, nor exclusion of any from their full and equal enjoyment. Here is pronounced the right of all men, and 'consequently', as the Quaker preacher said, 'of all women' to a voice in the government. And here, in this very first paragraph of the declaration, is the assertion of the natural right of all to the ballot; for, how can 'the consent of the governed' be given, if the right to vote be denied. Again: 'That whenever any form of government becomes destructive of these ends, it is the right of the people to alter or abolish it, and to institute a new government, laying its foundations on such principles, and organizing its powers in such forms as to them shall seem most likely to effect their safety and happiness.'

'One-half of the people of this nation today are utterly powerless'

Surely, the right of the whole people to vote is here clearly implied. For however destructive in their happiness this government might become, a disfranchised class could neither alter nor abolish it, nor institute a new one, except by the old brute force method of insurrection and rebellion. One-half of the people of this nation today are utterly powerless to blot from the statute books an unjust law, or to write there a new and a just one. The women, dissatisfied as they are with this form of government, that enforces taxation without representation – that compels them to obey laws to which they have never given their consent, that imprisons and hangs them without a trial by a jury of their peers, that robs them, in marriage, of the custody of their own persons, wages and children – are this half of the people left wholly at the mercy of the other half, in direct violation of the spirit and letter of the declarations of the framers of this government, every one of which was based on the immutable principle of equal rights to all.

. . . The preamble of the federal constitution says: 'We, the people of the United States, in order to form a more perfect union, establish justice, insure domestic tranquility, provide for the common defense, promote the general welfare and secure the blessings of liberty to ourselves and our posterity, do ordain and established this constitution for the United States of America.'

It was we, the people, not we, the white male citizens, nor yet we, the male citizens; but we, the whole people, who formed this Union. And we formed it, not to give the blessings or liberty, but to secure them; not to the half of ourselves and the half of our posterity, but to the whole people – women as well as men. And it is downright mockery to talk to women of their enjoyment of the blessings of liberty while they are denied the use of the only means of securing them provided by this democratic-republican government – the ballot.

. . . For any state to make sex a qualification that must ever result in the disfranchisement of one entire half of the people, is to pass a bill of attainder, or an ex post facto law, and is therefore a violation of the supreme law of the land. By it, the blessings of liberty are forever withheld from women and their female posterity. To them, this government has no just powers derived from the consent of the governed. To them this government is not a democracy. It is not a republic. It is an odious aristocracy; a hateful oligarchy of sex. The most hateful aristocracy ever established on the face of the globe . . . this oligarchy of sex, which makes father, brothers, husband, sons, the oligarchs over the mother and sisters, the wife and daughters of every household; which ordains all men sovereigns, all women subjects, carries dissension, discord and rebellion into every home of the nation.

'The only question left to be settled, now, is: Are women persons?'

. . . Though the words 'persons', 'people', 'inhabitants', 'electors', 'citizens' are all used indiscriminately in the national and state constitutions, there was always a conflict of opinion, prior to the war, as to whether they were synonymous terms . . . But, whatever there was for a doubt, under the old regime, the adoption of the Fourteenth Amendment settled that question forever, in its first sentence: 'All persons born or naturalized in the United States and subject to the jurisdiction thereof, are citizens of the United States and of the state wherein they reside.'

And the second settles the equal status of all persons – all citizens: 'No states shall make or enforce any law which shall abridge the privileges or immunities of citizens; nor shall any state deprive any person of life, liberty or property, without due process of law, nor deny to any person within its jurisdiction the equal protection of the laws.'

The only question left to be settled, now, is: Are women persons? And I hardly believe any of our opponents will have the hardihood to say they are not. Being persons, then, women are citizens, and no state has a right to make any new law, or to enforce any old law, that shall abridge their privileges or immunities. Hence, every discrimination against women in the constitutions and laws of the several states, is today null and void, precisely as is every one against negroes . . . .

'I am here
as a soldier'

EMMELINE PANKHURST

*Speech on the British campaign for women's suffrage,
13 November 1913*

THE CAMPAIGN FOR BRITISH WOMEN'S RIGHT to vote made its impact felt mainly in the first two decades of the 20th century. One of its leading lights was Emmeline Pankhurst. She acquired her surname through marriage to Richard Marsden Pankhurst, a radical Manchester barrister and socialist, who had been instrumental in framing reformist legislation concerning women's property rights. In 1889 Richard died; that same year, Emmeline founded the Women's Franchise League, and later, in 1903, she started the influential Women's Social and Political Union with her campaigning daughter Christabel (1880–1958).

The motto of the WSPU was 'deeds, not words', and its supporters embarked on demonstrations, petitions and disrupting political meetings – actions that in themselves raised eyebrows, especially when performed by middle-class women. In 1910, a hundred supporters led by Emmeline were arrested and brutally treated by police on 'Black Friday' after protesting at the House of Commons about the dropping of a bill that would have advanced their cause. The years that followed saw an intensification of the struggle as the government failed to enact reforms, especially in 1913 when the WSPU initiated a campaign of attacks on property – from post boxes to golf courses to politicians' houses. Emmeline herself was arrested on several occasions from 1908 onwards – for 'obstruction', for leading deputations, for smashing the prime minister's windows, for 'conspiracy', for 'inciting persons to commit offences'. Always she defended herself eloquently in court, and took full part in the hunger strikes that her jailed supporters carried out.

EMMELINE PANKHURST

Born Emmeline Goulden on 14 July 1858 in Manchester, England.

Her parents were politically progressive, and in 1879 she married the radical barrister Richard Marsden Pankhurst, sharing campaigns with him. She founded the Women's Franchise League in 1889, and later the Women's Social and Political Union (WSPU), which undertook an increasingly militant campaign for women's voting rights. She was first imprisoned for her actions in 1908. Undertook several speaking tours of the United States and Canada, from 1909. With the outbreak of the First World War, she began new campaigns to allow women to work and became increasingly hostile to left-wing politics. She adopted four 'war babies', and began a second home life with close female friends. She spent the years 1924–5 in Canada, Bermuda and France.

Died 14 June 1928 in London, while she was campaigning to become a Conservative Member of Parliament.

She also made a name for herself in the United States, beginning in 1909 when she introduced herself at New York's Carnegie Hall as a 'hooligan'. Her activist credentials ensured large American crowds to hear her speak – and, despite the 'deeds not words' motto, she made hundreds of speeches during her lifetime. In 1913, she was released from a three-year prison sentence temporarily to regain her health, as part of the government's so-called 'Cat and Mouse' policy to prevent hunger strikers dying in jail. Pankhurst took the opportunity to make another US trip. In Hartford, Connecticut, on 13 November, she gave a famous speech in which she presented herself 'as a soldier who has temporarily left the field of battle'. She went on to justify her 'revolutionary' tactics and to characterize the struggle as a life-and-death one. Indeed, by then Emily Wilding Davison had thrown herself, fatally, in front of the king's horse at the February 1913 Epsom

Derby: the single most startling suffragette action of the period. American suffragists absorbed the lessons, and by 1916 some were themselves on hunger strike.

The First World War changed everything. The British authorities released suffragettes unconditionally, and Emmeline began a patriotic Women's Right to Serve campaign. In June 1918, an Act of Parliament gave women over the age of 30 the right to vote (with restrictions). A Parliamentary bill giving British women equal voting rights to men became law in July 1928 – the month after Emmeline died.

I DO NOT COME HERE AS AN ADVOCATE, because whatever position the suffrage movement may occupy in the United States of America, in England it has passed beyond the realm of advocacy and it has entered into the sphere of practical politics. It has become the subject of revolution and civil war, and so tonight I am not here to advocate woman suffrage. American suffragists can do that very well for themselves. I am here as a soldier who has temporarily left the field of battle in order to explain – it seems strange it should have to be explained – what civil war is like when civil war is waged by women . . . If I were a man and I said to you, 'I come from a country which professes to have representative institutions and yet denies me, a taxpayer, an inhabitant of the country, representative rights,' you would at once understand that that human being, being a man, was justified in the adoption of revolutionary methods to get representative institutions. But since I am a woman it is necessary in the 20th century to explain why women have adopted revolutionary methods in order to win the rights of citizenship.

'Either women are to be killed or women are to have the vote'

. . . Now, I want to say to you who think women cannot succeed, we have brought the government of England to this position, that it has to face this alternative; either women are to be killed or women are to have the vote. I ask American men in this meeting, what would you say if in your State you were faced with that alternative, that you must either kill them or give them their citizenship – women, many of whom you respect, women whom you know have lived useful lives, women whom you know, even if you do not know them personally, are animated with the highest motives, women who are in pursuit of liberty and the power to do useful public service? Well, there is only one answer to that alternative; there is only one way out of it, unless you are prepared to put back civilization two or three generations; you must give those women the vote. Now that is the outcome of our civil war.

'Ireland unfree shall
never be at peace'

PATRICK PEARSE
Funeral oration for Jeremiah O'Donovan Rossa, 1 August 1915

I N THE EARLY 20TH CENTURY, the movement for Irish independence boasted a variety of parties and semi-secret groups. Broadly speaking, they varied from those who campaigned, constitutionally, for 'home rule' and those whose beliefs and actions took a more revolutionary course. For the latter, typified by the Irish Republican Brotherhood (IRB), the outbreak of the First World War in 1914 represented a dilemma. Should Irish republicans support the British war effort? When John Redmond, leader of the Irish National Party, called on the Irish to support Britain, the more radical republicans in the IRB and the paramilitary Irish Volunteers took little notice. Rather, they saw Britain's entanglement on the Western Front as an opportunity. It was a feeling that manifested itself in the Easter Rising of 1916, one of whose leaders was the writer-revolutionary Patrick Pearse.

Patrick Pearse began his career as a propagator of Irish language and culture. He became radicalized from home-rule sympathies to revolutionary republicanism and eventually rose to senior roles in the IRB (including on its military council) and the Irish Volunteers. By 1915 he had also established himself as a powerful public speaker, who could galvanize his audiences by interweaving romantic allusions to Irish history with the urgency of contemporary politics.

When Pearse was asked in 1915 to deliver a funeral oration for the republican hero Jeremiah O'Donovan Rossa, he brought just those qualities to his performance. A member of the revolutionary Fenian Society, O'Donovan Rossa (1831–1915) had spent time in a British prison before exile in the United States. There, he had raised funds for paramilitary operations and, in the early 1880s, organized a bombing campaign on the British mainland. With the Irish Volunteers already planning rebellion, the return of O'Donovan Rossa's body to Dublin for burial presented a well-timed opportunity for an event to boost their support.

PATRICK PEARSE

Born 10 November 1879, of English and Irish parentage, in Dublin, Ireland.

Joined the cultural Gaelic League, 1895, and later edited its newspaper. After studying languages, literature and law at University and Trinity colleges, Dublin, he was called to the Bar. He founded St Enda's boys' school in 1908, teaching in Gaelic and English and inculcating nationalist values, and wrote widely in both languages. In 1912 he joined the new Irish Volunteers and then the Irish Republican Brotherhood, and was further radicalized by visiting the Irish diaspora in the United States. He demonstrated his robust oratory at a commemoration of the 18th-century nationalist hero Wolfe Tone in 1912, and then at the funeral of O'Donovan Rossa in 1915. Having publicly called for an armed uprising, Pearse was 'commandant-general' and chief propagandist of the week-long Easter Rebellion, 1916.

Executed, following a court martial, 3 May 1916, in Kilmainham Gaol, Dublin.

In his opening lines, Pearce constrasted O'Donovan Rossa's age with his own relative youth to stress that a new generation was picking up the baton in the cause of 'freedom'. He invoked other luminaries in the revolutionary pantheon, and he proclaimed the inextricability of the Gaelic language and a free Ireland. Pearse mentioned religion too, a nod to the ancient sense of Ireland as a civilizing Christian nation. Finally, and most portentiously, he returned to the themes of death and burial to assert that the graves of Irish patriots would serve as constant reminders of the struggle – and would spur further action. He concluded with the speech's most celebrated declaration, that 'while Ireland holds these graves, Ireland unfree shall never be at peace'.

On 24 April 1916, Pearse made his next memorable public speech, proclaiming a new provisional republic from the steps of Dublin's General Post Office at the start of the Easter Rising. The insurrection launched by around 1200 Irish Volunteers and Citizens Army activists had little chance of lasting success; but the scale of it (and some inept British responses, along with the deaths of innocent civilians) was a sign of things to come. As for Pearse himself, he was tried and executed by firing squad the next month (as was his brother Willie), joining O'Donovan Rossa among the graves of 'the Fenian dead'.

IT HAS SEEMED RIGHT, before we turn away from this place in which we have hid the mortal remains of O'Donovan Rossa, that one among us should, in the name of all, speak the praise of that valiant man, and endeavour to formulate the thought and the hope that are in us as we stand around his grave. And if there is anything that makes it fitting that I, rather than some other, I rather than one of the grey-haired men who were young with him and shared in his labour and in his suffering, should speak here, it is perhaps that I may be taken as speaking on behalf of a new generation that has been rebaptized in the Fenian faith, and that has accepted the responsibility of carrying out the Fenian programme. I propose to you then that, here by the grave of this unrepentant Fenian, we renew our baptismal vows; that, here by the grave of this unconquered and unconquerable man, we ask of God, each one for himself, such unshakeable purpose, such high and gallant courage, such unbreakable strength of soul as belonged to O'Donovan Rossa.

'We only know one definition of freedom'

Deliberately here we avow ourselves, as he avowed himself in the dock, Irishmen of one allegiance only. We of the Irish Volunteers, and you others who are associated with us in today's task and duty, are bound together and must stand together henceforth in brotherly union for the achievement of the freedom of Ireland. And we know only one definition of freedom: it is [Wolfe] Tone's definition, it is [John] Mitchel's definition, it is Rossa's definition. Let no man blaspheme the cause that the dead generations of Ireland served by giving it any other name and definition than their name and their definition.

We stand at Rossa's grave not in sadness but rather in exaltation of spirit that it has been given to us to come thus into so close a communion with that brave and splendid Gael. Splendid and holy causes are served by men who are themselves splendid and holy. O'Donovan Rossa was splendid in the proud manhood of him, splendid in the heroic grace of him, splendid in the Gaelic strength and clarity and truth of him. And all that splendour and pride and strength was compatible with a humility and a simplicity of devotion to Ireland, to all that was olden and beautiful and Gaelic in Ireland, the holiness and simplicity of patriotism of a Michael O'Clery [a 17th-century chronicler] or of an Eoghan O'Growney [a 19th-century scholar-priest, co-founder of the Gaelic League]. The clear true eyes of this man almost alone in his day visioned Ireland as we of today would surely have her: not free merely, but Gaelic as well; not Gaelic merely, but free as well.

'The fools, the fools, the fools! – they have left us our Fenian dead'

In a closer spiritual communion with him now than ever before or perhaps ever again, in a spiritual communion with those of his day, living and dead, who suffered with him in English prisons, in communion of spirit too with our own dear comrades who suffer in English prisons today, and speaking on their behalf as well as our own, we pledge to Ireland our love, and we pledge to English rule in Ireland our hate. This is a place of peace, sacred to the dead, where men should speak with all charity and with all restraint; but I hold it a Christian thing, as O'Donovan Rossa held it, to hate evil, to hate untruth, to hate oppression, and, hating them, to strive to overthrow them. Our foes are strong and wise and wary but, strong and wise and wary as they are, they cannot undo the miracles of God who ripens in the hearts of young men the seeds sown by the young men of a former generation. And the seeds sown by the young men of '65 and '67 are coming to their miraculous ripening today. Rulers and defenders of realms had need to be wary if they would guard against such processes. Life springs from death; and from the graves of patriot men and women spring living nations. The defenders of this realm have worked well in secret and in the open. They think that they have pacified Ireland. They think that they have purchased half of us and intimidated the other half. They think that they have foreseen everything, think that they have provided against everything; but the fools, the fools, the fools! – they have left us our Fenian dead, and while Ireland holds these graves, Ireland unfree shall never be at peace.

'The world must
be made safe for
democracy'

THE UNITED STATES' LONG TRADITION of staying out of the struggles among Europe's nations had lasted for over a century by the time of the First World War. In 1915 though, the German sinking of the SS *Lusitania*, which was carrying Allied arms, killed 128 Americans and roused the country to anger. By 1917, the pressure to join the fray became unstoppable. In January of that year, British Intelligence intercepted the 'Zimmerman telegram', which revealed that the German military was planning unrestricted submarine warfare; US ships supplying the Allies would be considered fair game if they were in the wrong place, at the wrong time. The telegram also proposed an anti-US alliance between Germany and Mexico should the United

States declare war. In February, the German navy enacted its submarine policy, and within days the *Housatonic*, an American liner, had been sunk off the Italian coast. The United States broke off diplomatic relations with Germany, and by April America had entered the war.

The man charged with seeking Congressional approval for war was the country's 28th president, Thomas Woodrow Wilson. It was his second term as president, following a narrow victory in 1916. This former lawyer and academic was not a natural warmonger, and there were many Americans who remained opposed to entanglement in Europe's Great War. Since the eruption of the First World War in 1914, Wilson had actively – in the open and in secret – mediated for peace among the belligerent countries.

In addressing Congress, Wilson expressed himself as a patient man with 'a profound sense of the solemn', representing a nation goaded beyond its endurance. It was, for him, a 'distressing

WOODROW WILSON

Born 28 December 1856 in Staunton, Virginia, the son of a Presbyterian minister.

His later life was characterized by a strict personal code of conduct. After studying law and politics, and a brief legal career, he turned to academia: taught at Bryn Mawr and Princeton universities, becoming the latter's president in 1902, the year in which he published a history of the United States. He entered Democratic Party politics, becoming Governor of New Jersey (1911) before election as US president, serving two terms (1913–21). Under Wilson, amendments to the US Constitution introduced Prohibition and votes for women, his 'New Freedom' programme aimed to foster equality of opportunity for men, and he strengthened labour unions. Having tried, and failed, to broker peace among the warring European nations from 1914, he persuaded the United States to enter the war in support of the Allies. In 1918 his 14-point plan for peace became the basis for the Paris Peace Conference. After difficult negotiations, the resulting Treaty of Versailles created the League of Nations. Despite Wilson's determined campaign, the United States did not join the League.

Died 3 January 1924 in Washington, D.C.

and oppressive duty', but America's policy of 'armed neutrality' was now 'ineffectual at best'. Wilson not only represented war as necessary to protect the nation from aggression. He sought to claim the high moral ground and imbue the task ahead with American idealism – in the speech's most potent phrase, 'the world must be made safe for democracy'. For Wilson, an enduring peace demanded 'a partnership of democratic nations ... a league of honour'.

A postwar league – the League of Nations, precursor to the United Nations – was to be Wilson's great international project. It would be no easy task, since, in the aftermath of war, many of Europe's politicians had their own nationalistic agendas uppermost in their minds. Nevertheless, by the terms of the Treaty of Versailles in 1919–20, the multinational body came into existence, tasked with trying to solve international disputes before they developed into war. Wilson received the Nobel Peace Prize for his efforts. But his tragedy was that, despite exhausting efforts (which contributed to a stroke, in 1919), he failed to carry his country with him. The US Senate would not ratify the League's covenant. Wilson fought as tenaciously as he could for his dream, brooking no compromise and arguing that US membership was essential to world peace. But the matter was settled when the 1920 presidential election delivered victory to the anti-League Republican, Warren Harding.

GENTLEMEN OF THE CONGRESS: . . . The present German submarine warfare against commerce is a warfare against mankind. It is war against all nations . . . The challenge is to all mankind.

Each nation must decide for itself how it will meet it. The choice we make for ourselves must be made with a moderation of counsel and temperateness of judgement befitting our character and our motives as a nation. We must put excited feeling away. Our motive will not be revenge or the victorious assertion of the physical might of the nation, but only the vindication of right, of human right, of which we are only a single champion.

. . . Armed neutrality is ineffectual enough at best; in such circumstances and in the face of such pretensions it is worse than ineffectual; it is likely only to produce what it was meant to prevent; it is practically certain to draw us into the war without either the rights or the effectiveness of belligerents. There is one choice we cannot make, we are incapable of making: we will not choose the path of submission and suffer the most sacred rights of our nation and our people to be ignored or violated. The wrongs against which we now array ourselves are no common wrongs: they cut to the very roots of human life.

With a profound sense of the solemn and even tragical character of the step I am taking . . . I advise that the Congress declare the recent course of the Imperial German government to be in fact nothing less than war against the government and people of the United States; that it formally accept the status of belligerent which has thus been thrust upon it; and that it take immediate steps not only to put the country in a more thorough state of defence but also to exert all its power and employ all its resources to bring the government of the German Empire to terms and end the war.

. . . While we do these things, these deeply momentous things, let us be very clear, and make very clear to all the world what our motives and our objects are . . . Our object . . . is to vindicate the principles of peace and justice in the life of the world as against selfish and autocratic power and to set up amongst the really free and self-governed peoples of the world such a concert of purpose and of action as will henceforth ensure the observance of those principles.

. . . A steadfast concert for peace can never be maintained except by a partnership of democratic nations. No autocratic government could be trusted to keep faith within it or observe its covenants. It must be a league of honour, a partnership of opinion.

. . . The world must be made safe for democracy. Its peace must be planted upon the tested foundations of political liberty. We have no selfish ends to serve.

'The right is more precious than peace'

We desire no conquest, no dominion. We seek no indemnities for ourselves, no material compensation for the sacrifices we shall cheerfully make. We are but one of the champions of the rights of mankind. We shall be satisfied when those rights have been made as secure as the faith and the freedom of nations can make them.

. . . It is a distressing and oppressive duty, gentlemen of the Congress, which I have performed in thus addressing you. There are, it may be, many months of fiery trial and sacrifice ahead of us. It is a fearful thing to lead this great peaceful people into war, into the most terrible and disastrous of all wars, civilization itself seeming to be in the balance.

But the right is more precious than peace, and we shall fight for the things which we have always carried nearest our hearts, for democracy, for the right of those who submit to authority to have a voice in their own governments, for the rights and liberties of small nations, for a universal dominion of right by such a concert of free peoples as shall bring peace and safety to all nations and make the world at last free.

To such a task we can dedicate our lives and our fortunes, everything that we are and everything that we have, with the pride of those who know that the day has come when America is privileged to spend her blood and her might for the principles that gave her birth and happiness and the peace which she has treasured. God helping her, she can do no other.

'Power to the Soviets'

VLADIMIR ILYICH LENIN

*Speech advancing Bolshevik
political aims, September 1917*

VLADIMIR ILYICH LENIN PUBLISHED THIS SPEECH in September 1917, just weeks before his Bolshevik Party seized power in Russia's October Revolution. In the speech, Lenin attacked Russia's Provisional Government, a shaky coalition that included the Socialist Revolutionaries, and which was headed by Alexander Kerensky. It had replaced the tsarist regime in the February Revolution, earlier in 1917. Lenin, in accordance with his Marxist beliefs, regarded the February Revolution as just a first revolutionary stage. It would, and should, be followed by a second revolution, whereby power would pass to the working people (the proletariat) and the peasants, rather than being held by the bourgeoisie (the middle classes) – who, because of their class interests, would oppose any truly radical social transformation.

Since its establishment, the Provisional Government had faced competition from workers' councils or 'Soviets'. The Soviets controlled the transport system and national industrial resources. The Provisional Government lacked real power and could not resolve Russia's serious economic crisis, nor its food shortages, and its commitment to continuing the unsuccessful war against Germany remained unpopular.

Lenin had returned from exile to his native Russia only in April 1917, in a sealed train carriage (aided by Germany). He had swiftly established himself in the wake of the February Revolution as a revolutionary force to be reckoned with. His 'April Theses' propagated the slogan 'All Power to the Soviets', which he elaborated in the September speech. During July, demonstrations against the government and the war erupted in Petrograd (i.e. St Petersburg, then the Russian capital), and the slogan was shouted by protestors. But the protests were too disorganized to have a properly revolutionary impact, and they were crushed.

By the last months of 1917, though, Petrograd was in turmoil, workers were taking over factories and 'Power to the Soviets' seemed to be becoming a reality. Together with Leon Trotsky, head of the Petrograd Soviet, Lenin and other senior Bolsheviks hurriedly planned for an armed uprising. On the night of 6 November (24 October, in Russian Old Style dating), Lenin ordered his Red Guards to take over key institutions in Petrograd,

VLADIMIR ILYICH LENIN

Born Vladimir Ilyich Ulyanov into a middle-class family on 10 April 1870, in Ulianovsk, Russia.

Having gained a law degree, and become politically radicalized (his brother was executed for anti-tsarist activity), he practised law in the 1890s while absorbing the political writings of Karl Marx and Friedrich Engels. Arrested for subversion in 1895, he was exiled to Siberia in 1897–1900. During the next 17 years he lived mostly in Western Europe (mainly Switzerland), organizing the Bolshevik ('Majority') wing of the Russian Social Democratic Party. In 1903 he provoked a split between the Bolsheviks and the more moderate Mensheviks ('Minority') at their London Congress. He returned to Russia in 1905–7, but could not capitalize on the political changes enacted at that time. His final return to Russia, in April 1917, was followed by the Bolshevik October Revolution and his leadership of the new Soviet Russian state, which defeated its main counter-revolutionary opponents by 1922. He survived an assassination attempt in 1918, but suffered increasingly poor health.

Died 21 January 1924 in Moscow.

including the Provisional Government's headquarters in the tsar's old Winter Palace. With very little bloodshed, the Bolsheviks seized power. With the Provisional Government's ministers under arrest, and the more moderate Mensheviks sidelined, the Bolshevik Party created a new supreme authority in the shape of the Soviet of the People's Commissars. The Bolsheviks renamed themselves the Communist Party, and the 'dictatorship of the proletariat', promised in Lenin's speech, had arrived.

The Bolshevik revolution was not yet home and dry. Although Russia hurriedly extricated itself from one war, making enormous concessions to Germany in return for peace, the country descended into civil war in 1918–21 as the Bolshevik 'Reds' fought the 'White' counter-revolutionaries over Russia's future. But with the winning of the civil war, and the extinguishing of Tsar Nicholas II and his family, Russia was set for 70 years of Communist Party rule. Lenin himself had only a few more years to live. But he achieved permanence as the revered father of the Revolution, his body embalmed and displayed in a glass coffin in Moscow's Red Square.

THE KEY QUESTION OF EVERY REVOLUTION is undoubtedly the question of state power. Which class holds power decides everything. When *Dyelo Naroda* [People's Cause], the paper of the chief governing party in Russia, recently complained that, owing to the controversies over power, both the question of the Constituent Assembly and that of bread are being forgotten, the Socialist Revolutionaries [SRs] should have been answered: 'Blame yourselves. For it is the wavering and indecision of your party that are mostly to blame for "ministerial leapfrog", the interminable postponements of the Constituent Assembly, and the undermining by the capitalists of the planned and agreed measures of a grain monopoly and of providing the country with bread.'

The question of power cannot be evaded or brushed aside, because it is the key question determining *everything* in a revolution's development, and in its foreign and domestic policies. It is an undisputed fact that our revolution has 'wasted' six months in wavering over the system of power; it is a fact resulting from the wavering policy of the Socialist Revolutionaries and Mensheviks. In the long run, these parties' wavering policy was determined by the class position of the petty bourgeoisie, by their economic instability in the struggle between capital and labour.

The whole issue at present is whether the petty-bourgeois democrats have learned anything during these great, exceptionally eventful six months. If not, then the revolution is lost, and only a victorious uprising of the proletariat can save it. If they have learned something, the establishment of a stable, unwavering power must be begun immediately. Only if power is based, obviously and unconditionally, on a majority of the population can it be stable during a popular revolution, i.e., a revolution which rouses the people, the majority of the workers and peasants, to action. Up to now state power in Russia has virtually remained in the hands of the *bourgeoisie*, who are compelled to make only particular concessions (only to begin withdrawing them the following day), to hand out promises (only to fail to carry them out), to search for all sorts of excuses to cover their domination (only to fool the people by a show of 'honest coalition'), etc., etc. In words it claims to be a popular, democratic, revolutionary government, but in deeds it is an anti-popular, undemocratic, counter-revolutionary, bourgeois government. This is the contradiction which has existed so far and which has been a source of the complete instability and inconsistency of power, of that 'ministerial leapfrog' in which the SRs and Mensheviks have been engaged with such unfortunate (for the people) enthusiasm.

'It means removing this apparatus and substituting for it a new, popular one'

In early June 1917 I told the All-Russia Congress of Soviets that either the Soviets would be dispersed and die an inglorious death, or all power must be transferred to them . . . The slogan, 'Power to the Soviets', however, is very often, if not in most cases, taken quite incorrectly to mean a cabinet of the parties of the Soviet majority. We would like to go into more detail on this very false notion.

. . . 'Power to the Soviets' means radically reshaping the entire old state apparatus, that bureaucratic apparatus which hampers everything democratic. It means removing this apparatus and substituting for it a new, popular one, i.e., a truly democratic apparatus of Soviets, i.e., the organized and armed majority of the people – the workers, soldiers and peasants. It means allowing the majority of the people initiative and independence not only in the election of deputies, but also in state administration, in effecting reforms and various other changes.

To make this difference clearer and more comprehensible, it is worth recalling a valuable admission made some time ago by the paper of the governing party of the SRs, *Dyelo Naroda*. It wrote that even in those ministries which were in the hands of socialist ministers (this was written during the notorious coalition with the Cadets, when some Mensheviks and SRs were ministers), the entire administrative apparatus had remained unchanged, and hampered work.

Let those who say 'We have no apparatus to replace the old one, which inevitably gravitates towards the defence of the bourgeoisie' be ashamed of themselves. For this apparatus exists. It is the Soviets. Don't be afraid of the people's initiative and independence. Put your faith in their revolutionary organizations, and you will see in all realms of state affairs the same strength, majesty and invincibility of the workers and peasants as were displayed in their unity and their fury against Kornilov.*

'There is no middle course. This has been shown by experience.'

There is no middle course. This has been shown by experience. Either all power goes to the Soviets both centrally and locally, and all land is given to the peasants immediately, pending the Constituent Assembly's decision, or the landowners and capitalists obstruct every step, restore the landowners' power, drive the peasants into a rage and carry things to an exceedingly violent peasant revolt.

Only the dictatorship of the proletariat and the poor peasants is capable of smashing the resistance of the capitalists, of displaying truly supreme courage and determination in the exercise of power, and of securing the enthusiastic, selfless and truly heroic support of the masses both in the army and among the peasants.

'Power to the Soviets – this is the only way'

Power to the Soviets – this is the only way to make further progress gradual, peaceful and smooth, keeping perfect pace with the political awareness and resolve of the majority of the people and with their own experience. Power to the Soviets means the complete transfer of the country's administration and economic control into the hands of the workers and peasants, to whom nobody would dare offer resistance and who, through practice, through their own experience, would soon learn how to distribute the land, products and grain properly.

*General Lavr Kornilov (1870–1918), whose attempt to stiffen the Provisional Government's resolve saw him dismissed from his post amid fears of a military coup.

'I believe in the law of love'

CLARENCE DARROW

Closing speech in defence of Henry Sweet, 11 May 1926

ON 11 MAY 1926, IN A DETROIT COURTROOM, lawyer Clarence Darrow completed his seven-hour closing summary as he battled to save an African American man from a murder charge. For the unconventional defence attorney, the case was his latest to challenge received opinion and attack prejudice.

The background to the case is redolent of the racial tensions in the decades before civil rights legislation. In Detroit, the growing automobile industry brought an influx of African American workers in the early 1920s, and sometimes white mobs drove African Americans away from the largely white areas they were living in. The night that Dr Ossian Sweet and his family moved into their new home, an organized riot broke out and rocks were thrown at the house. The family fought back with a firearm from an upper window, and a white man, Leon Breiner, was killed.

CLARENCE DARROW

Born 18 April 1857 in Kinsman, Ohio, son of an agnostic undertaker.

He studied law, was admitted to the Bar in 1878, and initially practised law locally. He moved to Chicago in 1887, and was influenced by the liberal judge John Altgeld. Became active in local Democratic politics, and was appointed to Chicago's corporation counsel in 1890. And he acted as a general attorney to the Chicago and North Western Railway until 1894. He successfully defended socialist miners' leader Bill Hayward against a charge of ordering the assassination of Idaho's governor, 1907 and was acquitted on a charge of attempting to bribe a jury, 1912. He defended the Chicago student murderers Leopold and Loeb (1924) and the freedom to teach evolutionary theory in the Scopes 'Monkey' trial (1925). In 1932 he came out of retirement to defend Thomas Massie from the charge of murdering his wife's alleged rapist.

Died 13 March 1938 in Chicago.

Clarence Darrow first defended the whole Sweet family against a charge of murder but the jury failed to reach a verdict. Darrow then defended Ossian's younger brother, Henry Sweet (who admitted to firing the gun), in the first of what were planned to be individual trials of each family member. Darrow believed that if he could secure an acquittal for Sweet, then the case for the other trials would disappear.

In his long summing-up for the all-white jury, Darrow demonstrated his superb qualities as a lawyer – immense courtroom skill, strong dramatic instincts and powerful persuasive abilities. He argued that the case was about racism, not murder: 'I insist that there is nothing but prejudice in this case; that if it was reversed and eleven white men had shot and killed a black while protecting their home and their lives against a mob of blacks, nobody would have dreamed of having them indicted ... Now, that is the case, gentlemen, and that is all there is to this case. Take the hatred away, and you have nothing left.' The jury took four hours to reach a 'not guilty' verdict, and in July the other defendants' charges were dropped.

Darrow's freethinking, questioning disposition had its roots in a family background of social radicalism and agnosticism. Having moved into criminal law, he handled the notorious case of Leopold and Loeb, two University of Chicago students in thrall to the philosopher Nietzsche, who murdered a 14-year-old boy in an experiment to commit the 'perfect' crime. Firmly opposed to the death penalty, Darrow made innovative use of psychiatric theories about determinism in human behaviour to have the two teenagers' likely death sentence commuted to life imprisonment. In over 50 capital cases throughout his career, Darrow lost only his first client to the executioner.

In 1925, Darrow defended John T. Scopes in a test case. He was accused of violating Tennessee's laws by teaching the theory of evolution in public schools. The Scopes 'Monkey' trial won national attention and has gone down as a landmark debate between Old Testament literalism and scientific discovery. Although Scopes was found guilty, the verdict was overturned on a technicality, and Darrow was able to deliver penetrating cross-examinations of the fundamentalist worldview. It is no wonder that Darrow had a posthumous life as the subject of books, films and plays.

NOW, GENTLEMEN, JUST ONE MORE WORD, and I am through with this case. I do not live in Detroit. But I have no feeling against this city. In fact, I shall always have the kindest remembrance of it, especially if this case results as I think and feel that it will. I am the last one to come here to stir up race hatred, or any other hatred. I do not believe in the law of hate. I may not be true to my ideals always, but I believe in the law of love, and I believe you can do nothing with hatred. I would like to see a time when man loves his fellow man, and forgets his colour or his creed. We will never be civilized until that time comes.

I know the negro race has a long road to go. I believe the life of the negro race has been a life of tragedy, of injustice, of oppression. The law has made him equal, but man has not. And, after all, the last analysis is, what has man done? – and not what has the law done? I know there is a long road ahead of him, before he can take the place which I believe he should take. I know that before him there is suffering, sorrow, tribulation and death among the blacks, and perhaps the whites. I am sorry. I would do what I could to avert it. I would advise patience; I would advise toleration; I would advise understanding; I would advise all of those things which are necessary for men who live together. Gentlemen, what do you think is your duty in this case? I have watched, day after day, these black, tense faces that have crowded this court. These black faces that now are looking to you twelve whites, feeling that the hopes and fears of a race are in your keeping.

This case is about to end, gentlemen. To them, it is life. Not one of their colour sits on this jury. Their fate is in the hands of twelve whites. Their eyes are fixed on you, their hearts go out to you, and their hopes hang on your verdict.

This is all. I ask you, on behalf of this defendant, on behalf of these helpless ones who turn to you, and more than that – on behalf of this great state, and this great city which must face this problem, and face it fairly – I ask you, in the name of progress and of the human race, to return a verdict of not guilty in this case!

'I have faith in the righteousness of our cause'

MOHANDAS K. GANDHI
Speech on the eve of his 'Salt March', 11 March 1930

I N 1930, MOHANDAS KARAMCHAND GANDHI was already a figure of international fascination for the methods by which he challenged British rule in India. As he summarized it during his 1922 trial for sedition, 'non-violence is the first article of my faith. It is also the last article of my creed.' His commitment to *satyagraha* ('steadfastness in truth') and *ahimsa* ('non-violence'), concepts derived from the Hindu and Jain religious traditions, had been developed during his two decades as a lawyer and campaigner for Indians' civil rights in South Africa.

By the time of Gandhi's return to India, in 1915, he had already cast off the legal profession and Western pretensions in order to adopt the frugal, ascetic dress and behaviour that would create the enduring image of the man. These qualities, together with his idealization of an agrarian society and the ashrams (spiritual communes) he inhabited, would always distinguish him from his more orthodox colleagues in the Indian National Congress political movement. Nevertheless, the Mahatma ('Great Soul'), as he was dubbed, commanded a tremendous respect based on moral authority and a refusal to accede to any principle of ends justifying means. At first, these qualities were channelled into local and social campaigns, such as fighting for the rights of Dalits ('Untouchables'), the lowest caste of Indian society. But within a few years Gandhi had involved himself in the wider political struggle for *swaraj* – home rule.

By January 1930, Gandhi and other Congress leaders felt frustrated enough at the lack of political progress to move beyond demanding Dominion status for India (on a par with Canada or Australia, but still within the British Empire) to demand *purna swaraj*: complete independence. On 2 March 1930, Gandhi wrote to the British viceroy, Lord Irwin, announcing his intention to begin a new campaign of civil disobedience. And its focus would be a rebellion against the historic injustice of the British salt tax.

Since the 18th century, the British authorities had collected significant revenues from taxes on Indian salt production and sale – taxes which, at various times, had reached staggeringly high levels. At their worst, the salt laws were life-threatening, effectively denying the vital commodity to the poorer members of Indian society. At the

MOHANDAS K. GANDHI

Born 2 October 1869 in the Indian princely state of Porbandar, Gujarat, where his father was chief minister.

He travelled to London in 1888 to study law, and was called to the Bar in 1891. He lived in South Africa 1893–1914, working for a legal firm and then championing the civil rights of Indian immigrants; in the Transvaal, from 1906, he developed his brand of nonviolent protest and experienced his first spells in prison. In India, from 1915, he joined the Indian National Congress and commenced non-violent campaigning for social justice, agrarian values and civil rights. Gandhi advocated domestic crafts, including the spinning of textiles, to create Indian self-sufficiency: he was tried and imprisoned for 'sedition' in 1922 after fomenting a boycott of imported British goods, though he called off protests when violence began. He launched a much publicized campaign to evade the British salt tax in 1930, leading to a further arrest. Gandhi attended disappointing Round Table talks on India's future in London (1931). His 'Quit India' speech of 1942 reversed the previous moderate support for Britain's war effort, and he was imprisoned (with other Congress leaders) until 1944. Gandhi strongly opposed the partition of India at independence in 1947.

Assassinated 20 January 1948 by a Hindu extremist, who saw him as too accommodating to Muslims.

very least, it was a gross insult to make it illegal for Indians to make their own salt from the naturally abundant deposits. Politically, the salt tax was a vivid symbol of Indians' dispossession from their own land. Access to salt – such a basic human necessity – was also an issue that perfectly combined Gandhi's spiritual, social and political priorities.

On 12 March 1930, Gandhi and almost 80 *satyagrahis* (his followers), under the scrutiny of the world's media, embarked on a three-week march from their ashram in Ahmedabad to the salt deposits at Dandi, near Jalalpur, on the coast of Gujarat. At evening prayers the night before, Gandhi gave a speech outlining his hopes and fears for the march. Once he reached the shore at Dandi, Gandhi picked up a handful of earth and seawater, and began the symbolic act of evaporating it to make salt. It was a calculated act of transgression, and Gandhi confidently expected to be arrested for it.

Arrest finally came in early May 1930, and by this time the widespread civil disobedience campaign was well and truly under way. Thousands were engaged in the black-market selling and buying of tax-free salt, and there were other economic boycotts too.

The Dandi march, and the civil disobedience campaign that followed, represented the apex of Gandhi's mobilization of popular protest. The tax on salt remained until the end of the British Raj – but the Raj itself gave up in 1947.

IN ALL PROBABILITY THIS WILL BE MY LAST SPEECH to you. Even if the government allow me to march tomorrow morning, this will be my last speech on the sacred banks of the Sabarmati. Possibly these may be the last words of my life here.

I have already told you yesterday what I had to say. Today I shall confine myself to what you should do after my companions and I are arrested. The programme of the march to Jalalpur must be fulfilled as originally settled. The enlistment of the volunteers for this purpose should be confined to Gujarat only. From what I have been [*sic*] and heard during the last fortnight, I am inclined to believe that the stream of civil resisters will flow unbroken.

'You may choose any one or all of these devices to break the salt monopoly'

But let there be not a semblance of breach of peace even after all of us have been arrested. We have resolved to utilize all our resources in the pursuit of an exclusively non-violent struggle. Let no one commit a wrong in anger. This is my hope and prayer. I wish these words of mine reached every nook and corner of the land. My task shall be done if I perish and so do my comrades. It will then be for the Working Committee of the Congress to show you the way and it will be up to you to follow its lead. So long as I have reached Jalalpur, let nothing be done in contravention to the authority vested in me by the Congress. But once I am arrested, the whole responsibility shifts to the Congress. No one who believes in non-violence, as a creed, need, therefore, sit still. My compact with the Congress ends as soon as I am arrested. In that case . . . Wherever possible, civil disobedience of salt [laws] should be started. These laws can be violated in three ways. It is an offence to manufacture salt wherever there are facilities for doing so. The possession and sale of contraband salt, which includes natural salt or salt earth, is also an offence. The purchasers of such salt will be equally guilty. To carry away the natural salt deposits on the seashore is likewise violation of law. So is the hawking of such salt. In short, you may choose any one or all of these devices to break the salt monopoly.

'We can refuse to pay taxes if we have the requisite strength'

We are, however, not to be content with this alone. There is no ban by the Congress and wherever the local workers have self-confidence other suitable measures may be adopted. I stress only one condition, namely, let our pledge of truth and non-violence as the only means for the attainment of *swaraj* [i.e., home rule] be faithfully kept. For the rest, every one has a free hand. But, that does not give a license to all and sundry to carry on their own responsibility. Wherever there are local leaders, their orders should be obeyed by the people. Where there are no leaders and only a handful of men have faith in the programme, they may do what they can, if they have enough self-confidence. They have a right, nay it is their duty, to do so . . . history . . . is full of instances of men who rose to leadership, by sheer force of self-confidence, bravery and tenacity. We too, if we sincerely aspire to *swaraj* and are impatient to attain it, should have similar self-confidence. Our ranks will swell and our hearts strengthen, as the number of our arrests by the government increases.

Much can be done in many other ways besides these. The liquor and foreign cloth shops can be picketed. We can refuse to pay taxes if we have the requisite strength. The lawyers can give up practice. The public can boycott the law courts by refraining from litigation. Government servants can resign their posts. In the midst of the despair reigning all round people quake with fear of losing employment. Such men are unfit for *swaraj*. But why this despair? The number of government servants in the country does not exceed a few hundred thousands. What about the rest? Where are they to go? Even free India will not be able to accommodate a greater number of public servants. A collector then will not need the number of servants he has got today. He will be his own servant. Our starving millions can by no means afford this enormous expenditure. If, therefore, we are sensible enough, let us bid good-bye to government employment, no matter if it is the post of a judge or a peon. Let all who are cooperating with the government in one way or another, be it by paying taxes, keeping titles, or sending children to official schools, etc., withdraw their co-operation in all or as many ways as possible. Then there are women who can stand shoulder to shoulder with men in this struggle.

'I have faith in the righteousness of our cause and the purity of our weapons'

You may take it as my will. It was the message that I desired to impart to you before starting on the march or for the jail. I wish that there should be no suspension or abandonment of the war that commences tomorrow morning or earlier, if I am arrested before that time. I shall eagerly await the news that ten batches are ready as soon as my batch is arrested. I believe there are men in India to complete the work begun by me. I have faith in the righteousness of our cause and the purity of our weapons. And where the means are clean, there God is undoubtedly present with His blessings. And where these three combine, there defeat is an impossibility. A *satyagrahi*, whether free or incarcerated, is ever victorious. He is vanquished only when he forsakes truth and non-violence and turns a deaf ear to the inner voice. If, therefore, there is such a thing as defeat for even a *satyagrahi*, he alone is the cause of it.

God bless you all and keep off all obstacles from the path in the struggle that begins tomorrow.

'The only thing we
have to fear is fear itself'

Presidential inaugural address, 4 March 1933

'A date which will
live in infamy'

Speech to Congress seeking a declaration of war, 8 December 1941
FRANKLIN D. ROOSEVELT

FRANKLIN D. ROOSEVELT SERVED no less than four terms at the White House, from 1933 until his death in 1945. His tenure of the US presidency coincided with two of the cataclysmic events of the 20th century – the Great Depression and the Second World War – and history has judged him according to his handling of those two traumas. That judgement has been, in large measure, a positive one.

Analysts and economists of many political hues have recognized that his exercise of 'big government' from 1933 was necessary to dig the United States out of the economic crisis following the Wall Street Crash of 1929 and the collapse of the banking system. The New Deal – Roosevelt's many-faceted federal programme involving economic measures, a raft of new legislation (including the 1935 Social Security Act) and public works schemes – chimed with the kind of reassurance and practical help that ordinary Americans sorely needed from their government. It delivered him a landslide re-election victory in 1936 and helped shape America for the decades to come.

In an uncertain world, where other embattled nations were falling prey to the dark temptations of fascism or communism, Roosevelt sought to re-empower Americans in his 1933 inaugural speech. The tenor was captured in his historic phrase 'The only thing we have to fear is fear itself.' Rejecting, in almost biblical language, the malpractices of 'unscrupulous money changers', he invoked core pioneer values – the 'moral stimulation of work', 'the joy of achievement', 'discipline and direction under leadership', and above all 'action now'. He also asked for 'broad executive power' to put his ideas into practice, and a strenghtened office of the US presidency was part of his legacy. In truth, aspects of the language varied not so much from what Europe's demagogues and would-be dictators were shouting. But context is everything, and in Roosevelt's America the 'essential democracy' he spoke of had deep roots and endured, as it could not in Italy or Germany in the 1930s.

FRANKLIN D. ROOSEVELT

Born 30 January 1882 in New York, into a prominent family; he was fifth cousin to former President Theodore Roosevelt.

After attending Harvard University and Columbia University Law School, he was called to the Bar and worked for a New York law firm. Married Anna Eleanor Roosevelt, a distant relative, in 1905. He became a Democratic New York state senator (1910) and was appointed as Woodrow Wilson's Assistant Secretary of the Navy (1913–20). In 1921 he contracted polio, the effects of which were largely concealed from the public in later years. He was governor of New York state for three years (1929–32), before winning the first of his consecutive four terms as US president, 1933–45. His first presidency saw increased presidential powers and two phases (1933–4 and 1935–6) of the New Deal, embracing new legislation, public spending, and price support to counteract the Great Depression. He attempted, unsuccessfully, to enlarge the Supreme Court. He built up the US Navy, as fears of war grew, and from 1940 he offered Britain (and later Russia) substantial material assistance. He took the United States into war against Japan after the bombing of Pearl Harbor in 1941. In 1941, he and Winston Churchill produced the Atlantic Charter, declaring the Allies' war aims and laying the basis for the United Nations.

Died 12 April 1945 in Warm Springs, Georgia.

PRESIDENT HOOVER, MR CHIEF JUSTICE, MY FRIENDS: this is a day of national consecration, and I am certain that my fellow Americans expect that on my induction into the presidency I will address them with a candour and a decision which the present situation of our nation impels.

This is pre-eminently the time to speak the truth, the whole truth, frankly and boldly. Nor need we shrink from honestly facing conditions in our country today. This great nation will endure as it has endured, will revive and will prosper.

So first of all let me assert my firm belief that the only thing we have to fear is fear itself – nameless, unreasoning, unjustified terror which paralyses needed efforts to convert retreat into advance.

'The withered leaves of industrial enterprise lie on every side'

In every dark hour of our national life a leadership of frankness and vigour has met with that understanding and support of the people themselves which is essential to victory. I am convinced that you will again give that support to leadership in these critical days. In such a spirit on my part and on yours we face our common difficulties. They concern, thank God, only material things. Values have shrunken to fantastic levels. Taxes have risen, our ability to pay has fallen, government of all kinds is faced by serious curtailment of income, the means of exchange are frozen in the currents of trade, the withered leaves of industrial enterprise lie on every side, farmers find no markets for their produce, the savings of many years in thousands of families are gone.

More important, a host of unemployed citizens face the grim problem of existence, and an equally great number toil with little return. Only a foolish optimist can deny the dark realities of the moment.

Yet our distress comes from no failure of substance. We are stricken by no plague of locusts. Compared with the perils which our forefathers conquered because they believed and were not afraid, we have still much to be thankful for. Nature still offers her bounty and human efforts have multiplied it. Plenty is at our doorstep, but a generous use of it languishes in the very sight of the supply.

Primarily, this is because the rulers of the exchange of mankind's goods have failed through their own stubbornness and their own incompetence, have admitted their failures and abdicated. Practices of the unscrupulous money changers stand indicted in the court of public opinion, rejected by the hearts and minds of men.

True, they have tried, but their efforts have been cast in the pattern of an outworn tradition. Faced by failure of credit, they have proposed only the lending of more money. Stripped of the lure of profit by which to induce our people to follow their false leadership, they have resorted to exhortations, pleading tearfully for restored conditions. They know only the rules of a generation of self-seekers. They have no vision, and when there is no vision the people perish.

'This nation asks for action, and action now'

. . . Happiness lies not in the mere possession of money, it lies in the joy of achievement, in the thrill of creative effort. The joy and moral stimulation of work no longer must be forgotten in the mad chase of evanescent profits. These dark days will be worth all they cost us if they teach us that our true destiny is not to be ministered unto but to minister to ourselves and to our fellow-men . . . This nation asks for action, and action now.

Our greatest primary task is to put people to work. This is no unsolvable problem if we face it wisely and courageously. It can be accompanied in part by direct recruiting by the government itself, treating the task as we would treat the emergency of a war, but at the same time, through this employment, accomplishing greatly needed projects to stimulate and reorganize the use of our national resources.

Hand in hand with this, we must frankly recognize the over-balance of population in our industrial centres and, by engaging on a national scale in a redistribution, endeavour to provide a better use of the land for those best fitted for the land. The task can be helped by definite efforts to raise the values of agricultural products and with this the power to purchase the output of our cities. It can be helped by preventing realistically the tragedy of the growing loss, through foreclosure, of our small homes and our farms. It can be helped by insistence that the federal, state, and local governments act forthwith on the demand that their cost be drastically reduced. It can be helped by the unifying of relief activities which today are often scattered, uneconomical and unequal. It can be helped by national planning for and supervision of all forms of transportation and of communications and other utilities which have a definitely public character. There are many ways in which it can be helped, but it can never be helped merely by talking about it. We must act, and act quickly.

Finally, in our progress toward a resumption of work we require two safeguards against a return of the evils of the old order: there must be a strict supervision of all banking and credits and investments, there must be an end to speculation with other people's money, and there must be provision for an adequate but sound currency.

These are the lines of attack. I shall presently urge upon a new Congress in special session detailed measures for their fulfilment, and I shall seek the immediate assistance of the several states.

'We face the arduous days that lie before us in the warm courage of national unity'

. . . I am prepared under my constitutional duty to recommend the measures that a stricken nation in the midst of a stricken world may require. But in the event that the Congress shall fail to take one of these courses, and in the event that the national emergency is still critical, I shall not evade the clear course of duty that will then confront me. I shall ask the Congress for the one remaining instrument to meet the crisis . . . broad executive power to wage a war against the emergency as great as the power that would be given to me if we were in fact invaded by a foreign foe.

For the trust reposed in me I will return the courage and the devotion that befit the time. I can do no less.

We face the arduous days that lie before us in the warm courage of national unity, with the clear consciousness of seeking old and precious moral values, with the clean satisfaction that comes from the stern performance of duty by old and young alike. We aim at the assurance of a rounded and permanent national life.

We do not distrust the future of essential democracy. The people of the United States have not failed. In their need they have registered a mandate that they want direct, vigorous action. They have asked for discipline and direction under leadership. They have made me the present instrument of their wishes. In the spirit of the gift I will take it.

In this dedication of a nation we humbly ask the blessing of God. May He protect each and every one of us! May He guide me in the days to come.

I N NOVEMBER 1941, US–JAPANESE RELATIONS were extremely tense. The expanding Japanese Empire was still in possession of a swathe of China and had recently begun occupying French Indochina. The United States had reacted with an economic blockade. American spies now indicated that Japanese naval forces were moving towards Southeast Asia – including the oil-rich Dutch East Indies and Malaya – but reports that aircraft carriers were approaching Hawaiian islands were not taken seriously.

On 7 December 1941, Japanese aircraft surprised the US Pacific Fleet at its base in Pearl Harbor, Hawaii. By noon that day, 8 US battleships had been sunk or disabled and 2,403 Americans killed. At the same time, Japanese forces began invasions of Malaya and Siam (Thailand) and struck at other US Pacific possessions. The Pearl Harbor assault had aimed to pre-empt any effective retaliation by the United States. In the short term, it did just that. In the longer term, it woke the sleeping giant.

The Pearl Harbor attack had the effect of clarifying thoughts in a nation still divided between pro-war and isolationist sentiments. On 8 December, Roosevelt asked Congress for a declaration of war against Japan. The attack, which Roosevelt indelibly described as 'a date which will live in infamy' in his six-and-a-half minute address, had hushed the doubters, and only one member of Congress voted against war. Three days later, Germany and Italy declared war on the United States, and the scene was set for the two systems of alliances that determined the outcome of the Second World War.

MR VICE PRESIDENT, MR SPEAKER, Members of the Senate, and of the House of Representatives:

Yesterday, December 7th, 1941 – a date which will live in infamy – the United States of America was suddenly and deliberately attacked by naval and air forces of the Empire of Japan.

The United States was at peace with that nation and, at the solicitation of Japan, was still in conversation with its government and its emperor looking toward the maintenance of peace in the Pacific. Indeed, one hour after Japanese air squadrons had commenced bombing in the American island of Oahu, the Japanese Ambassador to the United States and his colleagues delivered to our Secretary of State a formal reply to a recent American message. And while this reply stated that it seemed useless to continue the existing diplomatic negotiations, it contained no threat or hint of war or of armed attack.

It will be recorded that the distance of Hawaii from Japan makes it obvious that the attack was deliberately planned many days or even weeks ago. During the intervening time, the Japanese government has deliberately sought to deceive the United States by false statements and expressions of hope for continued peace.

The attack yesterday on the Hawaiian islands has caused severe damage to American naval and military forces. I regret to tell you that very many American lives have been lost. In addition, American ships have been reported torpedoed on the high seas between San Francisco and Honolulu.

'The American people in their righteous might will win through to absolute victory'

Yesterday, the Japanese government also launched an attack against Malaya. Last night, Japanese forces attacked Hong Kong. Last night, Japanese forces attacked Guam. Last night, Japanese forces attacked the Philippine Islands. Last night, the Japanese attacked Wake Island. And this morning, the Japanese attacked Midway Island.

Japan has, therefore, undertaken a surprise offensive extending throughout the Pacific area. The facts of yesterday and today speak for themselves. The people of the United States have already formed their opinions and well understand the implications to the very life and safety of our nation.

As commander in chief of the army and navy, I have directed that all measures be taken for our defence. But always will our whole nation remember the character of the onslaught against us.

No matter how long it may take us to overcome this premeditated invasion, the American people in their righteous might will win through to absolute victory.

'Our interests are in grave danger'

I believe that I interpret the will of the Congress and of the people when I assert that we will not only defend ourselves to the uttermost, but will make it very certain that this form of treachery shall never again endanger us.

Hostilities exist. There is no blinking at the fact that our people, our territory, and our interests are in grave danger.

With confidence in our armed forces, with the unbounding determination of our people, we will gain the inevitable triumph – so help us God.

I ask that the Congress declare that since the unprovoked and dastardly attack by Japan on Sunday, December 7th, 1941, a state of war has existed between the United States and the Japanese Empire.

'My patience is now at an end'

Speech demanding the Sudetenland from Czechoslovakia, 26 September 1938

'I am from now on just first soldier of the Reich'

Speech announcing war with Poland, 1 September 1939
ADOLF HITLER

N THE EARLY 1930S, AMONG THE ISSUES propelling Adolf Hitler and the Nazi Party to power in Germany was a widespread resentment at the conditions imposed after the First World War. By the terms of the Treaty of Versailles, the Germany that had existed before 1918 found itself divided in two. The newly independent but landlocked Poland received the so-called 'Polish Corridor' of former German land, giving Poland a route to the North Sea. However, that meant that Germany's easternmost territory – East Prussia – was now disconnected from the rest of Germany.

For Hitler, such territorial loss was both a symbol of German humiliation and a denial of Germany's true greatness. Having rapidly 'Nazified' Germany itself after 1933, imposing party control over the nation's institutions and dispensing with democracy, Hitler and his entourage turned to the larger project of delivering to the German *Volk* (people) their rightful due in terms of *Lebensraum* – the innocuous-sounding 'living space'.

Hitler worked by diplomatic duplicity, brinksmanship and raising the stakes. The German *Volk* did not just mean citizens of the German state – Hitler's term had a much larger sense, implying all those people who might be regarded as culturally, ethnically and linguistically German – and this gave Hitler and the Nazi regime pretexts for their

ADOLF HITLER

Born 20 April 1889 in Braunau, Austria. His artistic ambitions were limited by his failure to gain a place at the Vienna Academy.

He combined casual work with occasional sales of his watercolours and postcards, 1909–13. In 1914 he joined a Bavarian regiment on the Western Front: acted as runner, rose to rank of corporal and was wounded, earning the Iron Cross for bravery. In 1920 he joined the tiny National Socialist German Workers Party (abbreviated to Nazi Party), and was soon leading it. An unsuccessful coup in Munich (1923), against the Bavarian state government, landed him in prison for nine months, where he dictated his political and racial philosophy in *Mein Kampf* (My Struggle). In elections of 1930, the Nazis emerged as the second largest party in Germany's Weimar Republic. Hitler became chancellor in 1933, initially leading a coalition. Within a year, the parliament building (the Reichstag) was burned down, opposition parties silenced, and the Enabling Acts gave Hitler absolute control. He took the presidency

too, on the death of President Hindenburg in 1934, creating the personality cult of the *Führer* (leader). The years 1935–8 saw German rearmament, the (illegal) remilitarization of the Rhineland, and the annexation of Austria and the Sudetenland. In September 1939, the German invasion of Poland triggered the Franco-British declarations of war, initiating the Second World War. Hitler's wartime leadership exhibited increasing distrust of his generals and overconfidence in his own instincts; and Nazi-occupied zones and client regimes perpetrated atrocities on a massive scale, notably the attempted genocide of European Jews in the Holocaust. With Germany facing defeat, Hitler narrowly survived assassination by German officers (July 1944). The *Führer* was reduced to commanding his shattered armies and people from the chancellory bunker in Berlin.

He married his long-term mistress Eva Braun before they committed suicide on the same day, 30 April 1945.

demands and actions. On 12 March 1938, after considerable pressure on the Austrian government, German troops crossed the Austro-German border, and the next day Hitler declared the *Anschluss* (annexation) of the country. It was, though, a move widely welcomed among Austrians, and to which other powers acquiesced.

For now, the situation with Poland was, at least superficially, stabilized through a Polish–German non-aggression pact of 1934. Quite different, though, was the situation of Czechoslovakia and its 'Sudeten Germans' – the German minority in the northwest of the country, who comprised almost a quarter of its population. Czechoslovakia had emerged as an independent republic from the ruins of the Austro-Hungarian Empire in 1918, and Hitler made plain his contempt for the country's 'illegal' existence, and its leader Edvard Beneš (1884–1948), in his speech at the Berlin Sportpalast on 26 September 1938. Having whipped up the grievances of the Sudetenland's Germans, Hitler used the speech for some unabashed sabre-rattling. His declaration that 'my patience is now at an end' could mean nothing less than the threat of war.

The British had already informed Beneš that they would not guarantee Czech security – indeed, France and Britain urged him to accommodate Hitler. By 30 September Hitler had got his way, as Italy, Britain and France gave the green light in the Munich Agreement for German absorption of the Sudetenland. (The Czech government was presented with a *fait accompli*, and had to evacuate the area.) For Britain and France, it was supposed to be an honourable price for a wider European peace. For Hitler, it proved another cost-free success.

. . . I HAVE REALLY IN THESE YEARS pursued a practical peace policy. I have approached all apparently impossible problems with the firm resolve to solve them peacefully even when there was the danger of making more or less serious renunciations on Germany's part. I myself am a front-line soldier and I know how grave a thing war is. I wanted to spare the German people such an evil. Problem after problem I have tackled with the set purpose to make every effort to render possible a peaceful solution.

The most difficult problem which faced me was the relation between Germany and Poland. There was a danger that the conception of a 'heredity enmity' might take possession of our people and of the Polish people. That I wanted to prevent. I know quite well that I should not have succeeded if Poland at that time had had a democratic constitution. For these democracies which are overflowing with phrases about peace are the most bloodthirsty instigators of war. But Poland at that time was governed by no democracy but by a man [General Pilsudski, who staged a military coup in 1926]. In the course of barely a year it was possible to conclude an agreement which, in the first instance for a period of ten years, on principle removed the danger of a conflict. We are all convinced that this agreement will bring with it a permanent pacification. We realize that here are two peoples which must live side by side and that neither of them can destroy the other. A state with a population of thirty-three millions will always strive for an access to the sea. A way to an understanding had therefore to be found.

. . . And now before us stands the last problem that must be solved and will be solved. It is the last territorial claim which I have to make in Europe, but it is the claim from which I will not recede and which, God willing, I will make good.

'The decision now lies in his hands: peace or war'

. . . I have only a few statements still to make. I am grateful to Mr Chamberlain for all his efforts. I have assured him that the German people desires nothing else than peace, but I have also told him that I cannot go back behind the limits set to our patience. I have further assured him, and I repeat it here, that when this problem is solved there is for Germany no further territorial problem in Europe. And I have further assured him that at the moment when Czechoslovakia solves her problems, that means when the Czechs have come to terms with their other minorities, and that peaceably and not through oppression, then I have no further interest in the Czech state. And that is guaranteed to him! We want no Czechs!

But in the same way I desire to state before the German people that with regard to the problem of the Sudeten Germans my patience is now at an end! I have made Mr Beneš an offer which is nothing but the carrying into effect of what he himself has promised. The decision now lies in his hands: peace or war. He will either accept this offer and now at last give to the Germans their freedom or we will go and fetch this freedom for ourselves.

BY MARCH 1939, CZECHOSLOVAKIA as an independent republic was no more. Hitler had shown his disregard for the 1938 Munich Agreement by swallowing up the regions of Bohemia and Moravia, while his ally Hungary had taken its own portion of the country, and Slovakia had adopted its own fascist government.

The lesson for Hitler seemed to be that concerted pressure paid off, and in 1939 that pressure was applied to Poland. Germany demanded land access to East Prussia and threatened the neutral status of the disputed Free City of Danzig (now Gdansk, in Poland), where Nazi influence was strong. Additionally, Hitler's racial theories regarded Slav peoples as 'sub-human', so Poland held the prospect of justifiable additional *Lebensraum* for German expansion. Poland refused to concede, and as with Czechoslovakia Nazi propaganda fuelled patriotic German resentment. In August, the path for action was cleared when Nazi Germany and the communist Soviet Union – bitter ideological foes – concluded a non-aggression pact of convenience, enabling the mutual division of Poland. By 1 September, German Nazis in Danzig were rebelling, and German soldiers had manufactured a counterfeit Polish border clash, giving Hitler the pretexts he needed for full-scale invasion. His speech on that day gave empty reassurance to Britain and France, announced the cynical rapprochement with the Soviet Union, menaced Poland, promised retribution to traitors at home, and demanded 'every sacrifice' from the German people.

Historians debate how far Hitler understood the implications of his actions. On the one hand, his vivid phraseology clearly anticipates a life-or-death struggle ahead. However, his foreign minister, Von Ribbentrop, assured him that Britain and France would appease him yet again over Poland, to avoid a wider war. He was wrong, and by 3 September Britain and France had declared war. But it was too late to save Poland.

I HAVE DECLARED THAT THE FRONTIER between France and Germany is a final one. I have repeatedly offered friendship and, if necessary, the closest cooperation to Britain, but this cannot be offered from one side only. It must find response on the other side. Germany has no interests in the west, and our western wall is for all time the frontier of the Reich on the west. Moreover, we have no aims of any kind there for the future. With this assurance we are in solemn earnest, and as long as others do not violate their neutrality we will likewise take every care to respect it.

I am happy particularly to be able to tell you of one event. You know that Russia and Germany are governed by two different doctrines. There was only one question that had to be cleared up. Germany has no intention of exporting its doctrine. Given the fact that Soviet Russia has no intention of exporting its doctrine to Germany, I no longer see any reason why we should still oppose one another. On both sides we are clear on that. Any struggle between our people would only be of advantage to others. We have, therefore, resolved to conclude a pact which rules out for ever any use of violence between us. It imposes the obligation on us to consult together in certain European questions. It makes possible for us economic cooperation, and above all it assures that the powers of both these powerful states are not wasted against one another. Every attempt of the West to bring about any change in this will fail.

At the same time I should like here to declare that this political decision means a tremendous departure for the future, and that it is a final one. Russia and Germany fought against one another in the World War. That shall and will not happen a second time. In Moscow, too, this pact was greeted exactly as you greet it. I can only endorse word for word the speech of the Russian Foreign Commissar, [Vyacheslav] Molotov.

I am determined to solve the Danzig question; the question of the Corridor and to see to it that a change is made in the relationship between Germany and Poland that shall ensure a peaceful co-existence. In this I am resolved to continue to fight until either the present Polish government is willing to bring about this change or until another Polish government is ready to do so. I am resolved to remove from the German frontiers the element of uncertainty, the everlasting atmosphere of conditions resembling civil war. I will see to it that in the East there is, on the frontier, a peace precisely similar to that on our other frontiers.

'I will not war against women and children'

In this I will take the necessary measures to see that they do not contradict the proposals I have already made known in the Reichstag itself to the rest of the world, that is to say, I will not war against women and children. I have ordered my air force to restrict itself to attacks on military objectives. If, however, the enemy thinks he can from that draw carte blanche on his side to fight by the other methods he will receive an answer that will deprive him of hearing and sight.

This night for the first time Polish regular soldiers fired on our own territory. Since 5.45 a.m. we have been returning the fire, and from now on bombs will be met with bombs. Whoever fights with poison gas will be fought with poison gas. Whoever departs from the rules of humane warfare can only expect that we shall do the same. I will continue this struggle, no matter against whom, until the safety of the Reich and its rights are secured.

'I now ask sacrifices of the German people'

For six years now I have been working on the building up of the German defences. Over 90 milliards have in that time been spent on the building up of these defence forces. They are now the best equipped and are above all comparison with what they were in 1914. My trust in them is unshakeable. When I called up these forces and when I now ask sacrifices of the German people and if necessary every sacrifice, then I have a right to do so, for I also am today absolutely ready, just as we were formerly, to make every personal sacrifice.

I am asking of no German man more than I myself was ready throughout four years at any time to do. There will be no hardships for Germans to which I myself will not submit. My whole life henceforth belongs more than ever to my people. I am from now on just first soldier of the German Reich. I have once more put on that coat that was the most sacred and dear to me. I will not take it off again until victory is secured, or I will not survive the outcome.

'My whole life has been nothing but one long struggle for my people . . . and for Germany'

As a National Socialist and as a German soldier I enter upon this struggle with a stout heart. My whole life has been nothing but one long struggle for my people, for its restoration, and for Germany. There was only one watchword for that struggle: faith in this people. One word I have never learned: that is, surrender.

If, however, anyone thinks that we are facing a hard time, I should ask him to remember that once a Prussian king, with a ridiculously small state, opposed a stronger coalition, and in three wars finally came out successful because that state had that stout heart that we need in these times. I would, therefore, like to assure all the world that a November 1918 will never be repeated in German history. Just as I myself am ready at any time to stake my life – anyone can take it for my people and for Germany – so I ask the same of all others.

Whoever, however, thinks he can oppose this national command, whether directly or indirectly, shall fall. We have nothing to do with traitors. We are all faithful to our old principle. It is quite unimportant whether we ourselves live, but it is essential that our people shall live, that Germany shall live. The sacrifice that is demanded of us is not greater than the sacrifice that many generations have made. If we form a community closely bound together by vows, ready for anything, resolved never to surrender, then our will will master every hardship and difficulty. And I would like to close with the declaration that I once made when I began the struggle for power in the Reich. I then said: 'If our will is so strong that no hardship and suffering can subdue it, then our will and our German might shall prevail.'

'Peace for our time'

NEVILLE CHAMBERLAIN

Statement following the Munich Conference, 30 September 1938

RARELY HAVE SO FEW WORDS decided a historical reputation as happened in the case of British Prime Minister Neville Chamberlain. The short statement he delivered as he stepped off a plane on 30 September 1938 would become a monument to his failure. He was returning from the summit in Munich, where, along with France's Prime Minister Edouard Daladier and Italy's dictator Benito Mussolini, he sought to address Hitler's demand to annexe Czechoslovakia's Sudetenland, with its ethnically German population. Hitler had already made clear that his 'patience was at an end', a threat of military action should his demands be rebuffed.

For Chamberlain, the prize was peace in Europe, which he announced on 30 September as 'peace for our time'. For him, as for many politicians of the era, the memories of the sheer terribleness of the First Word War remained vivid, and the task of a British statesman, facing a resurgent and nationalistic Germany, was to avoid such a disaster again. It was a widely shared goal, and one reinforced by Britain's military unpreparedness. But it became known, pejoratively, as the policy of 'appeasement'. The tangible results were that an ever-bolder Hitler was encouraged in his ambitions. These included remilitarizing the Rhineland area and massively building up the German armed forces (including, secretly, creating a new air force, the *Luftwaffe*) – all in contravention of the 1919 Treaty of Versailles – as well as annexing Austria in March 1938.

Chamberlain genuinely had misgivings about the Treaty of Versailles and regarded some of the terms imposed on Germany as over-harsh, so there was a reservoir of sympathy for German aspirations in general. Chamberlain also felt, with regard to the Sudetenland, that Hitler had a point. Czechoslovakia, as an independent republic, was created in 1918 out of the old Austro-Hungarian Empire, and the presence of such a large ethnically German minority within its borders did raise questions. On 24 March 1938, Britain declared that it would not guarantee the security of Czecho-slovakia, and Britain and France then put pressure on the Czech government to come to terms with Hitler, but successive plans foundered.

At Munich, on 27–29 September, an invasion of Czechoslovakia – and the prospect of any wider war – was averted by an agreement that Germany

NEVILLE CHAMBERLAIN

Born 18 March 1869 in Birmingham, England.

His father, Joseph, was a prominent 19th-century radical Liberal (and then Liberal Unionist), and his half-brother Austen was foreign secretary in 1924–7. After education at Rugby School, and an early career in industry, he became Birmingham's lord mayor in 1915 (as his father had been), and the next year briefly served Lloyd George's wartime coalition government as Director General of National Service. His Parliamentary career began in 1918, as a Conservative MP. In the 1920s he rose through successive government appointments as paymaster general, a competent minister for health, and on the formation of a coalition government in 1931 he became chancellor of the exchequer until 1937. He succeeded Stanley Baldwin as prime minister in May 1937 and, faced with the rise of Hitler, Mussolini and the Spanish Civil War, spent much of the time absorbed by foreign crises. His two years of negotiations – the policy of 'appeasement', intended to preserve peace – was bankrupt by March 1939. As war commenced, British military failures, notably the campaign to protect Norway, lost him the confidence of Parliament, forcing his resignation in May 1940. He remained for a while in Winston Churchill's Cabinet as Lord President of the Council of War.

Died 9 November 1940 in London.

could have the Sudetenland but not other parts of the country. (The Czechs were not represented at the conference.) The agreement sacrificed Czech security for the larger goal of Anglo-French peace with Germany. On his return to Britain, Chamberlain sought to represent the conference as a diplomatic success in his brief statement, casting an optimistic spin on Anglo-German relations. But even he privately thought Hitler was 'half-mad' by this time, and British rearmament stepped up a pace.

The Munich Agreement was appeasement's last gasp, patently so when, on 15 March 1939, Germany simply ignored it and sent troops into the Czech regions of Bohemia and Moravia. The fatal flaw of appeasement's logic was that it depended on Hitler being a man who honoured agreements and who told the truth about his ambitions. By the end of March, Britain drew a line in the sand and promised Poland – Hitler's next likely target – that any attack by Germany would prompt a British declaration of war. In April 1939, peacetime military conscription took place for the first time in British history. By August, war was all but inevitable, and in September that inevitability came to pass.

Perhaps surprisingly, Chamberlain, his reputation battered, continued as prime minister until May 1940, until the chorus of Members of Parliament demanding his resignation became too loud. Although efforts to rehabilitate his reputation have been made, he remains the apostle of the failed policy of appeasement.

WE, THE GERMAN *FÜHRER* and chancellor, and the British prime minister, have had a further meeting today and are agreed in recognizing that the question of Anglo-German relations is of the first importance for our two countries and for Europe.

We regard the agreement signed last night and the Anglo-German Naval Agreement as symbolic of the desire of our two peoples never to go to war with one another again.

We are resolved that the method of consultation shall be the method adopted to deal with any other questions that may concern our two countries, and we are determined to continue our efforts to remove possible sources of difference, and thus to contribute to assure the peace of Europe.

Later, in front of 10 Downing Street, he added:

MY GOOD FRIENDS, for the second time in our history, a British prime minister has returned from Germany bringing peace with honour. I believe it is peace for our time. Go home and get a nice quiet sleep.

‘It is imperative
that we agree to
conclude the pact’

JOSEPH STALIN
*Speech to the Politburo about the Nazi–Soviet Pact,
19 August 1939*

N THE POLARIZED POLITICAL ATMOSPHERE of Europe during the 1930s, adherents of left-wing and right-wing movements often fought tenaciously – mostly with words, but also with deeds. The clearest example was in Spain, which dissolved into brutal civil war in 1936. At a national level, two dictatorships epitomized the ideological divide: Hitler's Nazi Germany and Stalin's communist Soviet Union (USSR). In the democracies, many people who feared the spread of Soviet influence harboured approval of Hitler's ruthless political oppression at home, seeing him as a bulwark against international communism. But, with Britain and France attempting to appease Hitler's ambitions, others regarded the Soviet Union as the only reliable, determined foe of the fascist threat.

The whole world, whatever its shade of opinion, was therefore stunned when it was revealed that the Soviet Union and Hitler's Third Reich had concluded a non-aggression pact in August 1939. (It is known as the Nazi-Soviet Pact, the Hitler–Stalin Pact, and also as the Molotov–Ribbentrop Pact after the foreign ministers who signed it.) According to its terms, not only would Germany and the Soviet Union not threaten one another directly, they would also not support a third party that threatened either one of them. The cynical nature of this marriage of convenience, and its timing, became clear to all as German *Stuka* dive-bombers and *Panzer* tanks began their onslaught on Poland in September 1939. For Germany, which proposed the pact, it ensured Soviet acquiescence in the Polish attack and meant that the Soviet Union would not support an almost inevitable declaration of war on Germany by the British and French.

For Stalin, many of the pact's benefits were contained in its secret protocol, whereby Germany and the Soviet Union divided Central and Eastern Europe into the zones they intended to dominate. Poland was to be carved up at an agreed border, and

JOSEPH STALIN

Born Joseph Vissarionovich Dzhugashvili on 21 December 1879 in Gori, Georgia, the son of a cobbler.

After training as a priest, in 1898 he became active in the revolutionary underground, and was twice exiled to Siberia (1902, 1913). He adopted the symbolically resonant name Stalin ('man of steel') in 1910. He played an active role in the Russian October Revolution (1917), and in 1922 he became general secretary of the Party Central Committee and built up his influence and a reputation to go with his name. After Lenin's death (1924) he isolated and disgraced his political rivals, including Trotsky, and by 1928 had manoeuvred himself into a pre-eminent position of power. In 1928 he began the collectivization of agriculture in which millions of peasants perished, and the first five-year plan for the forced industrialization of the economy. Between 1934 and 1938 he purged the party, government, armed forces and intelligentsia, putting leading figures through predetermined 'show trials', depleting the military of its skilled officers, and imprisoning, exiling or shooting millions of so-called 'enemies of the people'. After the German invasion of the Soviet Union (1941), he joined Roosevelt and Churchill as one of the 'Big Three' Allied leaders, who determined the war's outcome. After 1945, he returned to patterns of domestic repression and fostered the installation of pro-Soviet governments in postwar Eastern Europe: East–West tensions laid the foundations of the Cold War alignment of power blocs that would persist for 50 years.

Died 5 March 1953 in Moscow.

on 17 September 1939 Soviet forces moved to swallow up the eastern part of Poland, on the bogus pretext of providing for its safety. December 1939 saw the Soviet invasion of Finland, followed in June 1940 by the forcible annexation of the Baltic States (Latvia, Estonia and Lithuania) – all allowed for in the pact. And if Hitler were to be believed, the pact also safeguarded a militarily unprepared Soviet Union from German encroachment.

Stalin's speech to the Soviet Politburo on 19 August 1939 reveals his deliberations over the pact, which was signed on 23 August. The speech was not made public until 1991. It is an exercise in ice-cold *Realpolitik* in its analysis of possible scenarios. War and revolution are couched purely in terms of geopolitical advantage or ideological benefit, rather than as issues of death, destruction and horror. Issues of morality and principle are entirely absent. But while there is a shrewd, clinical intelligence at work, there are also fatal flaws. First, there is an overestimation of the ability of foreign communist parties to foment revolutions. Second – and surprisingly, given the bottomless cynicism that is apparent – Stalin made the same error as did Europe's appeasing politicians. He invested trust in Hitler. When Germany invaded the Soviet Union in June 1941, the pact's worthlessness was plain to see.

THE QUESTION OF WAR AND PEACE has entered a critical phase for us. Its solution depends entirely on the position which will be taken by the Soviet Union. We are absolutely convinced that if we conclude a mutual assistance pact with France and Great Britain, Germany will back off from Poland and seek a modus vivendi with the Western Powers. War would be avoided, but further events could prove dangerous for the USSR.

On the other hand, if we accept Germany's proposal, that you know, and conclude a non-aggression pact with her, she will certainly invade Poland, and the intervention of France and England is then unavoidable. Western Europe would be subjected to serious upheavals and disorder. In this case we will have a great opportunity to stay out of the conflict, and we could plan the opportune time for us to enter the war.

The experience of the last 20 years has shown that in peacetime the communist movement is never strong enough for the Bolshevik Party to seize power. The dictatorship of such a party will only become possible as the result of a major war.

Our choice is clear. We must accept the German proposal and, with a refusal, politely send the Anglo-French mission home.

It is not difficult to envisage the importance which we would obtain in this way of proceeding. It is obvious, for us, that Poland will be destroyed even before England and France are able to come to her assistance. In this case Germany will cede to us a part of Poland . . . Our immediate advantage will be to take Poland all the way to the gates of Warsaw, as well as Ukrainian Galicia.

This is in the case that Germany would emerge victorious from the war. We must, however, envisage the possibilities that will result from the defeat as well as from the victory of Germany. In case of her defeat, a Sovietization of Germany will unavoidably occur and a communist government will be created. We should not forget that a Sovietized Germany would bring about great danger, if this Sovietization is the result of German defeat in a transient war. England and France will still be strong enough to seize Berlin and to destroy a Soviet Germany. We would be unable to come effectually to the aid of our Bolshevik comrades in Germany.

'The USSR will presently assist Germany economically'

Therefore, our goal is that Germany should carry out the war as long as possible so that England and France grow weary and become exhausted to such a degree that they are no longer in a position to put down a Sovietized Germany.

Our position is this. Maintaining neutrality and waiting for the right time, the USSR will presently assist Germany economically and supply her with raw materials and provisions. It goes without saying that our assistance should not exceed a certain limit; we must not send so much as to weaken our economy or the power of our army.

At the same time we must carry on active communist propaganda in the Anglo-French bloc, and predominantly in France. We must expect that in that country in times of war, the Party should quit the legal means of warfare and turn underground. We know that their work will demand great sacrifices, but our French comrades will not hesitate. Their first task will be to decompose and demoralize the army and the police. If this preparatory work is fulfilled properly, the safety of Soviet Germany will be assured, and this will contribute to the Sovietization of France.

For the realization of these plans it is essential that the war continue for as long as possible, and all forces, which we have available in Western Europe and the Balkans, should be directed toward this goal.

Now let us consider the second possibility, a German victory. Some think that this would confront us with a serious danger. There is some truth in this, but it would be a mistake to regard the danger as so close at hand or as great as has been proposed.

If Germany should prove to be victorious, she will leave the war too weakened to start a war with the USSR within a decade at least. She will have to supervise the occupation of France and England and restore herself.

'Germany will be too busy elsewhere to turn against us'

In addition, a victorious Germany will have vast colonies; the exploitation of those and their adaptation to German methods will also absorb Germany during several decades.

Obviously, this Germany will be too busy elsewhere to turn against us. There is one additional thing that will strengthen our safety. In a conquered France, the French Communist Party will always be very strong. A communist revolution will unavoidably break out, and we will be able to exploit the situation and to come to the aid of France and make her our ally. In addition, all the nations that fall under the 'protection' of a victorious Germany will become our allies. This presents for us a broad field of action for the initiation of world revolution.

'It is in the interest of the USSR ... that a war breaks out between the Reich and the capitalist Anglo-French bloc'

Comrades, I have presented my considerations to you. I repeat that it is in the interest of the USSR, the workers' homeland, that a war breaks out between the Reich and the capitalist Anglo-French bloc. Everything should be done so that it drags out as long as possible with the goal of weakening both sides. For this reason, it is imperative that we agree to conclude the pact proposed by Germany, and then work in such a way that this war, once it is declared, will be prolonged maximally. We must strengthen our propaganda work in the belligerent countries, in order to be prepared when the war ends.

'Blood, toil tears and sweat'

'We shall fight on the beaches'

'This was their finest hour'

'Never in the field of human conflict'

'An iron curtain has descended'

Speeches on the Second World War and its aftermath, 1940–6
WINSTON CHURCHILL

OF ALL BRITISH POLITICAL FIGURES of the 20th-century, one stands out as the pre-eminent speechmaker: Winston Churchill. To an extent, the continuing resonance of his Second World War speeches is a reflection of the turbulent times in which they were made. But beyond that, history has accorded them a central role in maintaining Britain's war effort, especially in 1940–1 when a relatively vulnerable country stood alone against the might of the German war machine. Churchill took the events of the war, often dispiriting in themselves, and interpreted them in a way that turned potential doom and despondency into self-belief, defiance and purposefulness. By stressing – even exaggerating – what was at stake, he cast his beloved British Empire in a global drama about saving civilization. There was a Messianic element, and it flattered and empowered his listeners, making them believe that war against Nazi Germany was a battle worth fighting and one which they could win.

Early on in his career, Churchill felt intellectually inferior to many of his peers because he had not pursued a university education. He regretted the lack of practice in public speaking that he would have gained in university debates. He also suffered from a slight lisp and a stammer, so from the beginning he set about drafting his speeches so as to avoid patterns of everyday speech that he found difficult. He visited speech therapists and practised words and gestures in front of a mirror. He sometimes spent weeks constructing speeches, refining and improving them, and he came up with a style that was unique. His vocabulary was extremely large, filled with inventive word play, alliteration, vivid imagery and metaphor.

WINSTON CHURCHILL

Born 30 November 1874 at Blenheim Palace, Oxfordshire, England, the eldest son of Lord Randolph Churchill and Jennie Jerome (daughter of an American tycoon).

Educated at Harrow School and the Royal Military Academy, Sandhurst. He served as a soldier and war correspondent, seeing action at the Battle of Omdurman (1897) in the Sudan and against the Boers in South Africa, where he escaped from captivity. Elected to Parliament as a Conservative MP in 1900, he switched to the governing Liberal Party in 1904, rising to become home secretary (1910) and then First Lord of the Admiralty (1911). In 1915, he took responsibility for the failed Gallipoli (Dardanelles) campaign against the Turks and left politics for the Western Front, before returning as minister of munitions (1917). He was secretary for war and air (1919–21) and then, supporting the Conservatives, a relatively unsuccessful chancellor of the exchequer (1924–9). After nearly a decade of alienation

from the Conservative Party leadership, he joined Chamberlain's War Cabinet in September 1939 as First Lord of the Admiralty, before succeeding him as prime minister in May 1940, when he created a new coalition government. A notably hands-on and energetic wartime leader, he established a mood of defiance through his speeches and worked hard for a transatlantic alliance: he and President Roosevelt elaborated their war aims in the 1941 Atlantic Charter. When peace returned, he became Leader of the Opposition after the Labour Party won the 1945 election; he spoke widely in support of the United Nations and warned about the Cold War and nuclear threats. He was returned to the premiership in 1951, knighted in 1953, and he retired in 1955. The 'greatest living Englishman', as he became known, enjoyed bricklaying, landscape painting, historical writing, and copious amounts of champagne and cigars.

Died 24 January 1965 in London; he received a state funeral.

His style did not always suit the mood of the times. His big set-piece speeches in the House of Commons, to which he was first elected in 1900, were often criticized as being out of touch. During his 'wilderness years' of the 1930s, as a backbench MP, he delivered apocalyptic messages so often that politicians and the public alike were tempted to ignore them. But his conviction about Nazi Germany – that it was insatiably expansionist – turned out to be well founded. As Britain declared war in September 1939, Churchill was recalled to the Cabinet. By 10 May 1940, with German forces invading the Low Countries, Prime Minister Neville Chamberlain's credibility was shattered and Churchill's moment had come. Chamberlain recommended to King George VI that Churchill take up the premiership. It was perhaps his best decision, and for Churchill it felt as though 'all my past life had been but a preparation for this hour'. On 13 May, he explained to the House of Commons what he had to offer the country.

ON FRIDAY EVENING LAST I RECEIVED FROM HIS MAJESTY the mission to form a new administration. It was the evident will of Parliament and the nation that this should be conceived on the broadest possible basis and that it should include all parties. I have already completed the most important part of this task.

. . . I now invite the House by a resolution to record its approval of the steps taken and declare its confidence in the new government. The resolution is: 'That this House welcomes the formation of a government representing the united and inflexible resolve of the nation to prosecute the war with Germany to a victorious conclusion.'

'I have nothing to offer but blood, toil, tears, and sweat'

To form an administration of this scale and complexity is a serious undertaking in itself. But we are in the preliminary phase of one of the greatest battles in history. We are in action at many other points – in Norway and in Holland – and we have to be prepared in the Mediterranean. The air battle is continuing, and many preparations have to be made here at home.

In this crisis I think I may be pardoned if I do not address the House at any length today, and I hope that any of my friends and colleagues or former colleagues who are affected by the political reconstruction will make all allowances for any lack of ceremony with which it has been necessary to act.

I say to the House as I said to ministers who have joined this government, I have nothing to offer but blood, toil, tears and sweat. We have before us an ordeal of the most grievous kind. We have before us many, many months of struggle and suffering.

You ask, what is our policy? I say it is to wage war by land, sea, and air. War with all our might and with all the strength God has given us, and to wage war against a monstrous tyranny never surpassed in the dark and lamentable catalogue of human crime. That is our policy.

You ask, what is our aim? I can answer in one word. It is victory. Victory at all costs – victory in spite of all terrors – victory, however long and hard the road may be, for without victory there is no survival.

Let that be realized. No survival for the British Empire, no survival for all that the British Empire has stood for, no survival for the urge, the impulse of the ages, that mankind shall move forward towards his goal.

I take up my task in buoyancy and hope. I feel sure that our cause will not be suffered to fail among men. I feel entitled at this juncture, at this time, to claim the aid of all and to say, 'Come then, let us go forward together with our united strength.'

WITHIN TWO WEEKS OF TAKING OFFICE, Churchill faced disaster. Belgium's King Leopold surrendered, opening his country to the German forces, and the Netherlands had been knocked out of the war. The British Expeditionary Force (BEF) and a large body of French troops were caught in a German pincer movement and cut off. France was losing battles and the will to fight, and without the troops of the BEF it was unlikely that Britain would be able to resist a German invasion of the homeland. Churchill dramatically told his Cabinet that 'if this long island story of ours is to end at last, let it end only when each of us lies choking in his own blood upon the ground'.

A miracle was called for – and it arrived, in the shape of the Dunkirk evacuation. As soldiers fought a rearguard action to hold the Germans at bay, over 850 Royal Navy, Merchant Navy and volunteer civilian boats risked the *Luftwaffe* planes overhead to ferry troops back to England from Dunkirk. Astonishingly, 335,000 British and French troops were rescued between 27 May and 4 June. But all their equipment was left behind, much of it destroyed so as not to be of use to the enemy. As Churchill observed in his speech to the House of Commons on 4 June, 'wars are not won by evacuations'. But Dunkirk seemed, nevertheless, a kind of deliverance. For Churchill it was a pretext for a show of defiance. It was also, in the final phrase of his speech, an appeal for transatlantic help, for a time when 'the New World . . . steps forth to the rescue'.

I HAVE, MYSELF, FULL CONFIDENCE that if all do their duty, if nothing is neglected, and if the best arrangements are made, as they are being made, we shall prove ourselves once again able to defend our island home, to ride out the storm of war, and to outlive the menace of tyranny, if necessary for years, if necessary alone. At any rate, that is what we are going to try to do. That is the resolve of His Majesty's government – every man of them. That is the will of Parliament and the nation. The British Empire and the French Republic, linked together in their cause and in their need, will defend to the death their native soil, aiding each other like good comrades to the utmost of their strength.

Even though large tracts of Europe and many old and famous states have fallen or may fall into the grip of the Gestapo and all the odious apparatus of Nazi rule, we shall not flag or fail. We shall go on to the end, we shall fight in France, we shall fight on the seas and oceans, we shall fight with growing confidence and growing strength in the air, we shall defend our island, whatever the cost may be, we shall fight on the beaches, we shall fight on the landing grounds, we shall fight in the fields and in the streets, we shall fight in the hills; we shall never surrender, and even if, which I do not for a moment believe, this island or a large part of it were subjugated and starving, then our empire beyond the seas, armed and guarded by the British fleet, would carry on the struggle, until, in God's good time, the New World, with all its power and might, steps forth to the rescue and the liberation of the old.

BY 16 JUNE 1940, a new French government under Marshal Pétain was desperately suing for peace with Germany. Opportunistically, Italy, under its fascist dictator Benito Mussolini, had joined the war on Germany's side, hoping to snap up French territory. Belgium, Denmark, the Netherlands and Norway were already under Nazi sway. Even Churchill's oratorical transformation of the Dunkirk evacuation into a 'miracle of deliverance' could not conceal the bleakness of the situation. A conquered France would mean German forces just across the English Channel – and so far, no country had withstood German attack. Having flown to France on 11 June, to plead in vain with French politicians to continue the fight, Churchill now addressed the House of Commons in a speech that was broadcast on 18 June. He made a last-ditch effort to bolster the Anglo-French alliance, referring to a rather fanciful union of the two countries; but, more realistically, he prepared the country for a 'Battle of Britain', in which victory would deliver 'broad, sunlit uplands', but defeat would mean 'a new Dark Age'.

WE DO NOT YET KNOW WHAT WILL HAPPEN in France or whether the French resistance will be prolonged, both in France and in the French Empire overseas. The French government will be throwing away great

SPEECHES THAT CHANGED THE WORLD

opportunities and casting adrift their future if they do not continue the war in accordance with their treaty obligations, from which we have not felt able to release them. The House will have read the historic declaration in which, at the desire of many Frenchmen – and of our own hearts – we have proclaimed our willingness at the darkest hour in French history to conclude a union of common citizenship in this struggle. However matters may go in France or with the French government, or other French governments, we in this island and in the British Empire will never lose our sense of comradeship with the French people. If we are now called upon to endure what they have been suffering, we shall emulate their courage, and if final victory rewards our toils they shall share the gains, aye, and freedom shall be restored to all. We abate nothing of our just demands; not one jot or tittle do we recede. Czechs, Poles, Norwegians, Dutch, Belgians have joined their causes to our own. All these shall be restored.

What General Weygand [the French commander-in-chief] called the Battle of France is over. I expect that the Battle of Britain is about to begin. Upon this battle depends the survival of Christian civilization. Upon it depends our own British life, and the long continuity of our institutions and our empire. The whole fury and might of the enemy must very soon be turned on us.

ʻHitler knows that he will have to break usʼ

Hitler knows that he will have to break us in this island or lose the war. If we can stand up to him, all Europe may be free and the life of the world may move forward into broad, sunlit uplands. But if we fail, then the whole world, including the United States, including all that we have known and cared for, will sink into the abyss of a new Dark Age made more sinister, and perhaps more protracted, by the lights of perverted science.

Let us therefore brace ourselves to our duties, and so bear ourselves that if the British Empire and its Commonwealth last for a thousand years, men will still say, 'This was their finest hour.'

TWO MONTHS LATER, the 'Battle of Britain' – the largest aerial battle in history – neared its climax. Hitler was cautious about a sea invasion, especially since Britain's navy remained strong. His pre-condition was absolute air superiority, and his sanguine *Luftwaffe* commander, Reichsmarschall Goering, assured him that this would be easy. It meant destroying Fighter Command – the branch of the RAF whose role was to shoot down enemy aircraft. Battle proper had commenced in mid-July, but the intensity had stepped up with the *Luftwaffe*'s mass attacks of *Adler Tag* (Eagle Day) on 13 August. By late August, German bombing raids against fighter airbases were relentless. They would stretch Britain's defensive capability almost to breaking point.

Britain's frontline air defence hinged on a very small number of men – the fighter pilots, whose life-and-death dogfights were often watched by the population below. Churchill had observed aerial action through his binoculars on several occasions, and on 16 August he was present in No. 11 Group's operations room, which coordinated fighter forces over Southeast England. He found himself deeply moved by the efforts put in by the pilots and their ground organization. That day, he began elaborating the speech he would give four days later, which would honour both the fighter pilots and their less 'glamorous' bomber colleagues. After the speech, the Battle of Britain pilots were known simply as 'the Few'.

THE GREAT AIR BATTLE which has been in progress over this island for the last few weeks has recently attained a high intensity. It is too soon to assign limits either to its scale or to its duration. We must certainly expect that greater efforts will be made by the enemy than any he has so far put forth.

. . . The gratitude of every home in our island, in our empire, and indeed throughout the world, except in the abodes of the guilty, goes out to the British airmen who, undaunted by odds, unwearied in their constant challenge and mortal danger, are turning the tide of the World War by their prowess and by their devotion. Never in the field of human conflict was so much owed by so many to so few. All hearts go out to the fighter pilots, whose brilliant actions we see with our own eyes day after day. But we must never forget that all the time, night after night, month after month, our bomber squadrons travel far into Germany, find their targets in the darkness by the highest navigational skill, aim their attacks, often under the heaviest fire, often with serious loss, with deliberate careful discrimination, and inflict shattering blows upon the whole of the technical and war-making structure of the Nazi power.

WHEN, FROM LATE 1944, the defeat of Nazi Germany looked inevitable, so the mutual interests of the Allies seemed set to diverge. One fact was undeniable: the western advance of the Soviet Red Army, combined with the Soviet Union's huge suffering in the war, meant Stalin would expect a large zone of influence in Central and Eastern Europe. Churchill – who, despite the wartime alliance, regarded communism as corrosive and dangerous – became increasingly alarmed at the extent to which Stalin began foisting puppet regimes onto the countries he had occupied or 'liberated', despite agreements to restore pre-war governments or hold free elections.

In the immediate aftermath of war, Churchill – no longer prime minister, but still a statesman of renown – set out to articulate the dangers of the emerging power-bloc divide, the threat of Soviet expansionism, and the necessity of finding a route for peaceful coexistence in the nuclear age. When visiting the United States in March 1946, he used a degree ceremony at Fulton, Missouri, to voice his hopes for the new United Nations Organization and the Anglo-American 'special relationship', as well as his fears about the 'iron curtain' that was descending across Europe.

A SHADOW HAS FALLEN upon the scenes so lately lighted by the Allied victory. Nobody knows what Soviet Russia and its communist international organization intends to do in the immediate future, or what are the limits, if any, to their expansive and proselytizing tendencies. I have a strong admiration and regard for the valiant Russian people and for my wartime comrade, Marshal Stalin. There is deep sympathy and goodwill in Britain – and I doubt not here also – towards the peoples of all the Russias and a resolve to persevere through many differences and rebuffs in establishing lasting friendships. We understand the Russian need to be secure on her western frontiers by the removal of all possibility of German aggression. We welcome Russia to her rightful place among the leading nations of the world. We welcome her flag upon the seas. Above all, we welcome, or should welcome, constant, frequent and growing contacts between the Russian people and our own people on both sides of the Atlantic. It is my duty however . . . to place before you certain facts about the present position in Europe.

From Stettin in the Baltic to Trieste in the Adriatic an iron curtain has descended across the continent. Behind that line lie all the capitals of the ancient states of Central and Eastern Europe. Warsaw, Berlin, Prague, Vienna, Budapest, Belgrade, Bucharest and Sofia, all these famous cities and the populations around them lie in what I must call the Soviet sphere, and all are subject in one form or another not only to Soviet influence but to a very high and, in some cases, increasing measure of control from Moscow. Athens alone – Greece with its immortal glories – is free to decide its future at an election under British, American and French observation. The Russian-dominated Polish government has been encouraged to make enormous and wrongful inroads upon Germany, and mass expulsions of millions of Germans on a scale grievous and undreamed-of are now taking place. The communist parties, which were very small in all these Eastern states of Europe, have been raised to pre-eminence and power far beyond their numbers and are seeking everywhere to obtain totalitarian control . . .

. . . The safety of the world . . . requires a new unity in Europe, from which no nation should be permanently outcast . . . Surely we should work with conscious purpose for a grand pacification of Europe, within the structure of the United Nations and in accordance with our Charter.

'The flame of French resistance must not and shall not die'

CHARLES DE GAULLE

Radio appeal to create the Free French forces, 18 June 1940

THE RAPID COLLAPSE OF THE FRENCH MILITARY in June 1940, in the face of the Nazi offensive, sent shock and panic throughout France. Winston Churchill pressed the French to continue fighting, and even proposed a formal union of the two countries, but it was grabbing at straws. On 14 June German soldiers entered Paris, which was undefended, and on 16 June the French Prime Minister Paul Reynaud resigned, to be replaced by a hero from a previous war – Marshal Philippe Pétain. His new government immediately set about negotiating surrender.

Despite the generally lacklustre performance of the French army, one commander of a tank division had distinguished himself: General Charles de Gaulle. In early May he was a colonel whose opinionated stance on the necessity for mechanized-warfare tactics (as the German used) had stunted his career path. But sudden, rapid promotion took him into the French Cabinet in early June as under-secretary of defence. Refusing to accept the defeatism of Pétain, he escaped to Britain, where thousands of French troops had landed after evacuation from Dunkirk in early June. With Churchill's backing, he set himself up as an alternative French leader to Pétain. On 18 June, the same day as Churchill proclaimed the approach of the 'Battle of Britain', de Gaulle made a broadcast to rally those French men and women in a position to continue the fight. Perhaps the most famous phrase associated with his appeal – 'France has lost a battle. But France has not lost the war!' – was never actually broadcast.

Marshal Pétain became head of the technically neutral (but increasingly collaborationist) Vichy French regime, in the south of France, an ignoble role that resulted in his standing trial for treason after the war. By contrast, de Gaulle became a symbol of French defiance and worked hard to persuade the British, the Americans and French Resistance groups to accept him as the head of the Free French forces. The prickly de Gaulle had a difficult relationship with Churchill, and an even more problematic one with US President Roosevelt, and he often felt (and was) sidelined by the Anglo-American

CHARLES DE GAULLE

Born 22 November 1890 in Lille, France. A career soldier, he graduated from the Military Academy St Cyr in 1912 and joined an infantry regiment.

He served as a lieutenant in the First World War, during which he was wounded several times and captured at Verdun. He served in Poland as a major and military adviser during the Russo-Polish War (1919–21), and then studied and lectured at war college. His book *The Army of the Future* (1934), advocating a mechanization of the infantry and the widespread use of tanks, made him unpopular with the military establishment. His talents belatedly recognized, he was promoted to general and hoisted into the French government as France fell to Nazi Germany, in June 1940. He fled to England and appealed for the French to continue fighting. By 1944 de Gaulle had gained supreme control of the French war effort outside France and was increasingly recognized as the legitimate leader of a French government in exile. During 1944–6, he led provisional French governments but resigned over new constitutional arrangements. When France faced a crisis over war in Algeria (1958), he became prime minister and later that year, after constitutional changes, the first President of the Fifth Republic. He pursued a nationalistic foreign policy, making France a nuclear power and stressing independence from Britain and the United States while developing close relations with West Germany. After what he took to be a no-confidence vote in him, following a referendum, he resigned in 1969.

He survived a number of assassination plots, and died 9 November 1970 in Colombey-les-Deux-Eglises, France.

axis. Nevertheless, in the end it was General de Gaulle who entered a liberated Paris in triumph on 26 August 1944, and who went on to become the country's president in 1958.

THE LEADERS WHO, FOR MANY YEARS PAST, have been at the head of the French armed forces, have set up a government. Alleging the defeat of our armies, this government has entered into negotiations with the enemy with a view to bringing about a cessation of hostilities. It is quite true that we were, and still are, overwhelmed by enemy mechanized forces, both on the ground and in the air. It was the tanks, the planes and the tactics of the Germans, far more than the fact that we were outnumbered, that forced our armies to retreat. It was the German tanks, planes and tactics that provided the element of surprise which brought our leaders to their present plight.

But has the last word been said? Must we abandon all hope? Is our defeat final and irremediable? To these questions I answer – No!

Speaking in full knowledge of the facts, I ask you to believe me when I say that the cause of France is not lost. The very factors that brought about our defeat may one day lead us to victory. For, remember this, France does not stand alone. She is not isolated. Behind her is a vast empire, and she can make common cause with the British Empire, which commands the seas and is continuing the struggle. Like England, she can draw unreservedly on the immense industrial resources of the United States.

'The destiny of the world is at stake'

This war is not limited to our unfortunate country. The outcome of the struggle has not been decided by the Battle of France. This is a world war. Mistakes have been made, there have been delays and untold suffering, but the fact remains that there still exists in the world everything we need to crush our enemies some day. Today we are crushed by the sheer weight of mechanized force hurled against us, but we can still look to a future in which even greater mechanized force will bring us victory. The destiny of the world is at stake.

I, General de Gaulle, now in London, call on all French officers and men who are at present on British soil, or may be in the future, with or without their arms. I call on all engineers and skilled workmen from the armaments factories who are at present on British soil, or may be in the future, to get in touch with me.

Whatever happens, the flame of French resistance must not and shall not die.

'Perfidy unparalleled in the history of civilized nations'

VYACHESLAV MOLOTOV
Radio broadcast condemning the Nazi invasion of the Soviet Union, 22 June 1941

IT WAS VYACHESLAV MOLOTOV – Joseph Stalin's foreign minister – who unwittingly inspired the 'Molotov cocktail', an improvised petrol bomb first used against Soviet tanks by Finns during their Winter War of 1939–40. It was the same Molotov who signed, at his master's bidding, the Nazi-Soviet non-aggression pact of August 1939. He was also doing his master's bidding when, on 22 June 1941, he was tasked with broadcasting the news to his countrymen and women that Germany had torn up that agreement and was invading the Soviet Union on a massive scale.

The pact had been suggested by Germany as an expedient to keep the Soviet Union out of any Anglo-French alliance, and to ensure that Stalin would not interfere in German plans to invade Poland. Stalin regarded it as being in Soviet interests to sign, and then, despite deteriorating Soviet–German relations, could not bring himself to believe that Hitler would, or could, renege on it so soon. But for Hitler, the invasion of the Soviet Union and expansion of Germany's *Lebensraum* (literally 'living space') eastwards was always a cherished project. The existence of the pact had done nothing to assuage the Nazi leader's contempt, ideologically and racially, for the communist system or for Slav peoples.

At 3 a.m. on the morning of 22 June 1941, 3.5 million German, Romanian, Finnish and other Axis troops flooded across the Soviet borders. Despite evidence of the build-up of troops, and despite explicit warnings to Stalin from Winston Churchill (which Stalin dismissed), Soviet defences were unprepared. Stalin himself, rather than taking the helm at the nation's hour of crisis, disappeared from view, leaving it to Molotov to try and rally the country in the name of 'our great leader and comrade, Stalin'.

Within the first fortnight of the invasion, the Soviet Union lost a million men, nearly all its aircraft and thousands of tanks. Stalin ordered retreating Russians to 'scorch the earth' in order to render the land incapable of supporting the advancing German army. Through the summer of 1941, the Axis forces gained rapid ground, taking Leningrad and Kiev, and thousands of civilian men, women and children died in the indiscriminate killing. Molotov had promised on 22 June that 'Victory will be ours', and in the end a resurgent Red Army turned the tables decisively. But

VYACHESLAV MOLOTOV

Born 9 March 1890 in Kukarka (also called Sovetsk), Russia.

His family name was Scriabin (and he was related to the composer Alexander Scriabin). He became politically active as a student, and adopted the pseudonym Molotov ('Hammer') on joining the Bolsheviks in 1906. He was arrested in 1909 for the first time and exiled in northern Russia until 1911. Afterwards, he joined the editorial board of *Pravda* ('Truth'), the Bolshevik newspaper, and around this time met Stalin. He was part of the military revolutionary committee that planned the Bolshevik seizure of power in the October Revolution (1917). After Lenin's death, he earned promotion to full Politburo membership (1926) and, with Stalin now pre-eminent, he helped purge the Moscow Communist Party of anti-Stalin members, 1928–30. Molotov served as foreign minister in 1939–49 and 1953–56, but the rise of Nikita Khrushchev as premier saw him dismissed from government posts and leading party bodies. He was given the lowly position of Ambassador to Mongolia and in 1962 expelled from the Communist Party (until reinstated in 1984).

Died 8 November 1986 in Moscow.

the bitterly fought 'Great Patriotic War', as it is known in Russia, consumed over 20 million Soviet lives.

As for Molotov, during the war he played a vital role in secret conferences with US representatives, such as W. Averell Harriman, to secure American arms. But his later career could not withstand his reputation as a Stalinist apparatchik, and though he lived to be 96 he was sidelined after 1956.

CITIZENS OF THE SOVIET UNION:

The Soviet government and its head, Comrade Stalin, have authorized me to make the following statement:

Today at 4 a.m., without any claims having been presented to the Soviet Union, without a declaration of war, German troops attacked our country, attacked our borders at many points and bombed from their airplanes our cities Zhitomir, Kiev, Sevastopol, Kaunas and some others, killing and wounding over 200 persons.

. . . This unheard of attack upon our country is perfidy unparalleled in the history of civilized nations. The attack on our country was perpetrated despite the fact that a treaty of non-aggression had been signed between the USSR and Germany and that the Soviet government most faithfully abided by all provisions of this treaty.

The attack upon our country was perpetrated despite the fact that during the entire period of operation of this treaty, the German government could not find grounds for a single complaint against the USSR as regards observance of this treaty.

'The German government had decided to launch war against the USSR

Entire responsibility for this predatory attack upon the Soviet Union fall fully and completely upon the German fascist rulers.

At 5.30 a.m., that is, after the attack had already been perpetrated, [Friedrich] Von der Schulenburg, the German Ambassador in Moscow, on behalf of his government made the statement to me as People's Commissar of Foreign Affairs to the effect that the German government had decided to launch war against the USSR in connection with the concentration of Red Army units near the eastern German frontier.

In reply to this I stated on behalf of the Soviet government that, until the very last moment, the German government had not presented any claims to the Soviet government, that Germany attacked the USSR despite the peaceable position of the Soviet Union, and that for this reason fascist Germany is the aggressor.

On instruction of the government of the Soviet Union I also stated that at no point had our troops or our air force committed a violation of the frontier and therefore the statement made this morning by the Romanian radio to the effect that Soviet aircraft allegedly had fired on Romanian aerodromes is a sheer lie and provocation.

. . . This war has been forced upon us, not by the German people, not by German workers, peasants and intellectuals, whose sufferings we well understand, but by the clique of bloodthirsty fascist rulers of Germany who have enslaved Frenchmen, Czechs, Poles, Serbians, Norway, Belgium, Denmark, Holland, Greece and other nations.

'This is not the first time that our people have had to deal with an attack of an arrogant foe'

. . . This is not the first time that our people have had to deal with an attack of an arrogant foe. At the time of Napoleon's invasion of Russia our people's reply was war for the fatherland, and Napoleon suffered defeat and met his doom.

It will be the same with Hitler, who in his arrogance has proclaimed a new crusade against our country. The Red Army and our whole people will again wage victorious war for the fatherland, for our country, for honour, for liberty.

. . . The government calls upon you, citizens of the Soviet Union, to rally still more closely around our glorious Bolshevik Party, around our Soviet government, around our great leader and comrade, Stalin. Ours is a righteous cause. The enemy shall be defeated. Victory will be ours.

'I am personally going to shoot that paper-hanging sonofabitch Hitler'

GEORGE S. PATTON, JR
Rallying speech to the US Third Army before D-Day, 5 June 1944

THERE IS A POPULAR IMAGE of a type of American military commander that is beloved of Hollywood: aggressive, blunt, bursting with foul-mouthed *machismo*, but determined, loyal and effective. The archetype is George Smith Patton, Jr, who rose to the rank of general and played a key role commanding the US Seventh and Third armies in Europe in 1943–5, as the tide of fortune in the Second World War turned against Nazi Germany. Nicknamed 'Old Blood and Guts' by his men, Patton was colourful and controversial. He was quick-tempered, tough-minded and outspoken. He was also a disciplinarian, but his own example gained him loyalty from his men.

By June 1944, Patton's reputation had been reinforced by his command of the US II Corps in North Africa and then, leading the Seventh Army, his contribution to the Anglo-American capture of Sicily in 1943. Now he was to lead the US Third Army as part of the D-Day (Deliverance Day) landings of 6 June 1944, the hazardous – but successful – attempt to gain an Allied footing in France. 'Operation Overlord', as the offensive was codenamed, was intended to open up a western front against the Germans, which Stalin – his Red Army bitterly fighting the Germans in the east – had long called for. On the evening before D-Day, Patton addressed his men at their camp 'somewhere in England', as the deliberately vague official description has it.

The speech is typical of Patton's forthright and profane style, which nevertheless portrayed battle as a great drama, 'the most magnificent competition in which a human being can indulge'. Never using notes, Patton always addressed his men in the most direct terms, focusing on practicalities such as the basics of survival. Patton himself said of his swearing, 'You can't run an army without profanity; and it has to be eloquent profanity.' He recognized the naturalness of fear in battle and the inevitability that not all men would survive. But for Patton, true soldiering was about overcoming fear through higher values, so that 'a real man will never let his fear of death overpower his honour, his sense of duty to his country and his innate manhood'. The speech, in various reports and partial records, passed into military folklore, and in 1970 a version of these words opened the feature film *Patton*, starring George C. Scott as the eponymous general.

GEORGE S. PATTON, JR

Born 11 November 1885 in San Gabriel, California, into a family with a military tradition.

He graduated from West Point Military Academy in 1909. He received a commission in the cavalry, and led a small armoured attack into Mexico (1916) as part of the US response to the incursions of 'Pancho' Villa. He also saw tank service during World War I, when he was wounded (1918). In the 1920s and 1930s he was a vigorous advocate of tank warfare, eventually leading to the formation of US armoured divisions. After US entry into the Second World War, he commanded the Western Task Force in capturing Casablanca (1942), and in March 1943, now a lieutenant-general, he took control of II Corps in North Africa. For the Allied campaign to capture Sicily (Operation Husky) in July–August 1943, he led the US Seventh Army supporting Montgomery's British Eighth Army. In 1944 he was given command of the US Third Army, which, after D-Day (6 June), thrust across France and into Germany. Postwar, after criticizing de-Nazification policies in Germany, he was removed from command of the Third Army.

Died 21 December 1945 in Germany, after his car struck a truck. He is buried in Luxembourg among the soldiers who died in the Battle of the Bulge.

From D-Day, the Third Army was to be involved in 281 days of combat, during which it achieved a spectacular sweep through France and across the Rhine, then into Germany and Czechoslovakia. The servicemen encountered determined resistance, notably at the Battle of the Bulge in December and January 1944–5 as the Germans attempted a counter-offensive.

Patton had warned his men in his 5 June speech that 'Death must not be feared. Death, in time, comes to all men.' It came to the general, though, not in the heat of battle, but as a result of a road accident soon after war ended, in December 1945. Patton may have barely outlived the war, but his larger-than-life personality and genuine military achievements established an enduring legend.

. . . You are here today for three reasons. First, because you are here to defend your homes and your loved ones. Second, you are here for your own self respect, because you would not want to be anywhere else. Third, you are here because you are real men and all real men like to fight. When you, here, every one of you, were kids, you all admired the champion marble player, the fastest runner, the toughest boxer, the big league ball players, and the All-American football players. Americans love a winner. Americans will not tolerate a loser. Americans despise cowards. Americans play to win all of the time. I wouldn't give a hoot in hell for a man who lost and laughed. That's why Americans have never lost nor will ever lose a war; for the very idea of losing is hateful to an American.

You are not all going to die. Only two per cent of you right here today would die in a major battle. Death must not be feared. Death, in time, comes to all men. Yes, every man is scared in his first battle. If he says he's not, he's a liar. Some men are cowards but they fight the same as the brave men or they get the hell slammed out of them watching men fight who are just as scared as they are.

'Battle is the most magnificent competition in which a human being can indulge'

The real hero is the man who fights even though he is scared. Some men get over their fright in a minute under fire. For some, it takes an hour. For some it takes days. But a real man will never let his fear of death overpower his honour, his sense of duty to his country and his innate manhood.

Battle is the most magnificent competition in which a human being can indulge. It brings out all that is best and removes all that is base. Americans pride themselves on being He Men and they *are* He Men. Remember that the enemy is just as frightened as you are, and probably more so. They are not supermen.

. . . All of the real heroes are not storybook combat fighters, either. Every single man in this army plays a vital role. Don't ever let up. Don't ever think that your job is unimportant. Every man has a job to do and he must do it. Every man is a vital link in the great chain. What if every truck driver suddenly decided that he didn't like the whine of those shells overhead, turned yellow, and jumped headlong into a ditch? The cowardly bastard could say, 'Hell, they won't miss me, just one man in thousands.' But, what if every man thought that way? Where in the hell would we be now? What would our country, our loved ones, our homes, even the world, be like? No, goddamnit, Americans don't think like that. Every man does his job. Every man serves the whole. Every department, every unit, is important in the vast scheme of this war.

'Son, your granddaddy rode with the great Third Army and a son-of-a-goddamned-bitch named Georgie Patton!'

. . . Sure, we want to go home. We want this war over with. The quickest way to get it over with is to go get the bastards who started it. The quicker they are whipped, the quicker we can go home. The shortest way home is through Berlin and Tokyo. And when we get to Berlin, I am personally going to shoot that paper-hanging sonofabitch Hitler. Just like I'd shoot a snake!

. . . There is one great thing that you men will all be able to say after this war is over and you are home once again. You may be thankful that 20 years from now when you are sitting by the fireplace with your grandson on your knee and he asks you what you did in the great World War II, you won't have to cough, shift him to the other knee and say, 'Well, your granddaddy shovelled shit in Louisiana.' No, sir, you can look him straight in the eye and say, 'Son, your granddaddy rode with the great Third Army and a son-of-a-goddamned-bitch named Georgie Patton!'

'Enduring the unendurable'

EMPEROR HIROHITO

Broadcast explaining Japan's surrender, 15 August 1945

ON 3 MAY 1945, NAZI GERMANY formally surrendered to the Allied powers. The Second World War in Europe was over. But hostilities ground on in the Far East, where the US and Allied forces continued a war of attrition against Japan. Despite the fact that the Japanese were being overwhelmed on land and at sea, and the Americans had already achieved air superiority, the Japanese preparedness to fight to the death suggested that an Allied victory would not be easy or quick. Indeed, the US capture of the island of Okinawa in June 1945 had taken three hard-fought weeks and cost the lives of almost 13,000 Americans.

Unlocking Japanese surrender required a radical solution. It began on 6 August 1945, when a US Air Force B-29 bomber, the *Enola Gay*, dropped the world's first atomic bomb on the Japanese military base of Hiroshima, killing between 75,000 and 100,000 people and obliterating the city. The Japanese made no immediate response. Three days later, as conventional bombs battered Tokyo, a second atomic bomb was dropped on the port city of Nagasaki, causing comparable devastation. Shortly afterwards, Japan's Emperor Hirohito broke imperial tradition by broadcasting a speech to his people; it announced Japan's acceptance of the Allies' terms for surrender.

The use of the atomic bomb was controversial even in US military circles. But President Truman, who had succeeded Roosevelt on his death in April 1945, argued that using it would prevent a massive loss of Allied lives, and save thousands of Allied prisoners of war from being used as slave labour or dying of disease and starvation. Geopolitically, with deteriorating US–Soviet relations over the configuration of postwar Europe, Truman also wanted to ensure that Japan would surrender before Stalin had time to intervene significantly in East Asia. (At the Potsdam Conference on 24 July, Truman had mentioned only briefly to Stalin that the United States had 'a new weapon of unusual destructive force'.) The Soviet Union finally declared war on Japan on 9 August, and invaded Japanese-occupied China, but it was too late to give Stalin leverage over the fate of Japan.

Emperor Michinomiya Hirohito was revered as the 'divine' figurehead of Japan, although in practice his executive power was limited to ratifying policies. Historians differ on his attitude to war and involvement in decisions, but his private inclinations

EMPEROR HIROHITO

Born 29 April 1901 in Tokyo, the eldest son of Crown Prince Yoshihito.

In 1921, he was the first Japanese crown prince to travel abroad, on a six-month visit to Europe. He married a Japanese princess in 1924. He succeeded as Japan's 124th emperor, on the death of his father, (1926): his reign carried the imperial name *Showa* ('Enlightened Peace'). In the 1930s, nationalist-militarists gained the upper hand in Japanese politics, resulting in the wars against China (1931–2 and 1937–45) and then the wider war against the US and Allied powers from 1941. In August 1945, he made an unprecedented broadcast to his people explaining Japan's surrender. He renounced his divine status in 1946, and his position as a constitutional monarch was formalized in Japan's new constitution. In other ways, the monarchy was modernized, and his son Crown Prince Akhito married a commoner in 1959, breaking ancient tradition. He visited the United States in 1972 and 1975.

Died 7 January 1989 in Tokyo.

before the 1937 Japanese invasion of China seemed to be for peace. Once war had begun, he did provide moral support for Japan's war effort. Now, with atomic bombs threatening annihilation, Prime Minister Suzuki asked Hirohito to decide the country's fate, and Hirohito made his historic announcement. It is notable for its formality, its euphemism, and its tragic yet stoic tone. As a message for the Japanese people, it interpreted the war nobly, as an attempted 'emancipation of East Asia'. But now war had to end, because 'a new and most cruel bomb' could destroy the nation. His people would therefore have to constrain their emotions, subdue the cultural tradition that regarded surrender as dishonourable, and endure 'the unendurable'.

Hirohito endured, too, as the postwar settlement preserved him as monarch, though his divine status was soon dispensed with. He settled into a modernized, constitutional arrangement, devoting much of his time to his beloved study of marine biology, while Japan evolved into an economic giant.

TO OUR GOOD AND LOYAL SUBJECTS. After pondering deeply the general trends of the world and the actual conditions obtaining in our empire today, we have decided to effect a settlement of the present situation by resorting to an extraordinary measure.

We have ordered our government to communicate to the governments of the United States, Great Britain, China and the Soviet Union that our empire accepts the provisions of their joint declaration. To strive for the common prosperity and happiness of all nations as well as the security and well-being of our subjects is the solemn obligation which has been handed down by our imperial ancestors and which we lay close to the heart.

Indeed, we declared war on America and Britain out of our sincere desire to ensure Japan's self-preservation and the stabilization of East Asia, it being far from our thought either to infringe upon the sovereignty of other nations or to embark upon territorial aggrandizement.

'An ultimate collapse and obliteration of the Japanese nation'

But now the war has lasted for nearly four years. Despite the best that has been done by everyone – the gallant fighting of our military and naval forces, the diligence and assiduity of our servants of the State and the devoted service of our 100 million people – the war situation has developed not necessarily to Japan's advantage, while the general trends of the world have all turned against her interest.

Moreover, the enemy has begun to employ a new and most cruel bomb, the power of which to do damage is, indeed, incalculable, taking the toll of many innocent lives. Should we continue to fight, it would not only result in an ultimate collapse and obliteration of the Japanese nation, but also it would lead to the total extinction of human civilization.

Such being the case, how are we to save the millions of our subjects, nor to atone ourselves before the hallowed spirits of our imperial ancestors? This is the reason why we have ordered the acceptance of the provisions of the joint declaration of the powers.

We cannot but express the deepest sense of regret to our allied nations of East Asia, who have consistently cooperated with the empire toward the emancipation of East Asia.

The thought of those officers and men as well as others who have fallen in the fields of battle, those who died at their posts of duty, or those who met with untimely death and all their bereaved families, pains our heart night and day.

The welfare of the wounded and the war sufferers, and of those who lost their homes and livelihood, are the object of our profound solicitude. The hardships and sufferings to which our nation is to be subjected hereafter will certainly be great.

'Beware most strictly of any outbursts of emotion'

We are keenly aware of the inmost feelings of all of you, our subjects. However, it is according to the dictates of time and fate that we have resolved to pave the way for a grand peace for all the generations to come by enduring the unendurable and suffering what is insufferable. Having been able to save and maintain the structure of the Imperial State, we are always with you, our good and loyal subjects, relying upon your sincerity and integrity.

Beware most strictly of any outbursts of emotion that may engender needless complications, or any fraternal contention and strife that may create confusion, lead you astray and cause you to lose the confidence of the world.

Let the entire nation continue as one family from generation to generation, ever firm in its faith of the imperishableness of its divine land, and mindful of its heavy burden of responsibilities, and the long road before it. Unite your total strength to be devoted to the construction for the future. Cultivate the ways of rectitude, nobility of spirit, and work with resolution so that you may enhance the innate glory of the imperial state and keep pace with the progress of the world.

'We are not only
scientists; we
are men, too'

J. ROBERT OPPENHEIMER
*Speech on the atomic age and scientific
responsibility, 2 November 1945*

THE ALLIES' RACE TO DEFEAT NAZI GERMANY in 1944–5 did not simply reflect a desire to bring the war to a victorious conclusion and to liberate the countries under Nazi domination. Among senior politicians, military planners, scientists and Intelligence chiefs there was fear that Germany might yet – given a little time – regain the upper hand through innovative weapons technology.

As early as 1939, Albert Einstein and Leo Szilard – both Jewish refugees from Nazi Europe – had outlined the dangers should German laboratories be the first to develop an atomic bomb. Once the United States had entered the war in 1941, President Roosevelt set up a research organization, the 'Manhattan Project'. As part of this, in 1942 J. (Julius) Robert Oppenheimer was asked to lead British and American physicists in finding a way to harness nuclear energy for a nuclear bomb at the Project's laboratory in Los Alamos, New Mexico. The result was the first atomic bomb test at Alamogordo, New Mexico, on 16 July 1945. Some years later, Oppenheimer described his reaction: 'We knew the world would not be the same. A few people laughed, a few people cried, most people were silent. I remembered the line from the Hindu scripture, the Bhagavad-Gita ... "Now, I am become Death, the destroyer of worlds".'

The real-life application of the scientists' work took place, unforgettably, in August 1945, when, in order to bring the potentially long, attritional war in East Asia to a conclusion, President Truman ordered the dropping of atomic bombs on the Japanese cities of Hiroshima (6 August) and then Nagasaki (9 August). The devastation was far more horrifying than had been anticipated; but it brought about Japan's surrender on 15 August. Three months later, Oppenheimer spoke to fellow scientists, attempting to explain why he and his colleagues had created the bomb. He also considered why the existence of the bomb meant that future cooperation between nations would now be more necessary than ever.

Oppenheimer was a brilliant leader and scholar, who had a gift for languages and a deep interest in Eastern religions and philosophy. Although he maintained that he felt no guilt for his work on atomic weapons, he never denied his sense of moral responsibility. In the early 1950s – in the era of the Korean War and the 'Red Scare' – his opposition to the development of the vastly more destructive hydrogen bomb, together with his sharp tongue and views on the need for shared arms control with

J. ROBERT OPPENHEIMER

Born 22 April 1904 in New York.

After studying physics at Harvard, and quantum mechanics and relativity theory at the University of Cambridge's Cavendish Laboratory, England, he took a Ph.D at the University of Göttingen in Germany. From 1929 he held posts at the University of California, Berkeley, and the California Institute of Technology, where he established large schools of theoretical physics. In 1942, he was asked to coordinate work on the atomic bomb at the Manhatten Project's Los Alamos lab, New Mexico. He resigned in October 1945. He was chairman of the board of scientific advisers of the Atomic Energy Commission in 1947–52: in 1949 the board refused to pass a proposal to begin the manufacture of hydrogen bombs, beginning his period of disaffection from the political and military authorities, including the loss of security clearance in 1953. He continued to work at the Institute for Advanced Study, Princeton University.

Died 18 February 1967 in New York.

the Soviet Union, brought him military and political enemies. When he was alleged to have contacts with communists, he was even denied security clearance, preventing his involvement in secret research. However, ten years later the Atomic Energy Commission awarded him the prestigious Fermi Award (1963), recognizing his scientific leadership and groundwork on many peaceful uses of atomic energy, and he spent his last years exploring the relationship between science and society.

I SHOULD LIKE TO TALK TONIGHT . . . as a fellow scientist, and at least as a fellow worrier about the fix we are in.

. . . It is not possible to be a scientist unless you believe that it is good to learn. It is not good to be a scientist, and it is not possible, unless you think that it is of the highest value to share your knowledge, to share it with anyone who is interested. It is not possible to be a scientist unless you believe that the knowledge of the world, and the power which this gives, is a thing which is of intrinsic value to humanity, and that you are using it to help in the spread of knowledge, and are willing to take the consequences.

'These are the strongest bonds in the world'

. . . I think it is true to say that atomic weapons are a peril which affect everyone in the world, and in that sense a completely common problem, as common a problem as it was for the Allies to defeat the Nazis. I think that in order to handle this common problem there must be a complete sense of community responsibility . . . the point I want to make, the one point I want to hammer home, is what an enormous change in spirit is involved. There are things which we hold very dear, and I think rightly hold very dear; I would say that the word democracy perhaps stood for some of them as well as any other word. There are many parts of the world in which there is no democracy. There are other things which we hold dear, and which we rightly should. And when I speak of a new spirit in international affairs I mean that even to these deepest of things which we cherish, and for which Americans have been willing to die – and certainly most of us would be willing to die – even in these deepest things, we realize that there is something more profound than that; namely, the common bond with other men everywhere.

. . . We are not only scientists; we are men, too. We cannot forget our dependence on our fellow men . . . These are the strongest bonds in the world, stronger than those even that bind us to one another, these are the deepest bonds – that bind us to our fellow men.

'At the stroke of the midnight hour . . . India will awake'

JAWAHARLAL NEHRU
Speech marking the independence of India, 14 August 1947

S INCE THE 18TH CENTURY, Britain had exerted control over the patchwork of
territories and princely states that made up the subcontinent of India. In 1858,
control passed from the East India Company directly to the British state, and the era
of the British 'Raj' began. Queen Victoria was proclaimed 'Empress of India' in Delhi,
and India – then including what is now Pakistan and Bangladesh – was the 'jewel in
the crown' of Britain's vast empire. That history ended 'at the stroke of midnight' on
14 August 1947, when India's new leader Jawaharlal Nehru announced the birth of an
independent nation – first in a speech to India's Parliament (the version reproduced
here), and then in a radio broadcast to the nation later that day. On 15 August, an
independent Pakistan was born as well. The two new nations would have an uneasy relationship, embracing several wars over disputed Kashmir and the threat of
nuclear confront-ation. But in the 21st century, India is beginning to realize its huge
potential on the world's political and economic stage.

JAWAHARLAL NEHRU

**Born 14 November 1889 in Allahabad, United
Provinces (now Uttar Pradesh), India, the son of
a wealthy lawyer.**

He was educated in England at Harrow School and
Trinity College, Cambridge; then studied law at London's
Inner Temple, and was called to the Bar in 1912. On
his return to India he practised law. He was working
for the Indian Congress Party by 1918 and supported
Gandhi's civil disobedience campaigns. Elected general
secretary of the Congress in 1923. He became more
politically radical after spending 1926–7 in Europe and
the Soviet Union, eventually persuading the Congress by
1930 to campaign for full independence. After several
periods of arrest and imprisonment (during which time
he wrote his autobiography), he was elected leader of
the Congress (1936). Although disposed to help Britain
fight fascism, political deadlock brought his rearrest
and imprisonment in 1940–1 and again after the 'Quit
India' campaign began, 1942–5. He was vice-president
of the provisional government in 1946 and reluctantly
agreed, with the Muslim League, to the partition of
India. On India's independence (1947), he became
prime minister until 1964. In power, he consolidated
democracy, attempted economic modernization, lost a
border war with China (1962), and co-created the non-
aligned movement to try and represent nations that did
not want to ally themselves with the Soviet Union or
United States.

**Popularly named Pandit ('wise man'), he died on
27 May 1964 in Delhi.**

It had been a long and difficult
struggle. In 1885, the Indian National Congress was formed, bringing
together groups seeking reforms to
British administration. At first, they
simply wanted more schools and
more representation for Indians in
the legislature. By 1907, however, the
Congress began to see a divergence
between moderates who wanted
gradual Dominion status within
the empire (on a par with Canada
or Australia) and radicals wanting
complete and immediate self-rule.
From 1906, there was also a religious
divergence, as Muslim leaders, dis-
contented with the Hindu majority's
domination of the Congress, formed
the All India Muslim League. Later,
the League campaigned for a separate Muslim state.

Some representation for Indians
was introduced in 1909, and between 1914 and 1918 India's political
groups generally supported Britain
in the First World War. But during
this period, 'Mahatma' Gandhi
arrived back in India from South
Africa, bringing his unique brand
of civil disobedience with him. At

a Congress meeting in 1916 he met the wealthy, British-educated lawyer Jawaharlal Nehru: the two very different men would become the pivotal figures of India's independence struggle. Nehru agreed with most of Gandhi's principles, except the agrarian ideal of the simple life; by contrast, the more worldly Nehru was in favour of modernization.

After the war, the Congress's militant faction was angered by Britain's slowness in responding to demands for self-rule. Indian nationalism was also aroused by the Amritsar massacre (1919) of pro-independence protestors, in which General Dyer ordered British troops to fire on unarmed Indians, killing 379 and wounding a further 1200.

The 1920s–30s saw increasingly effective mass campaigns orchestrated by the Congress, while the British alternately attempted suppression and negotiation. Gandhi was found guilty of 'sedition' in 1922, and Nehru spent many periods in jail, which he described as 'normal interludes in a life of abnormal political activity'. When Britain declared war on Nazi Germany in 1939, it was cautiously supported by the Congress. Britain was now inclined to negotiate Dominion status, but deadlock ensued and in 1942 Congress passed a 'Quit India' resolution. This led to the immediate imprisonment of Congress leaders, including Nehru.

By the end of the war, the tide of support for independence was undeniable – and the British Labour government, running an economically shattered Britain, knew that the 'jewel in the crown' was too impractical to maintain. After 50 years of struggle, independence, when it came, was negotiated in a matter of months under the last Viceroy of India, Lord Mountbatten. Thus, on 14 August 1947, Nehru announced that India's 'tryst with destiny' had finally come to pass, and the world's most populous democracy took flight. For the next 17 years Nehru was its leader, attempting to chart a course of industrialization and political non-alignment in the Cold War world.

LONG YEARS AGO WE MADE A TRYST WITH DESTINY, and now the time comes when we shall redeem our pledge, not wholly or in full measure, but very substantially.

At the stroke of the midnight hour, when the world sleeps, India will awake to life and freedom. A moment comes, which comes but rarely in history, when we step out from the old to the new, when an age ends, and when the soul of a nation, long suppressed, finds utterance. It is fitting that at this solemn moment we take the pledge of dedication to the service of India and her people and to the still larger cause of humanity.

At the dawn of history India started on her unending quest, and trackless centuries are filled with her striving and the grandeur of her success and her failures. Through good and ill fortune alike she has never lost sight of that quest or forgotten the ideals which gave her strength. We end today a period of ill fortune and India discovers herself again. The achievement we celebrate today is but a step, an opening of opportunity, to the greater triumphs and achievements that await us. Are we brave enough and wise enough to grasp this opportunity and accept the challenge of the future?

'The past is over and it is the future that beckons to us now'

Freedom and power bring responsibility. The responsibility rests upon this Assembly, a sovereign body representing the sovereign people of India. Before the birth of freedom we have endured all the pains of labour and our hearts are heavy with the memory of this sorrow. Some of those pains continue even now. Nevertheless, the past is over and it is the future that beckons to us now.

That future is not one of ease or resting but of incessant striving so that we may fulfil the pledges we have so often taken and the one we shall take today. The service of India means the service of the millions who suffer. It means the ending of poverty and ignorance and disease and inequality of opportunity. The ambition of the greatest man of our generation has been to wipe every tear from every eye. That may be beyond us, but as long as there are tears and suffering, so long our work will not be over.

'Join us with faith and confidence in this great adventure'

And so we have to labour and to work, and work hard, to give reality to our dreams. Those dreams are for India, but they are also for the world, for all the nations and peoples are too closely knit together today for any one of them to imagine that it can live apart. Peace has been said to be indivisible; so is freedom, so is prosperity now, and so also is disaster in this one world that can no longer be split into isolated fragments.

To the people of India, whose representatives we are, we make an appeal to join us with faith and confidence in this great adventure. This is no time for petty and destructive criticism, no time for ill will or blaming others. We have to build the noble mansion of free India where all her children may dwell.

'I have just left your fighting sons in Korea'

DOUGLAS MacARTHUR
Farewell address to Congress, 19 April 1951

I N 1950, THE GROWING EAST–WEST POLITICAL DIVIDE, between the communist and non-communist blocs, reached a crisis point. In that year, the Cold War turned hot as Soviet-backed North Korean forces surged across the 49th Parallel and into US-backed South Korea, in an attempt to unify the country under the North's communist regime. The temporary absence of the Soviet Union from the United Nations Security Council enabled a UN resolution to mount military counter-measures. It was the start of an American-dominated fight-back, and the man chosen to lead it was the United States' most glittering general, Douglas MacArthur.

After a distinguished record during the First World War, MacArthur rose to become chief of staff in 1930. He retired in 1937, but was called back to mastermind the US Army in the Far East shortly before the Japanese attack on Pearl Harbor brought war. It was MacArthur who oversaw Japan's formal surrender on 2 September 1945, and who presided over the country's US occupation and administration over the next five years. Although arrogant, aloof and egotistical, MacArthur was also warm-hearted, courageous, self-sacrificing and capable of inspiring loyalty. He was also staunchly anti-communist.

The counter-offensive in Korea was successful, with MacArthur landing forces audaciously behind enemy lines. The North Koreans were pushed back above the 49th Parallel, and by late October as far north as the Yalu River, the border with China. But it was perhaps too far, and – whether feeling threatened or just determined not to see a fellow communist regime toppled (historians differ) – China responded with massive force, sending over 1 million men pouring across the border, overwhelming the Americans and their allies, and re-taking the South Korean capital, Seoul.

The US leadership was faced with a new crisis, which would cause a deep rift. MacArthur felt that the route to victory was to take the war to mainland China using US airpower (potentially even including nuclear weapons) and co-opting the anti-communist Chinese forces on the island of Formosa (Taiwan). His political superior, Democratic President Truman, regarded this as over-adventurous: he feared that such a widening of the war risked direct conflict with the Soviet Union, the latter now a nuclear power. When MacArthur continued to propagate his

DOUGLAS MacARTHUR

Born 26 January 1880 in Little Rock, Arkansas, the son of a general.

He graduated first in his class at West Point Military Academy (1903), becoming a second lieutenant, and was stationed in the Philippines and Japan. He was much-decorated in the First World War, serving as Chief of Staff of the famous Rainbow Division and later as Commander of the 84th Infantry Brigade. In 1919 he became Superintendent of West Point: he broadened the curriculum and raised standards. He was Commander in the Philippines (1922–5) and US Chief of Staff (1930–5). MacArthur returned to the Philippines in 1935 to prepare the islands against possible Japanese invasion, becoming Field Marshal of the Philippine Army (1936). Retired from the US Army in December 1937, until recalled in July 1941 to command of all the US Army forces in the Far East: he liberated the Philippines in spring 1945. Having witnessed Japan's formal surrender, he became *de facto* governor of postwar Japan until 1949. He commanded UN forces in the Korean War in 1950–1, before his dismissal (and retirement) for ostensible insubordination. He settled in New York, and was frequently consulted by US presidents.

Died 5 April 1964 in New York.

views in letters and statements, including to Republican politicians, it appeared to the president as subordination, a contradiction of the democratic principle that military commanders defer to their elected politicians. MacArthur was dismissed from his command. It seemed an ignominious end to a glittering career.

MacArthur remained, however, hugely popular at home, and he was courted by the Republican Party as a possible presidential candidate. Congress invited him to give a televised speech on 19 April 1951, where – constantly interrupted by applause and ovations – he made a farewell address after 50 years of soldiering.

I ADDRESS YOU WITH NEITHER RANCOUR nor bitterness in the fading twilight of life, with but one purpose in mind: to serve my country.

. . . While I was not consulted prior to the president's decision to intervene in support of the Republic of Korea, that decision from a military standpoint, proved a sound one, as we hurled back the invader and decimated his forces. Our victory was complete, and our objectives within reach, when Red China intervened with numerically superior ground forces.

This created a new war and an entirely new situation, a situation not contemplated when our forces were committed against the North Korean invaders; a situation which called for new decisions in the diplomatic sphere to permit the realistic adjustment of military strategy. Such decisions have not been forthcoming.

While no man in his right mind would advocate sending our ground forces into continental China, and such was never given a thought, the new situation did urgently demand a drastic revision of strategic planning if our political aim was to defeat this new enemy as we had defeated the old.

Apart from the military need, as I saw it, to neutralize the sanctuary protection given the enemy north of the Yalu, I felt that military necessity in the conduct of the war made necessary: first, the intensification of our economic blockade against China; two, the imposition of a naval blockade against the China coast; three, removal of restrictions on air reconnaissance of China's coastal areas and of Manchuria; four, removal of restrictions on the forces of the Republic of China on Formosa, with logistical support to contribute to their effective operations against the common enemy.

For entertaining these views, all professionally designed to support our forces committed to Korea and bring hostilities to an end with the least possible delay and at a saving of countless American and allied lives, I have been severely criticized in lay circles, principally abroad, despite my understanding that from a military standpoint the above views have been fully shared in the past by practically every military leader concerned with the Korean campaign, including our own Joint Chiefs of Staff.

I called for reinforcements but was informed that reinforcements were not available. I made clear that if not permitted to destroy the enemy built-up bases north of the Yalu, if not permitted to utilize the friendly Chinese Force of some 600,000 men on Formosa, if not permitted to blockade the China coast to prevent the Chinese Reds from getting succour from without, and if there were to be no hope of major reinforcements, the position of the command from the military standpoint forbade victory.

'There are some who, for varying reasons, would appease Red China'

. . . Efforts have been made to distort my position. It has been said, in effect, that I was a warmonger. Nothing could be further from the truth. I know war as few other men now living know it, and nothing to me is more revolting. I have long advocated its complete abolition, as its very destructiveness on both friend and foe has rendered it useless as a means of settling international disputes.

There are some who, for varying reasons, would appease Red China. They are blind to history's clear lesson, for history teaches with unmistakable emphasis that appeasement but begets new and bloodier war …

I have just left your fighting sons in Korea. They have met all tests there, and I can report to you without reservation that they are splendid in every way.

. . . I am closing my 52 years of military service. When I joined the army, even before the turn of the century, it was the fulfilment of all of my boyish hopes and dreams. The world has turned over many times since I took the oath on the plain at West Point, and the hopes and dreams have long since vanished, but I still remember the refrain of one of the most popular barrack ballads of that day which proclaimed most proudly that 'old soldiers never die; they just fade away'.

And like the old soldier of that ballad, I now close my military career and just fade away, an old soldier who tried to do his duty as God gave him the light to see that duty.

Goodbye.

'The cult of the individual'

NIKITA KHRUSHCHEV

Secret speech denouncing Stalin at the 20th Communist Party Congress, 25 February 1956

ON 25 FEBRUARY 1956, THE FIRST SECRETARY of the Soviet Communist Party, Nikita Khrushchev, addressed over 1300 delegates in a closed session of the party's 20th Congress. In a speech lasting several hours, Khrushchev delivered to his gripped, sometimes indignant, but often exhilarated audience nothing less than an assassination of the character, behaviour, policies and self-delusions of the man who had ruled the Soviet Union for 30 years: Joseph Stalin.

NIKITA KHRUSHCHEV

Born 17 April 1894 in Kalinovka, Russia, near the Ukrainian border.

Poorly educated, he trained as a metalworker. He joined the Bolshevik Party in 1918, fought in the Russian Civil War, and afterwards rose in the Ukrainian Communist Party, transferring to become Second Secretary, then First Secretary, of the Moscow Party. He held the post of First Secretary of the Ukrainian Communist Party, 1938–47, and entered the Politburo. He experienced disfavour and temporary demotion for suspected nationalist and pro-peasant sympathies. After Stalin's death in 1953, he outmanoeuvred Politburo rivals in 1957 to establish himself as the nation's leader. Domestically, he pursued campaigns to decentralize decision-making, increase agricultural output and consumer goods, and to suppress religion (though generally he liberalized freedom of expression), promising a true communist state within 20 years. Elsewhere, successive crises – rebellion in Hungary, trouble in Poland, and his attempt to place nuclear weapons on Cuba (capable of hitting the United States) – were partly ameliorated by the 1963 Nuclear Test Ban Treaty. In 1964, unpopular with colleagues, the military and state institutions, he was removed from power. He subsequently compiled his memoirs, published in the West.

Died 11 September 1971 in Moscow.

With a mastery of forensic detail as well as the rhetoric of big ideas – and astutely ensuring his ideological adherence to the father of the Russian Revolution, Lenin – Khrushchev demolished the official version of the Stalinist state. He painted a picture of rampant, brutal megalomania, in which Stalin had effectively stolen the Soviet leadership after Lenin's death and then perverted revolutionary principles to create a 'cult of the individual'. Khrushchev described how Stalin embraced state violence – vendettas, purges, show-trials, mass deportations, illegal executions, imprisonments – as a *modus vivendi,* whose prime rationale (when it had one) was not to defeat genuine threats to the Soviet people or the Communist Party, but to assuage the paranoia of the despot.

To an extent, Khrushchev could rely on his audience breathing (or rather gasping) a sigh of relief. The sufferings he recounted would have resonated with many of them, if not personally then through the experiences of family and friends. Yet to have these things laid bare was in itself shocking, and Khrushchev – often satirized as a blunt-speaking peasant – was relentless in revealing hitherto unknown, startling details of loyal party members destroyed.

One reason it was all so shocking was that the 'cult of the individual' had in many respects succeeded. Stalin had been publicly (and internationally) 'Uncle Joe', whose ostensibly wise, steadfast leadership had ensured victory in the 'Great Patriotic War' with Nazi Germany. And Stalin had gone on to expand Soviet power and prestige through the formation of the Soviet bloc in Eastern and Central Europe. But here, too, Khrushchev allowed his target no refuge. In some of the best-received passages, he lambasted Stalin for stealing the credit for victory in war from the true heroes – the Soviet people and the armed forces. Furthermore, he provided documentary evidence for Stalin's catastrophic errors in laying the country open to invasion in the first place.

The speech had many purposes. Khrushchev was still manoeuvring to cement his own position, and it was to his advantage to undermine pro-Stalinist colleagues. He also passed over quietly his own earlier acquiescence in some of the evils and policies he described when he was running the Communist Party in the Ukraine. Nevertheless, the Khrushchev era of Soviet history, which lasted until 1964, is not unfairly known as 'the Thaw' for the extent to which it liberalized political and social life.

Khrushchev's words were soon leaked internationally, appearing in the *New York Times* and elsewhere, and they produced profound – and often unintended – consequences. Reformers and nationalists in the Soviet bloc felt spurred on, but in Hungary the attempt to liberalize the regime and withdraw from the Warsaw Pact brought about Soviet military intervention. For Chairman Mao's China, the speech contributed to a growing split with the Soviet Union over the direction of worldwide communism. For Khrushchev, such consequences contributed to his downfall in 1964, when he was moved forcibly into political retirement.

COMRADES! IN THE PARTY CENTRAL COMMITTEE's report at the 20th Congress and in a number of speeches by delegates to the congress … quite a lot has been said about the cult of the individual and about its harmful consequences.

After Stalin's death, the Central Committee began to implement a policy of explaining concisely and consistently that it is impermissible and foreign to the spirit of Marxism-Leninism to elevate one person, to transform him into a superman possessing supernatural characteristics, akin to those of a god. Such a man supposedly knows everything, sees everything, thinks for everyone, can do anything, is infallible in his behaviour.

Such a belief about a man, and specifically about Stalin, was cultivated among us for many years . . .

Because not all as yet realize fully the practical consequences resulting from the cult of the individual, the great harm caused by violation of the principle of collective party direction and by the accumulation of immense and limitless power in the hands of one person, the Central Committee considers it absolutely necessary to make material pertaining to this matter available to the 20th Congress of the Communist Party of the Soviet Union . . .

Fearing the future fate of the party and of the Soviet nation, V.I. Lenin made a completely correct characterization of Stalin. He pointed out that it was necessary to consider transferring Stalin from the position of general secretary because Stalin was excessively rude, did not have a proper attitude toward his comrades, and was capricious and abused his power . . .

'Stalin originated the concept 'enemy of the people''

Stalin acted not through persuasion, explanation and patient cooperation with people, but by imposing his concepts and demanding absolute submission to his opinion. Whoever opposed these concepts or tried to prove his viewpoint and the correctness of his position was doomed to removal from the leadership collective and to subsequent moral and physical annihilation . . .

Stalin originated the concept 'enemy of the people'. This term automatically made it unnecessary that the ideological errors of a man or men engaged in a controversy be proven. It made possible the use of the cruellest repression, violating all norms of revolutionary legality, against anyone who in any way disagreed with Stalin, against those who were only suspected of hostile intent, against those who had bad reputations. The concept 'enemy of the people' actually eliminated the possibility of any kind of ideological fight or the making of one's views known on this or that issue . . . On the whole, the only proof of guilt actually used, against all norms of current legal science, was the 'confession' of the accused himself. As subsequent probing has proven, 'confessions' were acquired through physical pressures against the accused.

'Often violating all existing norms of morality and of Soviet laws'

. . . He discarded the Leninist method of convincing and educating, he abandoned the method of ideological struggle for that of administrative violence, mass repressions and terror. He acted on an increasingly larger scale and more stubbornly through punitive organs, at the same time often violating all existing norms of morality and of Soviet laws.

Arbitrary behaviour by one person encouraged and permitted arbitrariness in others. Mass arrests and deportations of many thousands of people, execution without trial and without normal investigation created conditions of insecurity, fear and even desperation.

. . . The commission has presented to the Central Committee's presidium [Politburo] lengthy and documented materials pertaining to mass repressions against the delegates to the 17th Party Congress and against members of the Central Committee elected at that congress. These materials have been studied by the presidium.

It was determined that of the 139 members and candidates of the Central Committee who were elected at the 17th congress [in 1934], 98 persons, i.e., 70 per cent, were arrested and shot . . . The only reasons . . . were because honest communists were slandered, accusations against them were fabricated, and revolutionary legality was gravely undermined.

. . . When we look at many of our novels, films and historical-scientific studies, the role of Stalin in the Patriotic War [Second World War] appears to be entirely improbable. Stalin had foreseen everything . . . The epic victory gained through the armed might of the land of the Soviets, through our heroic people, is ascribed in this type of novel, film and 'scientific study' as being completely due to the strategic genius of Stalin.

'Not Stalin, but the party as a whole . . .
the whole Soviet nation . . . assured
victory in the Great Patriotic War'

. . . During the war and after the war, Stalin advanced the thesis that the tragedy our nation experienced in the first part of the war was the result of an 'unexpected' attack by the Germans against the Soviet Union. But, comrades, this is completely untrue. As soon as Hitler came to power in Germany he assigned to himself the task of liquidating communism. The fascists were saying this openly. They did not hide their plans . . . Not Stalin, but the party as a whole, the Soviet government, our heroic army, its talented leaders and brave soldiers, the whole Soviet nation – these are the ones who assured victory in the Great Patriotic War.

. . . And was it without Stalin's knowledge that many of the largest enterprises and towns were named after him? Was it without his knowledge that Stalin monuments were erected in the whole country – these 'memorials to the living'?

Comrades! We must abolish the cult of the individual decisively . . . .

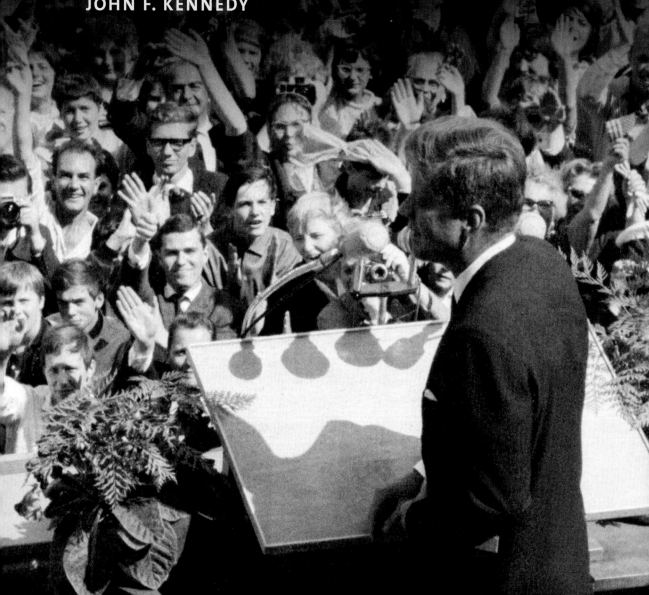

'Ask not what your country can do for you'

Presidential inaugural address, 20 January 1961

'Ich bin ein Berliner'

Speech at the Berlin Wall defending democracy, 26 June 1963
JOHN F. KENNEDY

THE BRIEF PRESIDENCY OF JOHN F. KENNEDY basks in a kind of afterglow in the modern American memory. It continues to represent a strand of idealism, even though much more is now known about Kennedy's personal flaws. One reason for his enduring appeal is that while his actual deeds were curtailed by his assassination in 1963, his words have expanded to fill the gap. They represent his potential, what he might have achieved, had he had the time.

At 43 years of age he was the youngest man, and the first Roman Catholic, to be elected president. His arrival in the White House on 20 January 1961 followed a narrow electoral victory over his Republican rival Richard Nixon, who had been vice-president for eight years. Kennedy promoted his 'New Frontier' to combat the economic slump, advocated robust foreign and defence policies (claiming President Eisenhower had allowed a decline in America's influence), and gained African American support by helping to get Martin Luther King released from jail following his civil rights activities in Georgia. Once in office, Kennedy appointed a Cabinet of young able men, including his 35-year-old brother Robert (as attorney general) and some Republicans. Together with his glamorous First Lady Jacqueline, the good-looking Jack Kennedy presided over a White House dubbed 'Camelot', encouraging intellectual and artistic activity. It looked like a renaissance, of an America that was assertive, forward-looking, yet liberal.

JOHN F. KENNEDY

Born in Brookline, Massachusetts, into a wealthy Irish-American family.

He was educated at Choate School and (from 1936) Harvard University, and visited Britain in 1938, where his father, Joseph, was ambassador. Joined the US Navy in 1940, and his actions in saving his torpedo-boat crew in 1943 earned him a decoration for bravery. Representing Massachusetts' 11th District as a Democrat, he served his first term (of three) in the US House of Representatives before being elected to the Senate in 1952. In 1953 he married Jacqueline Bouvier, and in 1957 he won the Pulitzer Prize for the book *Profiles in Courage*. After his victorious presidential election, he was inaugurated in 1961. His presidency saw the failed attempt to topple Fidel Castro in Cuba (the 'Bay of Pigs' fiasco), crisis in Berlin and the building of the Berlin Wall, the introduction of a civil rights bill in Congress, the Cuban Missile Crisis and signing of the Nuclear Test Ban treaty, the serious beginnings of a US space programme and a plan to combat poverty.

Assassinated (shot) 22 November 1963 in Dallas, Texas, by Lee Harvey Oswald.

Kennedy was an admirer of fine oratory, and he refined and edited his inaugural address for two months before he gave it. The speech says much about the Cold War world he faced, and it is largely concerned with America's place in that world. Kennedy accepted his 'role of defending freedom in its hour of maximum danger'. He promised that 'this hemisphere intends to remain the master of its own house', and – presciently – warned the Soviet Union (though it was not named) to beware lest 'the dark powers of destruction unleashed by science engulf all humanity in planned or accidental destruction'. But he also capitalized on his own image of freshness to propose that it was possible, in good faith, to 'begin anew'. He concluded with his patriotic appeal to his countrymen and women: 'Ask not what America will do for you; ask what you can do for your country.' Less well known is that he continued, 'My fellow citizens of the world, ask not what America will do for you, but what together we can do for the freedom of man'.

Thirty-four months later, it was all over, when the president was shot dead in Texas. By then he had indeed tangled with the 'dark powers of destruction' during the Cuban Missile Crisis, in October 1962. During those 13 days, he faced down his more hawkish advisers, who – in response to the Soviet deployment of nuclear missiles to Cuba – favoured military retaliation. This was followed by the signing of the historic Nuclear Test Ban treaty in 1963. The American economy was greatly improving, civil rights laws were now on the agenda and Kennedy (reacting to recent Soviet success in space technology) promised to put a man on the moon by the end of the decade. However, American involvement in Vietnam was becoming a major issue, which Kennedy referred to as 'the worst problem we've got'.

VICE PRESIDENT [LYNDON] JOHNSON, Mr Speaker, Mr Chief Justice, President Eisenhower, Vice-President Nixon, President Truman, reverend clergy, fellow citizens: We observe today not a victory of party but a celebration of freedom, symbolizing an end as well as a beginning, signifying renewal as well as change. For I have sworn before you and Almighty God the same solemn oath our forebears prescribed nearly a century and three-quarters ago.

The world is very different now. For man holds in his mortal hands the power to abolish all forms of human poverty and all forms of human life. And yet the same revolutionary beliefs for which our forebears fought are still at issue around the globe – the belief that the rights of man come not from the generosity of the state but from the hand of God.

We dare not forget today that we are the heirs of that first revolution. Let the word go forth from this time and place, to friend and foe alike, that the torch has been passed to a new generation of Americans – born in this century, tempered by war, disciplined by a hard and bitter peace, proud of our ancient heritage – and unwilling to witness or permit the slow undoing of those human rights to which this nation has always been committed, and to which we are committed today at home and around the world.

Let every nation know, whether it wishes us well or ill, that we shall pay any price, bear any burden, meet any hardship, support any friend, oppose any foe to assure the survival and the success of liberty.

This much we pledge – and more.

To those old allies whose cultural and spiritual origins we share, we pledge the loyalty of faithful friends. United there is little we cannot do in a host of cooperative ventures. Divided there is little we can do, for we dare not meet a powerful challenge at odds and split asunder.

To those new states whom we welcome to the ranks of the free, we pledge our word that one form of colonial control shall not have passed away merely to be replaced by a far more iron tyranny. We shall not always expect to find them supporting our view. But we shall always hope to find them strongly supporting their own freedom – and to remember that, in the past, those who foolishly sought power by riding the back of the tiger ended up inside.

'If a free society cannot help the many who are poor, it cannot save the few who are rich'

To those people in the huts and villages of half the globe struggling to break the bonds of mass misery, we pledge our best efforts to help them help themselves, for whatever period is required – not because the communists may be doing it, not because we seek their votes, but because it is right.

If a free society cannot help the many who are poor, it cannot save the few who are rich.

To our sister republics south of our border, we offer a special pledge: to convert our good words into good deeds, in a new alliance for progress, to assist free men and free governments in casting off the chains of poverty. But this peaceful revolution of hope cannot become the prey of hostile powers. Let all our neighbours know that we shall join with them to oppose aggression or subversion anywhere in the Americas.

And let every other power know that this hemisphere intends to remain the master of its own house.

To that world assembly of sovereign states, the United Nations, our last best hope in an age where the instruments of war have far outpaced the instruments of peace, we renew our pledge of support – to prevent it from becoming merely a forum for invective, to strengthen its shield of the new and the weak, and to enlarge the area in which its writ may run.

Finally, to those nations who would make themselves our adversary, we offer not a pledge but a request: that both sides begin anew the quest for peace – before the dark powers of destruction unleashed by science engulf all humanity in planned or accidental self-destruction.

We dare not tempt them with weakness. For only when our arms are sufficient beyond doubt can we be certain beyond doubt that they will never be employed. But neither can two great and powerful groups of nations take comfort from our present course – both sides overburdened by the cost of modern weapons, both rightly alarmed by the steady spread of the deadly atom, yet both racing to alter that uncertain balance of terror that stays the hand of mankind's final war. So let us begin anew – remembering on both sides that civility is not a sign of weakness, and sincerity is always subject to proof.

> 'Let us never negotiate out of fear. But let us never fear to negotiate.'

Let us never negotiate out of fear. But let us never fear to negotiate.

Let both sides explore what problems unite us instead of belabouring those problems which divide us.

Let both sides, for the first time, formulate serious and precise proposals for the inspection and control of arms, and bring the absolute power to destroy other nations under the absolute control of all nations.

Let both sides seek to invoke the wonders of science instead of its terrors. Together let us explore the stars, conquer the deserts, eradicate disease, tap the ocean depths, and encourage the arts and commerce.

Let both sides unite to heed, in all corners of the earth, the command of Isaiah – to 'undo the heavy burdens . . . and let the oppressed go free'.

And if a beachhead of cooperation may push back the jungle of suspicion, let both sides join in creating a new endeavour – not a new balance of power, but a new world of law – where the strong are just, and the weak secure, and the peace preserved.

All this will not be finished in the first one hundred days. Nor will it be finished in the first one thousand days; nor in the life of this Administration; nor even perhaps in our lifetime on this planet. But let us begin.

In your hands, my fellow citizens, more than mine, will rest the final success or failure of our course. Since this country was founded, each generation of Americans has been summoned to give testimony to its national loyalty. The graves of young Americans who answered the call to service surround the globe.

Now the trumpet summons us again – not as a call to bear arms, though arms we need – not as a call to battle, though embattled we are – but a call to bear the burden of a long twilight struggle, year in and year out, rejoicing in hope, patient in tribulation, a struggle against the common enemies of man: tyranny, poverty, disease and war itself.

Can we forge against these enemies a grand and global alliance, North and South, East and West, that can assure a more fruitful life for all mankind? Will you join in that historic effort?

In the long history of the world, only a few generations have been granted the role of defending freedom in its hour of maximum danger. I do not shrink from this responsibility – I welcome it. I do not believe that any of us would exchange places with any other people or any other generation. The energy, the faith, the devotion which we bring to this endeavour will light our country and all who serve it. And the glow from that fire can truly light the world.

'Ask what you can do for your country'

And so, my fellow Americans, ask not what your country can do for you; ask what you can do for your country.

My fellow citizens of the world, ask not what America will do for you, but what together we can do for the freedom of man.

Finally, whether you are citizens of America or citizens of the world, ask of us here the same high standards of strength and sacrifice which we ask of you. With a good conscience our only sure reward, with history the final judge of our deeds, let us go forth to lead the land we love, asking His blessing and His help, but knowing that here on earth God's work must truly be our own.

THE CITY OF BERLIN HAD BEEN, since 1945, the crucible of the Cold War. It was divided after the Second World War into US, Soviet, British and French zones, but later the Soviet zone was merged into the communist client state of East Germany, leaving the rest – West Berlin – as a capitalist, democratic outpost surrounded by East Germany. As freedoms and living standards deteriorated in East Germany compared to the 'economic miracle' of West Germany, migrants flowed into West Berlin from the East Berlin sector, across the still open dividing lines. In order to stop the exodus, the East Germans built the Berlin Wall in summer 1961, just inside their sector. A physical barrier of concrete, barbed wire and watchtowers now surrounded West Berlin.

For the Western democracies, the Berlin Wall became a potent symbol of the failures of the communist system, and West Berlin a vital expression of the defence of free peoples. On 26 June 1963, Kennedy emphasized this symbolism in a rousing speech to West Berliners, where he identified with the city's people, famously declaring *'Ich bin ein Berliner'* – I am a Berliner.

I AM PROUD TO COME TO THIS CITY as the guest of your distinguished mayor, who has symbolized throughout the world the fighting spirit of West Berlin. And I am proud to visit the Federal Republic [i.e West Germany] with your distinguished chancellor who for so many years has committed Germany to democracy and freedom and progress, and to come here in the company of my fellow American, General Clay, who has been in this city during its great moments of crisis and will come again if ever needed.

Two thousand years ago, the proudest boast was *civis Romanus sum* [I am a Roman citizen]. Today, in the world of freedom, the proudest boast is *Ich bin ein Berliner.*

. . . There are many people in the world who really don't understand, or say they don't, what is the great issue between the free world and the communist world. Let them come to Berlin.

There are some who say that communism is the wave of the future. Let them come to Berlin.

'Freedom has many difficulties and democracy is not perfect'

And there are some who say, in Europe and elsewhere, we can work with the communists. Let them come to Berlin.

And there are even a few who say that it is true that communism is an evil system, but it permits us to make economic progress. *Lass' sie nach Berlin kommen.* Let them come to Berlin.

Freedom has many difficulties and democracy is not perfect. But we have never had to put a wall up to keep our people in – to prevent them from leaving us. I want to say on behalf of my countrymen who live many miles away on the other side of the Atlantic, who are far distant from you, that they take the greatest pride, that they have been able to share with you, even from a distance, the story of the last 18 years. I know of no town, no city, that has been besieged for 18 years that still lives with the vitality and the force, and the hope, and the determination of the city of West Berlin.

While the wall is the most obvious and vivid demonstration of the failures of the communist system – for all the world to see – we take no satisfaction in it; for it is, as your mayor has said, an offence not only against history but an offence against humanity, separating families, dividing husbands and wives and brothers and sisters, and dividing a people who wish to be joined together.

'Lift your eyes beyond the dangers of today, to the hopes of tomorrow'

What is true of this city is true of Germany: real, lasting peace in Europe can never be assured as long as one German out of four is denied the elementary right of free men, and that is to make a free choice. In 18 years of peace and good faith, this generation of Germans has earned the right to be free, including the right to unite their families and their nation in lasting peace, with good will to all people.

You live in a defended island of freedom, but your life is part of the main. So let me ask you, as I close, to lift your eyes beyond the dangers of today, to the hopes of tomorrow, beyond the freedom merely of this city of Berlin, or your country of Germany, to the advance of freedom everywhere, beyond the wall to the day of peace with justice, beyond yourselves and ourselves to all mankind.

Freedom is indivisible, and when one man is enslaved, all are not free. When all are free, then we can look forward to that day when this city will be joined as one and this country and this great Continent of Europe in a peaceful and hopeful globe. When that day finally comes, as it will, the people of West Berlin can take sober satisfaction in the fact that they were in the front lines for almost two decades.

All free men, wherever they may live, are citizens of Berlin.

And, therefore, as a free man, I take pride in the words *Ich bin ein Berliner*.

'I have a dream'

Civil rights speech at the Lincoln Memorial, 28 August 1963

'I've seen the promised land'

Civil rights speech on the eve of his assassination, 3 April 1968

MARTIN LUTHER KING, JR

IN 1955, IN THE TOWN OF MONTGOMERY, Alabama, an African American seamstress took a seat in a section of a bus reserved for whites. When the driver asked Rosa Parks to move to the back, under the state's segregation laws, she refused. Her subsequent arrest propelled an African American boycott of Montgomery's buses, which in turn produced a historic US Supreme Court decision outlawing racial segregation on public transport. The leader of the boycott was a young Baptist minister with a Ph.D in theology under his belt: Dr Martin Luther King, Jr.

Eight years later, as President of the Southern Christian Leadership Conference and figurehead of America's civil rights movement, King addressed more than 250,000 supporters on the steps of the Lincoln Memorial in Washington, D.C., at the culmination of the 'March on Washington for Jobs and Freedom'. The campaign called for an end to segregation in schools and discrimination in the workplace, along with other measures to improve the fortunes of African Americans, and it is credited with easing the passage of the 1964 Civil Rights Act and the 1965 National Voting Rights Act. How far King had a sense of his place in history is something that later commentators would speculate about. But his 'I have a dream' speech was timely in 1963, and for many not even born then, it resonates more deeply than any other modern American speech.

The speech itself is redolent of the phrasing and cadences of the Bible and the pulpit, from its opening – the deliberately archaic 'Five score years ago', which purposely echoes Lincoln's Gettyburg Address. It creates a picture of an America that is failing to live up

MARTIN LUTHER KING, JR

Born Michael King on 15 January 1929 in Atlanta, Georgia: his name was changed by his father to honour the reformation theologian Martin Luther.

He studied sociology at Morehouse College, Atlanta, and then obtained a Ph.D in theology from Boston University. He became a Baptist minister in Montgomery, Alabama, and led the Montgomery Bus Boycott in 1955–6. He co-founded a civil rights organization, the Southern Christian Leadership Conference (1957), and in 1958 he survived a stabbing at a book signing. In 1960 he became pastor of Ebenezer Baptist Church in his home neighbourhood in Atlanta. He addressed 250,000 supporters of the 'March on Washington' in 1963, and in 1964 he received the Nobel Peace Prize. In 1968, he began a new 'Poor People's' campaign.

Assassinated (shot) 4 April 1968 in Memphis, Tennessee. In 2000, the United States adopted Martin Luther King Day (in January) as a federal holiday.

to its promise as a New Jerusalem, as a home for all of 'God's children'. King dramatized 'a shameful condition' of African Americans, 'on a lonely island of poverty in the midst of a vast ocean of material prosperity', in terms of economic need, of constitutional obligations towards them, of a battle against unjust laws and unjust law-enforcers. As he built to his climax – a vision of racial equality – he reached further into Old Testament imagery and New World idealism to create a landscape of 'prodigious hills' and 'mighty mountains', where 'one day every valley shall be exalted' and the 'crooked places will be made straight'. It remains a rhetorical triumph.

FIVE SCORE YEARS AGO, a great American, in whose symbolic shadow we stand today, signed the Emancipation Proclamation. This momentous decree came as a great beacon light of hope to millions of negro slaves, who had been seared in the flames of withering injustice. It came as a joyous daybreak to end the long night of their captivity.

But one hundred years later, the negro still is not free. One hundred years later, the life of the negro is still sadly crippled by the manacles of segregation and the chains of discrimination. One hundred years later, the negro lives on a lonely island of poverty in the midst of a vast ocean of material prosperity. One hundred years later, the negro is still languished in the corners of American society and finds himself an exile in his own land. And so we've come here today to dramatize a shameful condition.

'But we refuse to believe that the bank of justice is bankrupt'

In a sense we have come to our nation's capital to cash a cheque. When the architects of our republic wrote the magnificent words of the Constitution and the Declaration of Independence, they were signing a promissory note to which every American was to fall heir. This note was a promise that all men, yes, black men as well as white men, would be guaranteed the unalienable rights of life, liberty, and the pursuit of happiness. It is obvious today that America has defaulted on this promissory note, insofar as her citizens of colour are concerned. Instead of honouring this sacred obligation, America has given the negro people a bad cheque, a cheque which has come back marked 'insufficient funds'.

But we refuse to believe that the bank of justice is bankrupt. We refuse to believe that there are insufficient funds in the great vaults of opportunity of this nation. And so we have come to cash this cheque, a cheque that will give us upon demand the riches of freedom and the security of justice.

We have also come to this hallowed spot to remind America of the fierce urgency of Now. This is no time to engage in the luxury of cooling off or to take the tranquillizing drug of gradualism. Now is the time to make real the promises of democracy. Now is the time to rise from the dark and desolate valley of segregation to the sunlit path of racial justice. Now is the time to lift our nation from the quicksands of racial injustice to the solid rock of brotherhood. Now is the time to make justice a reality for all of God's children.

It would be fatal for the nation to overlook the urgency of the moment. This sweltering summer of the negro's legitimate discontent will not pass until there is an invigorating autumn of freedom and equality. Nineteen sixty-three is not an end but a beginning. Those who hope that the negro needed to blow off steam and will now be content will have a rude awakening if the nation returns to business as usual. There will be neither rest nor tranquillity in America until the negro is granted his citizenship rights. The whirlwinds of revolt will continue to shake the foundations of our nation until the bright day of justice emerges.

But there is something that I must say to my people who stand on the warm threshold which leads into the palace of justice. In the process of gaining our rightful place we must not be guilty of wrongful deeds. Let us not seek to satisfy our thirst for freedom by drinking from the cup of bitterness and hatred. We must ever conduct our struggle on the high plane of dignity and discipline. We must not allow our creative protest to degenerate into physical violence. Again and again we must rise to the majestic heights of meeting physical force with soul force.

The marvellous new militancy which has engulfed the negro community must not lead us to a distrust of all white people, for many of our white brothers, as evidenced by their presence here today, have come to realize that their destiny is tied up with our destiny. And they have come to realize that their freedom is inextricably bound to our freedom. We cannot walk alone.

'No, no, we are not satisfied and we will not be satisfied until justice rolls down like waters'

And as we walk, we must make the pledge that we shall always march ahead. We cannot turn back. There are those who are asking the devotees of civil rights, 'When will you be satisfied?' We can never be satisfied as long as the negro is the victim of the unspeakable horrors of police brutality. We can never be satisfied as long as our bodies, heavy with the fatigue of travel, cannot gain lodging in the motels of the highways and the hotels of the cities. We cannot be satisfied as long as a negro in Mississippi cannot vote and a negro in New York believes he has nothing for which to vote. No, no, we are not satisfied and we will not be satisfied until justice rolls down like waters and righteousness like a mighty stream.

I am not unmindful that some of you have come here out of great trials and tribulations. Some of you have come fresh from narrow jail cells.

Some of you have come from areas where your quest for freedom left you battered by the storms of persecutions and staggered by the winds of police brutality. You have been the veterans of creative suffering. Continue to work with the faith that unearned suffering is redemptive. Go back to Mississippi, go back to Alabama, go back to South Carolina, go back to Georgia, go back to Louisiana, go back to the slums and ghettos of our northern cities, knowing that somehow this situation can and will be changed. Let us not wallow in the valley of despair, I say to you today, my friends. And so even though we face the difficulties of today and tomorrow, I still have a dream. It is a dream deeply rooted in the American dream.

I have a dream that one day this nation will rise up and live out the true meaning of its creed: We hold these truths to be self-evident that all men are created equal.

I have a dream that one day on the red hills of Georgia the sons of former slaves and the sons of former slave owners will be able to sit down together at the table of brotherhood.

I have a dream that one day even the state of Mississippi, a state sweltering with the heat of injustice, sweltering with the heat of oppression, will be transformed into an oasis of freedom and justice.

I have a dream that my four little children will one day live in a nation where they will not be judged by the colour of their skin but by the content of their character. I have a dream today!

I have a dream that one day, down in Alabama, with its vicious racists, with its governor having his lips dripping with the words of interposition and nullification; one day right down in Alabama little black boys and black girls will be able to join hands with little white boys and white girls as sisters and brothers. I have a dream today!

I have a dream that one day every valley shall be exalted, and every hill and mountain shall be made low, the rough places will be made plain, and the crooked places will be made straight, and the glory of the Lord shall be revealed and all flesh shall see it together.

This is our hope. This is the faith that I will go back to the South with. With this faith we will be able to hew out of the mountain of despair a stone of hope. With this faith we will be able to transform the jangling discords of our nation into a beautiful symphony of brotherhood. With this faith we will be able to work together, to pray together, to struggle together, to go to jail together, to stand up for freedom together, knowing that we will be free one day. And this will be the day, this will be the day when all of God's children will be able to sing with new meaning, 'My country 'tis of thee, sweet land of liberty, of thee I sing. Land where my fathers died, land of the Pilgrim's pride, from every mountainside, let freedom ring!' And if America is to be a great nation, this must become true.

'Let freedom ring from every hill and molehill of Mississippi'

And so let freedom ring from the prodigious hilltops of New Hampshire.

Let freedom ring from the mighty mountains of New York.

Let freedom ring from the heightening Alleghenies of Pennsylvania.

Let freedom ring from the snow-capped Rockies of Colorado.

Let freedom ring from the curvaceous slopes of California.

But not only that. Let freedom ring from Stone Mountain of Georgia.

Let freedom ring from Lookout Mountain of Tennessee.

Let freedom ring from every hill and molehill of Mississippi, from every mountainside, let freedom ring!

And when this happens, when we allow freedom to ring, when we let it ring from every village and every hamlet, from every state and every city, we will be able to speed up that day when all of God's children, black men and white men, Jews and Gentiles, Protestants and Catholics, will be able to join hands and sing in the words of the old negro spiritual, 'Free at last, free at last. Thank God Almighty, we are free at last.'

FOUR YEARS AFTER THE 'MARCH ON WASHINGTON', King embarked on a new Poor People's Campaign. As part of that project he arrived in Memphis, Tennessee, in April 1968, intending to lead a march supporting striking garbage collectors. He gave an informal speech on 3 April that was personal, poignant and eerily prophetic, in which he remembered his recovery after a stabbing in 1958 and reflected on his own mortality in the context of his campaigns, past and present. His final serene words contained the possibility that the evening would be his last: 'Longevity has its place. But I'm not concerned about that now . . . I'm happy, tonight. I'm not worried about anything. I'm not fearing any man.' The next day he was killed by a bullet while standing on the balcony of the Lorraine Motel.

YOU KNOW, SEVERAL YEARS AGO, I was in New York City autographing the first book that I had written. And while sitting there autographing books, a demented black woman came up. The only question I heard from her was, 'Are you Martin Luther King?' And I was looking down writing, and I said yes. And the next minute I felt something beating on my chest. Before I knew it I had been stabbed by this demented woman. I was rushed to Harlem Hospital. It was a dark Saturday afternoon. And that blade had gone through, and the X-rays revealed that the tip of the blade was on the edge of my aorta, the main artery. And once that's punctured, you drown in your own blood – that's the end of you.

'If I had sneezed, I would have died'

It came out in the *New York Times* the next morning that if I had sneezed, I would have died. Well, about four days later, they allowed me, after the operation, after my chest had been opened, and the blade had been taken out, to move around in the wheelchair in the hospital. They allowed me to read some of the mail that came in, and from all over the states, and the world, kind letters came in. I read a few, but one of them I will never forget. I had received one from the president and the vice-president. I've forgotten what those telegrams said. I'd received a visit and a letter from the Governor of New York, but I've forgotten what the letter said. But there was another letter that came from a little girl, a young girl who was a student at the White Plains High School. And I looked at that letter, and I'll never forget it. It said simply, 'Dear Dr King: I am a ninth-grade student at the White Plains High School.' She said, 'While it should not matter, I would like to mention that I am a white girl. I read in the paper of your misfortune, and of your suffering. And I read that if you had sneezed, you would have died. And I'm simply writing you to say that I'm so happy that you didn't sneeze.'

'The black people of Birmingham, Alabama, aroused the conscience of this nation'

And I want to say tonight, I want to say that I am happy that I didn't sneeze. Because if I had sneezed, I wouldn't have been around here in 1960, when students all over the South started sitting-in at lunch counters. And I knew that as they were sitting in, they were really standing up for the best in the American dream. And taking the whole nation back to those great wells of democracy which were dug deep by the Founding Fathers in the Declaration of Independence and the Constitution. If I had sneezed, I wouldn't have been around in 1962, when negroes in Albany, Georgia, decided to straighten their backs up. And whenever men and women straighten their backs up, they are going somewhere, because a man can't ride your back unless it is bent. If I had sneezed, I wouldn't have been here in 1963, when the black people of Birmingham, Alabama, aroused the conscience of this nation, and brought into being the Civil Rights Bill. If I had sneezed, I wouldn't have had a chance later that year, in August, to try to tell America about a dream that I had had. If I had sneezed, I wouldn't have been down in Selma, Alabama, to see the great movement there. If I had sneezed, I wouldn't have been in Memphis to see a community rally around those brothers and sisters who are suffering. I'm so happy that I didn't sneeze.

And they were telling me, now it doesn't matter now. It really doesn't matter what happens now. I left Atlanta this morning, and as we got started on the plane, there were six of us, the pilot said over the public address system, 'We are sorry for the delay, but we have Dr Martin Luther King on the plane. And to be sure that all of the bags were checked, and to be sure that nothing would be wrong with the plane, we had to check out everything carefully. And we've had the plane protected and guarded all night.'

And then I got into Memphis. And some began to say that threats, or talk about the threats that were out. What would happen to me from some of our sick white brothers?

'We, as a people will get to the promised land'

Well, I don't know what will happen now. We've got some difficult days ahead. But it doesn't matter with me now. Because I've been to the mountaintop. And I don't mind. Like anybody, I would like to live a long life. Longevity has its place. But I'm not concerned about that now. I just want to do God's will. And He's allowed me to go up to the mountain. And I've looked over. And I've seen the promised land. I may not get there with you. But I want you to know tonight, that we, as a people will get to the promised land. And I'm happy, tonight. I'm not worried about anything. I'm not fearing any man. Mine eyes have seen the glory of the coming of the Lord.

'An ideal for which I am prepared to die'

Trial speech defending his actions and goals, 20 April 1964

'Free at last'

Speech after ANC election victory, 2 May 1994
NELSON MANDELA

ON 20 APRIL 1964, THE FUTURE LEADER of South Africa, Nelson Mandela, was facing a bleak future. He was on trial in Pretoria for committing sabotage and treason against the white-minority ruled state and its segregationist apartheid policies. Of the former charge, he was indeed guilty, for he was a co-founder and leader of *Umkhonto we Sizwe* (Spear of the Nation), the paramilitary wing of the banned anti-apartheid African National Congress, which had been conducting a campaign of sabotage against industrial and other targets. Mandela was already in prison, serving a five-year sentence for leading a strike and travelling abroad without permission. Now, the so-called 'Rivonia Trial', named after the Johannesburg suburb where his co-defendants had been arrested, moved to hearing the defence, and Mandela spoke at length.

It was not a novel experience for him, and he was able to use his legal training to good effect. He presented an eloquent, dispassionate analysis of the iniquities of South Africa. He traced the history of the Sharpeville massacre (of protesting blacks) in 1960 and the subsequent banning of the ANC. He spoke plainly of the creation of *Umkhonto we Sizwe* as an effort to marshal the violent resentment that black South Africans were feeling and direct it to a type of constructive destruction – sabotage of official installations rather than the killing of people. He lauded the British Parliament and the American Congress as models of representative government. With a possible death sentence awaiting him, he also declared that in order to achieve the society he aspired to he would be 'prepared to die'.

Mandela acknowledged that a commonality of interests in fighting white minority rule had brought the ANC and the South African Communist Party in close proximity – and the government liked to lump them together as the common enemy. But, he

NELSON MANDELA

Born 18 July 1918 in Umtata (now in Eastern Cape Province), South Africa, the eldest son of a Xhosa-speaking Tempu chief.

He attended a Methodist school (from 1937), took correspondence courses with the University of South Africa, and studied law at the University of the Witwatersrand, Johannesburg. He joined the African National Congress in 1943, helping to found its youth league. The apartheid era proper began in 1948, following the National Party's election victory. In 1952, he opened a legal practice with Oliver Tambo, who later led the ANC while Mandela was in prison. In 1956 he was arrested with others for treason, but acquitted after a long trial. After the Sharpeville massacre (1960) and a government state of emergency, he co-founded *Umkhonto we Sizwe*, the ANC's armed wing. He received a five-year prison sentence in 1962 for fomenting strikes and breaking travel restrictions, and in 1964, at the 'Rivonia Trial', he and others received life sentences for sabotage and treason. He remained in prison for 26 years, the majority spent on Robben Island. He was released in 1990 and became leader of the now legalized ANC, beginning negotiations with President F.W. De Klerk towards black majority rule: they jointly won the Nobel Peace Prize in 1993. With the historic ANC victory in South Africa's first fully free elections, Mandela became President of South Africa (1994) until retiring in 1999; he remained an active elder statesman until his death. He was praised for ensuring that stability and reconciliation prevailed in South Africa rather than civil war or retribution.

Died 5 December 2013 in Johannesburg.

stated that the ANC did not plan to overturn capitalism. On the question of black majority rule, he asserted that 'the ANC has spent half a century fighting against racialism. When it triumphs, it will not change that policy . . .'. The seeds of the statesmanlike Mandela, who would emerge on the world's stage 30 years later, were present in 1964.

I AM THE FIRST ACCUSED.

I hold a Bachelor's Degree in Arts and practised as an attorney in Johannesburg for a number of years in partnership with Oliver Tambo. I am a convicted prisoner serving five years for leaving the country without a permit and for inciting people to go on strike at the end of May 1961.

. . . The lack of human dignity experienced by Africans is the direct result of the policy of white supremacy. White supremacy implies black inferiority. Legislation designed to preserve white supremacy entrenches this notion. Menial tasks in South Africa are invariably performed by Africans. When anything has to be carried or cleaned the white man will look around for an African to do it for him, whether the African is employed by him or not. Because of this sort of attitude, whites tend to regard Africans as a separate breed. They do not look upon them as people with families of their own; they do not realize that they have emotions – that they fall in love like white people do; that they want to be with their wives and children like white people want to be with theirs; that they want to earn enough money to support their families properly, to feed and clothe them and send them to school. And what 'house-boy' or 'garden-boy' or labourer can ever hope to do this?

Pass laws [limiting black South Africans' freedom of movement], which to the Africans are among the most hated bits of legislation in South Africa, render any African liable to police surveillance at any time. I doubt whether there is a single African male in South Africa who has not at some stage had a brush with the police over his pass. Hundreds and thousands of Africans are thrown into jail each year under pass laws. Even worse than this is the fact that pass laws keep husband and wife apart and lead to the breakdown of family life.

Poverty and the breakdown of family life have secondary effects. Children wander about the streets of the townships because they have no schools to go to, or no money to enable them to go to school, or no parents at home to see that they go to school, because both parents (if there be two) have to work to keep the family alive. This leads to a breakdown in moral standards, to an alarming rise in illegitimacy, and to growing violence which erupts not only politically, but everywhere. Life in the townships is dangerous. There is not a day that goes by without somebody being stabbed or assaulted. And violence is carried out of the townships in the white living areas. People are afraid to walk alone in the streets after dark. Housebreakings and robberies are increasing, despite the fact that the death sentence can now be imposed for such offences. Death sentences cannot cure the festering sore.

'Above all, we want equal political rights'

Africans want to be paid a living wage. Africans want to perform work which they are capable of doing, and not work which the government declares them to be capable of. Africans want to be allowed to live where they obtain work, and not be endorsed out of an area because they were not born there. Africans want to be allowed to own land in places where they work, and not to be obliged to live in rented houses which they can never call their own. Africans want to be part of the general population, and not confined to living in their own ghettoes. African men want to have their wives and children to live with them where they work, and not be forced into an unnatural existence in men's hostels. African women want to be with their menfolk and not be left permanently widowed in the Reserves. Africans want to be allowed out after eleven o'clock at night and not to be confined to their rooms like little children. Africans want to be allowed to travel in their own country and to seek work where they want to and not where the Labour Bureau tells them to. Africans want a just share in the whole of South Africa; they want security and a stake in society.

Above all, we want equal political rights, because without them our disabilities will be permanent. I know this sounds revolutionary to the whites in this country, because the majority of voters will be Africans. This makes the white man fear democracy.

But this fear cannot be allowed to stand in the way of the only solution which will guarantee racial harmony and freedom for all. It is not true that the enfranchisement of all will result in racial domination. Political division, based on colour, is entirely artificial and, when it disappears, so will the domination of one colour group by another. The ANC has spent half a century fighting against racialism. When it triumphs it will not change that policy.

This then is what the ANC is fighting. Their struggle is a truly national one. It is a struggle of the African people, inspired by their own suffering and their own experience. It is a struggle for the right to live.

During my lifetime I have dedicated myself to this struggle of the African people. I have fought against white domination, and I have fought against black domination. I have cherished the ideal of a democratic and free society in which all persons live together in harmony and with equal opportunities. It is an ideal which I hope to live for and to achieve. But if needs be, it is an ideal for which I am prepared to die.

AFTER HIS RELEASE FROM PRISON IN 1991, Mandela succeeded Oliver Tambo as President of the ANC. He travelled widely to maintain international support for the ending of apartheid, acquiring a huge and admiring following. After negotiations with the last National Party President of South Africa, F.W. De Klerk, paved the way for the historic elections of May 1994, Mandela assumed the country's presidency. The speech he gave on the evening of his victory is characteristic of his easy, mature style. It was a measure of the man and the national transformation that he could commend the security forces for their 'sterling work'. In an echo of Martin Luther King's 'I have a dream' speech, Mandela could proclaim that his people were 'free at last', and with a particular poignancy given his long years of incarceration. Appropriately, his autobiography, published in the same year, was titled *Long Walk to Freedom*.

MY FELLOW SOUTH AFRICANS – the people of South Africa: This is indeed a joyous night. Although not yet final, we have received the provisional results of the election, and are delighted by the overwhelming support for the African National Congress.

To all those in the African National Congress and the democratic movement who worked so hard these last few days and through these many decades, I thank you and honour you. To the people of South Africa and the world who are watching: this is a joyous night for the human spirit. This is your victory too. You helped end apartheid, you stood with us through the transition.

I watched, along with all of you, as the tens of thousands of our people stood patiently in long queues for many hours. Some sleeping on the open ground overnight waiting to cast this momentous vote. South Africa's heroes are legend across the generations. But it is you, the people, who are our true heroes.

This is one of the most important moments in the life of our country. I stand here before you filled with deep pride and joy: pride in the ordinary, humble people of this country . . . And joy that we can loudly proclaim from the rooftops – free at last!

I stand before you humbled by your courage, with a heart full of love for all of you. I regard it as the highest honour to lead the ANC at this moment in our history, and that we have been chosen to lead our country into the new century. I pledge to use all my strength and ability to live up to your expectations of me as well as of the ANC. I am personally indebted and pay tribute to some of South Africa's greatest leaders. They should have been here to celebrate with us, for this is their achievement too.

Tomorrow, the entire ANC leadership and I will be back at our desks. We are rolling up our sleeves to begin tackling the problems our country faces. We ask you all to join us – go back to your jobs in the morning. Let's get South Africa working. For we must, together and without delay, begin to build a better life for all South Africans. This means creating jobs, building houses, providing education and bringing peace and security for all.

The calm and tolerant atmosphere that prevailed during the elections depicts the type of South Africa we can build. It set the tone for the future. We might have our differences, but we are one people with a common destiny in our rich variety of culture, race and tradition.

'Join together to celebrate the birth of democracy'

People have voted for the party of their choice and we respect that. This is democracy. I hold out a hand of friendship to the leaders of all parties and their members, and ask all of them to join us in working together to tackle the problems we face as a nation. An ANC government will serve all the people of South Africa, not just ANC members.

We also commend the security forces for the sterling work done. This has laid a solid foundation for a truly professional security force, committed to the service of the people and loyalty to the new constitution.

Now is the time for celebration, for South Africans to join together to celebrate the birth of democracy. I raise a glass to you all for working so hard to achieve what can only be called a small miracle. Let our celebrations be in keeping with the mood set in the elections, peaceful, respectful and disciplined, showing we are a people ready to assume the responsibilities of government.

I promise that I will do my best to be worthy of the faith and confidence you have placed in me and my organization, the African National Congress. Let us build the future together, and toast a better life for all South Africans.

'You can't hate the roots of a tree and not hate the tree'

MALCOLM X
Speech celebrating African descent, 14 February 1965

F MARTIN LUTHER KING, JR, represented one route towards African American self-realization in the 1960s – rooted in the language and morality of the Bible, the community of the Southern Baptist Church, and aspiring for integration – then Malcolm X represented a very different version. A Muslim convert born in Nebraska, his family history embraced unexplained death (his father committed suicide or was killed), committal to a mental institution (his mother), the burning of his house (by Ku Klux Klan members) and, according to his *Autobiography*, the racist murder of three uncles. His own early life comprised periods at a detention centre, various menial jobs, and petty crime leading to his arrest and imprisonment in 1946 for burglary. It was in prison that he found Islam, or a version of it, and his life took a very different course.

By 1954 Malcolm Little, as he was born, had changed his name to Malcolm X, to symbolize his new life as an 'ex-smoker, ex-drinker, ex-Christian, ex-slave'. He was also now minister of Temple No. 7, in New York's Harlem district, part of the Elijah Muhammad's Nation of Islam (NOI). The NOI was an organization founded by Muhammad's predecessor, Wallace Fard, and which combined elements of Islam with a form of black separatism, even black supremacy. During the ten years he spent pro-moting the Nation of Islam, Malcolm X became its most powerful spokesperson. He was also more politically engaged than was comfortable for the NOI, with his muscular views that African Americans should assert their own identities, create their own institutions and defend themselves against white racism. In 1963, after he described President Kennedy's assassination as 'chickens coming home to roost', there was an outcry and the NOI stopped him giving speeches.

In 1964, Malcolm X made a decisive break with Muhammad and the NOI, incurring their enduring antipathy, and founded his own organization. This last reinvention saw him become an orthodox Sunni Muslim and reject what he saw as the NOI's insular black nationalism in favour of an engagement with civil rights activism and a broader battle against racism. He visited Britain and spoke on the subject at Oxford University, he addressed heads of state in Cairo, and back in America he created an Organization of Afro-American Unity to advance his evolving perspective, perhaps summed up in his new phrase 'more African than American'.

His difference from the civil rights mainstream was embodied in a *Life* magazine photo of 1964, in which he clutched a rifle. And his language remained pungent, spiky,

MALCOLM X

Born 19 May 1925 in Omaha, Nebraska.

In 1938, with his father dead and his mother in a mental institution, he moved to a foster home. In 1941 he was 'mentally disqualified' for the draft, which he later said he concocted. After a variety of jobs and criminal activities, he was imprisoned for burglary (1946–52). He converted to Islam, and after release joined the Nation of Islam, becoming minister of Temple No. 7 in Harlem, New York, in 1954. After becoming the most high-profile, but controversial, public figure within the NOI, he left it in 1964 after disagreements and disillusionments. He worked with Alex Haley to publish his *Autobiography of Malcolm X* in 1964. The same year he visited Mecca (and became a Sunni Muslim), Africa, France and Britain, and founded the Organization of Afro-American Unity.

Assassinated (shot) 21 February 1965 in New York, while giving a speech.

challenging. But his life became increasingly endangered because of hostility not just from white racist groups but from the NOI. In the speech reproduced here, given in Detroit on 14 February 1965, he elaborated on his differences with the NOI and on his Afro-American perspective. A week later, he was beginning another speech at his regular venue in New York's Audubon Ballroom. He did not get far before NOI gunmen in the audience shot him dead.

. . . I AM NOT A RACIST in any form whatsoever. I don't believe in any form of racism. I don't believe in any form of discrimination or segregation. I believe in Islam.

. . . Elijah Muhammad had taught us that the white man could not enter into Mecca in Arabia and all of us who followed him, we believed it … When I got over there and went to Mecca and saw these people who were blond and blue-eyed and pale-skinned and all those things, I said 'Well,' but watched them closely. And I noticed that though they were white, and they would call themselves white, there was a difference between them and the white ones over here. And that basic difference was this: In Asia or the Arab world or in Africa, where the Muslims are, if you find one who says he's white, all he's doing is using an adjective to describe something that's incidental about him, one of his incidental characteristics; there is nothing else to it, he's just white.

But when you get the white man over here in America and he says he's white, he means something else. You can listen to the sound of his voice – when he says he's white, he means he's boss. That's right. That's what white means in this language. You know the expression 'free, white and twenty-one'. He made that up. He's letting you know that white means free, boss. He's up there, so that when he says he's white he has a little different sound in his voice. I know you know what I'm talking about …

Despite the fact that I saw that Islam was a religious brotherhood, I also had to face reality. And when I got back into this American society, I'm not in a society that practises brotherhood. I'm in a society that might preach it on Sunday, but they don't practise it on any day . . .This society is controlled primarily by the racists and segregationists who are from Washington, D.C., in positions of power.

. . . Now what effect does the struggle over Africa have on us? Why should the black man in America concern himself since he's been away from the African continent for three or four hundred years? Why should we concern ourselves? What impact does what happens to them have upon us? Number one, you have to realize that up until 1959 Africa was dominated by the colonial powers. Having complete control over Africa, the colonial powers of Europe projected the image of Africa negatively.

They always project Africa in a negative light: jungle savages, cannibals, nothing civilized. Why then naturally it was so negative that it was negative to you and me, and you and I began to hate it. We didn't want anybody telling us anything about Africa, much less calling us Africans. In hating Africa and in hating the Africans, we ended up hating ourselves, without even realizing it. Because you can't hate the roots of a tree, and not hate the tree. You can't hate your origin and not end up hating yourself. You can't hate Africa and not hate yourself.

'He is still more African than he is American'

To the same degree that your understanding of and attitude toward Africa become positive, you'll find your understanding of and your attitude toward yourself will also become positive. And this is what the white man knows. So they very skilfully make you and me hate our African identity, our African characteristics.

. . . One of the things that made the black Muslim movement grow was its emphasis upon things African. African blood, African origin, African culture, African ties. And you'd be surprised – we discovered that deep within the subconscious of the black man in this country, he is still more African than he is American. He thinks that he's more American than African, because the man is jiving him, the man is brainwashing him every day.

'You haven't enjoyed those fruits. You've enjoyed the thorns.'

. . . Just because you're in this country doesn't make you an American. No, you've got to go farther than that before you can become an American. You've got to enjoy the fruits of Americanism. You haven't enjoyed those fruits. You've enjoyed the thorns. You've enjoyed the thistles.

. . . I say again that I am not a racist. I don't believe in any form of segregation or anything like that. I'm for brotherhood for everybody, but I don't believe in forcing brotherhood upon people who don't want it. Let us practise brotherhood among ourselves, and then if others want to practise brotherhood with us, we're for practising it with them also. But I don't think that we should run around trying to love somebody who doesn't love us.

'Who are the kidnap victims?'

PIERRE TRUDEAU

Address during Quebec separatist crisis, 16 October 1970

I N CANADIAN POLITICS OF THE SECOND HALF of the 20th century, two speeches stand out. Both of them are rooted in the continuing question of French-speaking Quebec and its relationship with the rest of the country. The first speech was not even given by a Canadian, but by French President Charles de Gaulle. Visiting Quebec City in 1967, he provocatively uttered the words 'Vivre le Québec libre!' – translating as 'Long live free Quebec!' It sounded like unalloyed support for those who wanted to take the province out of Canada altogether, and it was taken up as a slogan by Quebec's separatists. By the mid-1960s, some of these had turned to violent action, notably the Front de Libération du Québec (FLQ), which mounted a campaign of bombings through the decade.

The second speech, three years later, was an impassioned broadcast by Canadian Prime Minister Pierre Trudeau, on the unprecedented invoking of the War Measures Act – effectively a state of emergency – in response to a domestic occurrence: the 'October Crisis'. On 5 October an FLQ cell had kidnapped the British trade commissioner, James Cross, in Montreal, and five days later the group also captured Pierre Laporte, Quebec's minister of labour and immigration. The group's demands included the freeing of FLQ members in prison and the publicizing of its manifesto.

Despite his Quebec origins, his liberal, modernizing instincts, and his support for Francophone rights, Trudeau believed in a strong federal government and had no sympathies for militant secessionism. But his decision to invoke the 1914 War Measures Act was controversial, for the Act suspended civil liberties and gave the federal government powers to rule by decree. It had last been invoked during the Second World War. In his speech, Trudeau refused to bow to the kidnappers' demands. For the prime minister, at stake was the 'unity and freedom of Canada'.

PIERRE TRUDEAU

Born 18 October 1919 in Montreal, Quebec.

He attended the elite Jesuit Collège Jean-de Brébeuf in Montreal, and studied law at the University of Montreal (1943) before being conscripted. After graduate study at Harvard University, the Institut d'Etudes Politiques (Paris) and the London School of Economics in the later 1940s, he returned to Quebec, becoming involved in local opposition politics, before teaching law (1961–5). He joined the Liberal Party, and was elected to the federal parliament in 1965, becoming minister of justice in 1967, where he introduced a bill of rights protecting the French language. After election as party leader, he was appointed prime minister in 1968, a position he held almost continuously over intervening elections until his resignation in 1984. Under his governments, Canada became officially bilingual, legalized homosexuality and abortion, saw off violent Quebec secessionism (after the 1970 October Crisis), controversially introduced controls on prices and energy resources in the 1970s, and modernized the constitution (including a Charter of Rights and Freedoms) in 1982.

Died 28 September 2000 in Montreal.

Cross was later rescued, but Laporte was murdered by his captors. In the wake of the crisis, over 400 secessionists and suspected FLQ members were arrested, and by the early 1970s violent secessionism had petered out, giving way to non-violent political action, notably the emergence of the Parti Québécois.

Bilingual, cultured, suave and stylish, Trudeau was a charismatic figure who dominated Canadian national politics over the 1970s and early 1980s. He was sometimes careless with his public remarks (as when he described farmers as 'professional complainers'), but he nonetheless achieved an enduring popularity. His death in 2000 occasioned a state funeral. In 2015 his son, Justin Trudeau, was elected Prime Minister of Canada.

I AM SPEAKING TO YOU at a moment of grave crisis, when violent and fanatical men are attempting to destroy the unity and the freedom of Canada. One aspect of that crisis is the threat which has been made on the lives of two innocent men. These are matters of the utmost gravity and I want to tell you what the government is doing to deal with them.

What has taken place in Montreal in the past two weeks is not unprecedented. It has happened elsewhere in the world on several recent occasions; it could happen elsewhere within Canada. But Canadians have always assumed that it could not happen here and as a result we are doubly shocked that it has.

Our assumption may have been naive, but it was understandable; understandable because democracy flourishes in Canada; understandable because individual liberty is cherished in Canada.

Notwithstanding these conditions – partly because of them – it has now been demonstrated to us by a few misguided persons just how fragile a democratic society can be, if democracy is not prepared to defend itself, and just how vulnerable to blackmail are tolerant, compassionate people.

'But I ask them whose attention are they seeking to attract?'

The governments of Canada and Quebec have been told by groups of self-styled revolutionaries that they intend to murder in cold blood two innocent men unless their demands are met. The kidnappers claim they act as they do in order to draw attention to instances of social injustice. But I ask them whose attention are they seeking to attract? The government of Canada? The government of Quebec? Every government in this country is well aware of the existence of deep and important social problems. And every government to the limit of its resources and ability is deeply committed to their solution. But not by kidnappings and bombings. By hard work. And if any doubt exists about the good faith or the ability of any government, there are opposition parties ready and willing to be given an opportunity to govern. In short there is available everywhere in Canada an effective mechanism to change governments by peaceful means. It has been employed by disenchanted voters again and again.

Who are the kidnap victims? To the victims' families they are husbands and fathers. To the kidnappers their identity is immaterial. The kidnappers' purposes would be served equally well by having in their grip you or me, or perhaps some child. Their purpose is to exploit the normal, human feelings of Canadians and to bend those feelings of sympathy into instruments for their own violent and revolutionary ends.

'They also want money. Ransom money.'

What are the kidnappers demanding in return for the lives of these men? Several things. For one, they want their grievances aired by force in public on the assumption, no doubt, that all right-thinking persons would be persuaded that the problems of the world can be solved by shouting slogans and insults.

They want more, they want the police to offer up as a sacrificial lamb a person whom they assume assisted in the lawful arrest and proper conviction of certain of their criminal friends.

They also want money. Ransom money.

They want still more. They demand the release from prison of 17 criminals, and the dropping of charges against six other men, all of whom they refer to as 'political prisoners'. Who are these men who are held out as latter-day patriots and martyrs? Let me describe them to you.

Three are convicted murderers; five others were jailed for manslaughter; one is serving a life imprisonment after having pleaded guilty to numerous charges related to bombings; another has been convicted of 17 armed robberies; two were once paroled but are now back in jail awaiting trial on charges of robberies.

Yet we are being asked to believe that these persons have been unjustly dealt with, that they have been imprisoned as a result of their political opinions, and that they deserve to be freed immediately, without recourse to due process of law.

The responsibilty of deciding whether to release one or other of these criminals is that of the federal goverment . . . To bow to the pressures of these kidnappers . . . would not only be an abdication of responsibilty, it would lead to an increase in terrorist activities in Quebec. It would be as well as an invitation to kidnapping and terrorism across the country.

. . . If a democratic society is to continue to exist, it must be able to root out the cancer of an armed, revolutionary movement that is bent on destroying the very basis of our freedom. For that reason the government, following an analysis of the facts, including requests of the government of Quebec and the city of Montreal for urgent action, decided to proclaim the War Measures Act. It did so at 4.00 a.m. this morning, in order to permit the full weight of government to be brought quickly to bear on all those persons advocating or practising violence as a means of achieving political ends.

The War Measures Act gives sweeping powers to the government. It also suspends the operation of the Canadian Bill of Rights. I can assure you that the government is most reluctant to seek such powers, and did so only when it became crystal clear that the situation could not be controlled unless some extraordinary assistance was made available on an urgent basis.

The authority contained in the Act will permit governments to deal effectively with the nebulous yet dangerous challenge to society represented by the terrorist organizations. The criminal law as it stands is simply not adequate to deal with systematic terrorism.

'These are strong powers and I find them as distasteful as I am sure you do'

The police have therefore been given certain extraordinary powers necessary for the effective detection and elimination of conspiratorial organizations which advocate the use of violence. These organizations, and membership in them, have been declared illegal. The powers include the right to search and arrest without warrant, to detain suspected persons without the necessity of laying specific charges immediately, and to detain persons without bail.

These are strong powers and I find them as distasteful as I am sure do you. They are necessary, however, to permit the police to deal with persons who advocate or promote the violent overthrow of our democratic system. In short, I assure you that the government recognizes its grave responsibilities in interfering in certain cases with civil liberties, and that it remains answerable to the people of Canada for its actions. The government will revoke this proclamation as soon as possible . . . .

'There can be no whitewash at the White House'

RICHARD NIXON

National address promising transparency over the Watergate affair, 30 April 1973

ONE OF THE MOST PSYCHOLOGICALLY COMPLEX individuals to occupy the Oval Office, the highly experienced Richard Milhous Nixon came to power with a reputation as a zealous anti-communist and a ruthless political streetfighter. His subsequent attempts to bomb the North Vietnamese (and Cambodians) into ending the Vietnam War made him a figure of hate to antiwar protestors, and America's support of an army coup against the left-wing President Allende of Chile made liberals scorn him. That impression is complicated by the fact that he promoted civil rights, accelerated desegregation in Southern schools, created the Environmental Protection Agency, opened diplomatic relations with communist China (and made a groundbreaking visit there), pursued arms-control agreements with the Soviet Union, and ultimately did manage to extract the United States from Vietnam. While re-evaluations of Nixon have begun, one event still largely determines his historical reputation: the Watergate scandal.

During the 1972 presidential campaign, which delivered a landslide re-election victory to Nixon, there was a break-in at the offices of the Democratic Party's National Committee, at Washington's Watergate building. There had been an attempt to wiretap telephones. It was revealed – partly through some clever investigative journalism and an FBI informant known as 'Deep Throat' – that the perpetrators had been commissioned by high-ranking Republican officials working to re-elect Nixon. Criminal prosecutions commenced against some presidential aides, but thus far the president himself remained aloof, asserting his ignorance of the events. Attempting to put some clear blue water between himself and 'this whole sordid affair', he made a national television address which memorably concluded that 'There can be no whitewash at the White House.' Unfortunately, there was.

In the months that followed, the president's credibility disintegrated. After legal tussles, going up to the Supreme Court, Congressional investigators eventually secured unedited tapes of White House conversations held in 1972: Nixon, it turned out,

RICHARD NIXON

Born 9 January 1913 into a Quaker family in Yorba Linda, California.

He studied at Whittier College and at Duke University Law School, where he excelled, going on to practise law in Whittier. During the Second World War, he enlisted in the US Navy, serving in the Pacific as a lieutenant-commander. He was elected as a Republican to the US House of Representatives (1946) and played a prominent role as a member of the House Committee on Un-American Activities, exposing the spy Alger Hiss. He entered the US Senate (1951), and in 1952 President Eisenhower chose him as his running mate: Nixon was vice-president until 1960, when he challenged John F. Kennedy for the presidency, narrowly losing. After an unsuccessful attempt to win the California governorship in 1962, he left politics, embittered, for law practice in New York; but he returned to finally win the presidency in 1968, and then defeated George McGovern by a wide margin in 1972. As president, he worked with Henry Kissinger to end the US presence in Vietnam 'with honour', recognized the People's Republic of China, signed the Anti-Ballistic Missile Treaty with the Soviet Union, and pursued some important social, economic and environmental legislation. From 1972, the Watergate break-in and its repercussions dogged his presidency, forcing his resignation in 1974.

Died 18 April 1994 in New York.

habitually had his conversations recorded. Not only did the tapes reveal a hitherto unknown foul-mouthed side to the president, there also transpired one conversation – the so-called 'smoking gun' tape from just days after the break-in – which proved that Nixon had encouraged his aides to try and hinder the FBI investigation into the incident. Nixon faced almost certain impeachment, having lost the support of even most Republicans in Congress. He resigned instead, making his farewell address to his staff, admitting 'Mistakes, yes. But for personal gain, never.'

Vice-President Ford now assumed the presidency, and he issued a controversial pardon to Nixon, saving him from criminal charges. Nixon's full, posthumous rehabilitation – if it is to happen – awaits a future date.

GOOD EVENING.

I want to talk to you tonight from my heart on a subject of deep concern to every American.

In recent months, members of my Administration and officials of the Committee for the Re-Election of the President – including some of my closest friends and most trusted aides – have been charged with involvement in what has come to be known as the Watergate affair. These include charges of illegal activity during and preceding the 1972 presidential election and charges that responsible officials participated in efforts to cover up that illegal activity.

The inevitable result of these charges has been to raise serious questions about the integrity of the White House itself. Tonight I wish to address those questions.

Last June 17, while I was in Florida trying to get a few days rest after my visit to Moscow, I first learned from news reports of the Watergate break-in. I was appalled at this senseless, illegal action, and I was shocked to learn that employees of the Re-Election Committee were apparently among those guilty.

I immediately ordered an investigation by appropriate government authorities. On September 15, as you will recall, indictments were brought against seven defendants in the case.

As the investigations went forward, I repeatedly asked those conducting the investigation whether there was any reason to believe that members of my Administration were in any way involved. I received repeated assurances that there were not. Because of these continuing reassurances, because I believed the reports I was getting, because I had faith in the persons from whom I was getting them, I discounted the stories in the press that appeared to implicate members of my Administration or other officials of the campaign committee.

Until March of this year, I remained convinced that the denials were true and that the charges of involvement by members of the White House Staff were false. The comments I made during this period, and the comments made by my press secretary on my behalf, were based on the information provided to us at the time we made those comments. However, new information then came to me which persuaded me that there was a real possibility that some of these charges were true, and suggesting further that there had been an effort to conceal the facts both from the public, from you, and from me.

'The truth should be fully brought out – no matter who was involved'

As a result, on March 21, I personally assumed the responsibility for coordinating intensive new inquiries into the matter, and I personally ordered those conducting the investigations to get all the facts and to report them directly to me, right here in this office.

I again ordered that all persons in the government or at the Re-Election Committee should cooperate fully with the FBI, the prosecutors and the grand jury. I also ordered that anyone who refused to cooperate in telling the truth would be asked to resign from government service. And, with ground rules adopted that would preserve the basic constitutional separation of powers between the Congress and the presidency, I directed that members of the White House staff should appear and testify voluntarily under oath before the Senate committee which was investigating Watergate.

I was determined that we should get to the bottom of the matter, and that the truth should be fully brought out – no matter who was involved.

'One of the most difficult decisions of my presidency'

At the same time, I was determined not to take precipitate action and to avoid, if at all possible, any action that would appear to reflect on innocent people. I wanted to be fair. But I knew that in the final analysis, the integrity of this office – public faith in the integrity of this office – would have to take priority over all personal considerations.

Today, in one of the most difficult decisions of my presidency, I accepted the resignations of two of my closest associates in the White House – Bob Haldeman [chief of staff], John Ehrlichman [domestic adviser] and – two of the finest public servants it has been my privilege to know.*

I want to stress that in accepting these resignations, I mean to leave no implication whatever of personal wrongdoing on their part, and I leave no implication tonight of implication on the part of others who have been charged in this matter. But in matters as sensitive as guarding the integrity of our democratic process, it is essential not only that rigorous legal and ethical standards be observed but also that the public, you, have total confidence that they are both being observed and enforced by those in authority and particularly by the President of the United States. They agreed with me that this move was necessary in order to restore that confidence.

. . . Whatever may appear to have been the case before, whatever improper activities may yet be discovered in connection with this whole sordid affair, I want the American people, I want you to know beyond the shadow of a doubt that during my term as president, justice will be pursued fairly, fully and impartially, no matter who is involved. This office is a sacred trust and I am determined to be worthy of that trust.

'I owe it to this great office that I hold, and I owe it to you – to my country'

In any organization, the man at the top must bear the responsibility. That responsibility, therefore, belongs here, in this office. I accept it. And I pledge to you tonight, from this office, that I will do everything in my power to ensure that the guilty are brought to justice and that such abuses are purged from our political processes in the years to come, long after I have left this office.

. . . Since March, when I first learned that the Watergate affair might in fact be far more serious than I had been led to believe, it has claimed far too much of my time and my attention. Whatever may now transpire in the case, whatever the actions of the grand jury, whatever the outcome of any eventual trials, I must now turn my full attention – and I shall do so – once again to the larger duties of this office. I owe it to this great office that I hold, and I owe it to you – to my country . . . There is vital work to be done toward our goal of a lasting structure of peace in the world – work that cannot wait, work that I must do . . . .

*Both men were subsequently found guilty of conspiracy and obstruction of justice.

There is also vital work to be done right here in America: to ensure prosperity, and that means a good job for everyone who wants to work; to control inflation, that I know worries every housewife, everyone who tries to balance a family budget in America; to set in motion new and better ways of ensuring progress toward a better life for all Americans.

When I think of this office – of what it means – I think of all the things that I want to accomplish for this nation, of all the things I want to accomplish for you.

On Christmas Eve, during my terrible personal ordeal of the renewed bombing of North Vietnam, which after 12 years of war finally helped to bring America peace with honour, I sat down just before midnight. I wrote out some of my goals for my second term as president. Let me read them to you:

'We must maintain the integrity of the White House'

To make it possible for our children, and for our children's children, to live in a world of peace.

To make this country be more than ever a land of opportunity – of equal opportunity, full opportunity for every American.

To provide jobs for all who can work, and generous help for those who cannot work.

To establish a climate of decency and civility, in which each person respects the feelings and the dignity and the God-given rights of his neighbour.

To make this a land in which each person can dare to dream, can live his dreams – not in fear, but in hope – proud of his community, proud of his country, proud of what America has meant to himself and to the world.

These are great goals. I believe we can, we must work for them. We can achieve them. But we cannot achieve these goals unless we dedicate ourselves to another goal.

We must maintain the integrity of the White House, and that integrity must be real, not transparent. There can be no whitewash at the White House.

'The special responsibility of the women of India'

INDIRA GANDHI

Speech on the value of women's education, 23 November 1974

BETWEEN THE MID-1960s AND EARLY 1980s, Indira Gandhi was one of the most powerful and controversial women in the world. For much of the period she was India's prime minister and, being the daughter of Jawaharlal Nehru, she carried the authority and expectations that go with a political dynasty. At first though, not much was expected of her, and critics labelled her *goongi gudiya* ('dumb doll'). But she came to dominate the politics of the period as a determined leader, sometimes imposing her will ruthlessly.

'Gandhi' was Indira's married name – she had no relation to 'Mahatma' Gandhi, her father's close collaborator in the struggle for Indian independence. Indira had politics in her blood, and she managed her father's re-election in 1951. After the death of Nehru in 1964, Bahadur Shastri became prime minister and appointed Indira as minister of information. But Shastri died only two years later and at this point Gandhi became prime minister, leading the world's largest democracy with its large discrepancies between the wealthy minority and a poor majority. She shared her father's goals of modernizing India.

In the 1974 speech she gave at Indraprastha College for Women, she elaborated the importance of education – especially women's education – as a vital part of India becoming 'a modern, rational society'. She recognized the difficulties of synthesizing 'what has been valuable and timeless in our ancient traditions with what is good and valuable in modern thought', but saw education as the key to making that judgement. She also criticized the 'superstition' – implicitly the caste system – that consigned the lowest social groups, and most obviously the Dalits or 'Untouchables', to the most menial work while at the same time looking down on that work.

While she continued Nehru's policy of maintaining India as one of the leading non-aligned countries – in theory, separate from the power politics of the Western and Soviet blocs – regional politics caused her to agree a mutual defence arrangement with the Soviet Union as a counterweight to Pakistan's close relations with the United States. In 1971, as East Pakistan rebelled and refugees flooded into India, Gandhi intervened militarily,

INDIRA GANDHI

Born 19 November 1917 in Allahabad, Uttar Pradesh, India, the daughter of lawyer and future prime minister Jawaharlal Nehru.

Attended universities of Visva-Bharati (West Bengal) and Oxford (England). In 1942 she married an Indian National Congress radical, Feroze Gandhi. British authorities briefly imprisoned her in 1943, after the Congress began its 'Quit India' policy. She worked for her father once he became independent India's prime minister, and managed his re-election (1951). She became president of the Congress Party (1959), and minister for information (1964). As prime minister (1966–71) she moved India closer to the Soviet Union, attempted modernizing reforms and intervened in East Pakistan's independence war, which produced Bangladesh. Her election victory in 1972 brought accusations of malpractice, and court rulings against her in 1975 provoked her to impose a state of emergency until 1977. She lost the 1977 election, but was re-elected in 1980. In 1984, she ordered troops to forcibly remove armed Sikh separatists from the Golden Temple in Amritsar, with much bloodshed.

Assassinated 31 October 1984 by two of her Sikh bodyguards. In 1991, her son and political heir Rajiv Gandhi was assassinated by a suicide bomber from Sri Lanka's Tamil Tigers.

with the result that East Pakistan achieved independence as Bangladesh. President Richard Nixon loathed Gandhi for her Soviet leanings and intervention in East Pakistan, referring to her in private as an 'old witch'.

In 1972 she led the Congress Party to a landslide victory, but she would be dogged by accusations of violating election laws and she faced being barred from politics. In response, she imprisoned opponents and ruled by decree for 21 months until, having called an election, the voters threw her out. She won power again in 1980, and now built closer ties with the United States and a good relationship with President Ronald Reagan. But her confrontation with Sikh separatists, resulting in a bloody battle to eject them from Amritsar's Golden Temple, brought about her 1984 assassination.

AN ANCIENT SANSKRIT saying says, woman is the home and the home is the basis of society. It is as we build our homes that we can build our country. If the home is inadequate – either inadequate in material goods and necessities or inadequate in the sort of friendly, loving atmosphere that every child needs to grow and develop – then that country cannot have harmony and no country which does not have harmony can grow in any direction at all.

That is why women's education is almost more important than the education of boys and men. We – and by 'we' I do not mean only we in India but all the world – have neglected women's education. It is fairly recent. Of course, not to you but when I was a child, the story of early days of women's education in England, for instance, was very current. Everybody remembered what had happened in the early days.

. . . Now, we have got education and there is a debate all over the country whether this education is adequate to the needs of society or the needs of our young people. I am one of those who always believe that education needs a thorough overhauling. But at the same time, I think that everything in our education is not bad, that even the present education has produced very fine men and women, specially scientists and experts in different fields, who are in great demand all over the world and even in the most affluent countries. Many of our young people leave us and go abroad because they get higher salaries, they get better conditions of work.

. . . One of the biggest responsibilities of the educated women today is how to synthesize what has been valuable and timeless in our ancient traditions with what is good and valuable in modern thought. All that is modern is not good just as all that is old is neither all good nor all bad. We have to decide, not once and for all but almost every week, every month what is coming out that is good and useful to our country and what of the old we can keep and enshrine in our society. To be modern, most people think that it is something of a manner of dress or a manner of speaking or certain habits and customs, but that is not really being modern. It is a very superficial part of modernity.

. . . Now, for India to become what we want it to become with a modern, rational society and firmly based on what is good in our ancient tradition and in our soil, for this we have to have a thinking public, thinking young women who are not content to accept what comes from any part of the world but are willing to listen to it, to analyze it and to decide whether it is to be accepted or whether it is to be thrown out and this is the sort of education which we want, which enables our young people to adjust to this changing world and to be able to contribute to it.

Some people think that only by taking up very high jobs, you are doing something important or you are doing national service. But we all know that the most complex machinery will be ineffective if one small screw is not working as it should and that screw is just as important as any big part. It is the same in national life. There is no job that is too small; there is no person who is too small. Everybody has something to do. And if he or she does it well, then the country will run well.

'Everything, whether dirty or small, had a purpose'

In our superstition, we have thought that some work is dirty work. For instance, sweeping has been regarded as dirty. Only some people can do it; others should not do it. Now we find that manure is the most valuable thing that the world has today and many of the world's economies are shaking because there is not enough fertilizer – and not just the chemical fertilizer but the ordinary manure, night-soil and all that sort of thing, things which were considered dirty. Now it shows how beautifully balanced the world was with everything fitted in with something else. Everything, whether dirty or small, had a purpose.

. . . So, I hope that all of you who have this great advantage of education will not only do whatever work you are doing keeping the national interests in view, but you will make your own contribution to creating peace and harmony, to bringing beauty in the lives of our people and our country. I think this is the special responsibility of the women of India. We want to do a great deal for our country, but we have never regarded India as isolated from the rest of the world. What we want to do is to make a better world. So, we have to see India's problems in the perspective of the larger world problems.

'Hate, ignorance and evil'

CHAIM HERZOG

United Nations address condemning anti-Semitism, 10 November 1975

I N NOVEMBER 1975, UNITED NATIONS RESOLUTION 3379 asserted that 'Zionism is a form of racism and racial discrimination'. It was proposed by a group of mainly Arab and North African countries, and it passed on a majority vote. Its supporters comprised a collection of African and Soviet-bloc states. The passage of the resolution provoked a stinging and eloquent denunciation from Israel's Ambassador to the United Nations, Chaim Herzog.

Herzog's life had given him a good basis for describing the Jewish experience in the 20th century. Born in Northern Ireland, he moved with his family to Palestine in the 1930s, where his father became chief rabbi. Herzog served with the Jewish underground, the Haganah, supporting the British against Arabs who were rebelling against Jewish immigration. In the closing stages of the Second World War he headed British Military Intelligence in northern Germany, where he saw concentration camps for himself and helped identify the captured Nazi war criminal Heinrich Himmler, who had been instrumental in the attempt to liquidate Europe's Jews. He fought in the first Arab–Israeli war of 1948, which saw Israel establish itself, and then continued his work in Israeli Military Intelligence. The central part of his eventful life had thus witnessed the calamities of the Holocaust and the difficult birth of a Jewish state.

Now, Herzog threw the full weight of that history into his stinging rebuke of 'the two great evils which menace society' – 'hatred and ignorance'. He invoked the Nazi brutality and vandalism of *Kristallnacht* in 1938, the death camps of the Holocaust, the 'malicious falsehoods' of the *Protocols of the Elders of Zion* (a forgery, purportedly a plan for Jewish world domination) and recent statements by Yasser Arafat, leader of the Palestinian Liberation Organization. By these means he characterized Jews and Israelis as victims of racism, not perpetrators of racism. He also struck an unabashedly proud note with regard to 'the moral and historical values of the Jewish people'. Furthermore, Herzog suggested that the very fact that the United Nations could pass this resolution called into doubt the credibility of the organization. Finally, and perhaps most powerfully, he moderated his outrage by contrasting the often tragic Jewish experience in the 20th century with the present resolution, which, given the weight of history, was 'but a passing episode'.

Of course, the resolution reflected the Cold War divide of the time, whereby Israel was regarded as staunch partner of the West, hence the Soviet support

CHAIM HERZOG

Born 17 September 1918 in Belfast, Northern Ireland, where his father was chief rabbi.

Moved to Palestine in 1935, which was under British administration, and served with the Haganah (the Jewish underground irregulars) during the Palestinian Arab Revolt. He studied in Jerusalem, Cambridge and London, graduating in law, and was called to the Bar. During the Second World War he served the British Army as a tank commander and later as head of Intelligence in northern Germany. He returned to Palestine, fought in the War of Independence (1948), and served twice as head of the Israeli Defence Force's Military Intelligence (1948–50, 1959–62). He spent the years 1950–4 as defence attaché at the US Israeli Embassy. After Israel occupied the West Bank (1967), he acted as its first military governor. In 1975–8, he represented Israel as its UN Ambassador, and in 1981 he entered politics proper as a Labour Party member of the Knesset (parliament). A widely respected figure, he served two five-year terms as Israel's president, 1983–93.

Died 17 April 1997 in Tel Aviv, Israel.

for the resolution. By contrast, the United States, Western Europe, Australasia and much of South America voted against it. In 1991, as the Soviet Union petered out, a new UN resolution overwhelmingly revoked the 1975 one.

Mr President.

It is symbolic that this debate, which may well prove to be a turning point in the fortunes of the United Nations and a decisive factor in the possible continued existence of this organization, should take place on November 10. Tonight, thirty-seven years ago, has gone down in history as *Kristallnacht*, the Night of the Crystals. This was the night in 1938 when Hitler's Nazi stormtroopers launched a coordinated attack on the Jewish community in Germany, burned the synagogues in all its cities and made bonfires in the streets of the Holy Books and the Scrolls of the Holy Law and Bible. It was the night when Jewish homes were attacked and heads of families taken away, many of them never to return. It was the night when the windows of all Jewish businesses and stores were smashed, covering the streets in the cities of Germany with a film of broken glass which dissolved into the millions of crystals which gave that night its name. It was the night which led eventually to the crematoria and the gas chambers, Auschwitz-Birkenau, Dachau, Buchenwald, Theresienstadt and others. It was the night which led to the most terrifying holocaust in the history of man.

. . . I do not come to this rostrum to defend the moral and historical values of the Jewish people. They speak for themselves. They have given to mankind much of what is great and eternal. They have done for the spirit of man more than can readily be appreciated by a forum such as this one.

I come here to denounce the two great evils which menace society in general and a society of nations in particular. These two evils are hatred and ignorance. These two evils are the motivating force behind the proponents of this resolution and their supporters. These two evils characterize those who would drag this world organization, the ideals of which were first conceived by the prophets of Israel, to the depths to which it has been dragged today.

We are seeing here today but another manifestation of the bitter anti-Semitic, anti-Jewish hatred which animates Arab society. Who would have believed that in this year, 1975, the malicious falsehoods of the 'Elders of Zion' would be distributed officially by Arab governments? Who would have believed that we would today contemplate an Arab society which teaches the vilest anti-Jewish hate in the kindergartens? . . . We are being attacked by a society which is motivated by the most extreme form of racism known in the world today. This is the racism which was expressed so succinctly in the words of the leader of the PLO [Palestine Liberation Organization], Yasser Arafat, in his opening address at a symposium in Tripoli, Libya: 'There will be no presence in the region other than the Arab presence . . . .' In other words, in the Middle East from the Atlantic Ocean to the Persian Gulf only one presence is allowed, and that is Arab presence. No other people, regardless of how deep are its roots in the region, is to be permitted to enjoy its right to self-determination.

As I stand on this rostrum, the long and proud history of my people unravels itself before my inward eye. I see the oppressors of our people over the ages as they pass one another in evil procession into oblivion. I stand here before you as the representative of a strong and flourishing people which has survived them all and which will survive this shameful exhibition and the proponents of this resolution.

'This resolution based on hatred, falsehood and arrogance'

The great moments of Jewish history come to mind as I face you, once again outnumbered and the would-be victim of hate, ignorance and evil. I look back on those great moments. I recall the greatness of a nation which I have the honour to represent in this forum. I am mindful at this moment of the Jewish people throughout the world wherever they may be, be it in freedom or in slavery, whose prayers and thoughts are with me at this moment.

I stand here not as a supplicant. Vote as your moral conscience dictates to you. For the issue is neither Israel nor Zionism. The issue is the continued existence of this organization, which has been dragged to its lowest point of discredit by a coalition of despots and racists.

The vote of each delegation will record in history its country's stand on anti-Semitic racism and anti-Judaism. You yourselves bear the responsibility for your stand before history, for as such will you be viewed in history. We, the Jewish people, will not forget.

For us, the Jewish people, this is but a passing episode in a rich and event-filled history. We put our trust in our providence, in our faith and beliefs, in our time-hallowed tradition, in our striving for social advance and human values, and in our people wherever they may be. For us, the Jewish people, this resolution based on hatred, falsehood and arrogance, is devoid of any moral or legal value.

'We accept to live with you in permanent peace'

ANWAR AL-SADAT

Address to Israeli Knesset offering peace negotiations, 20 November 1977

WHEN ANWAR AL-SADAT SUCCEEDED the fiery Gamal abd al-Nasser as Egyptian president in 1970, there were few signs that he would last long as leader let alone turn out to be a peacemaker. Rivals at first considered him little more than a mediocre Nasser placeman, until he outmanoeuvred opponents and replaced many of the Nasser-era officials with a network of officials loyal to him.

As President of Egypt, the most populous and most militarily significant Arab state, Sadat was expected to lead Arab opposition to Israel. His country, along with Syria and Jordan, had been humiliated by Israel's swift victory during the 1967 Six Day War, a conflict that had given Israel the Golan Heights (from Syria), the West Bank (from Jordan) and the Sinai Peninsula (from Egypt). At first though, and to the surprise of many, Sadat backed a UN-sponsored peace plan, though this received short shrift from Israel.

It was too early for Egyptian–Israeli rapprochement, and instead, in 1973, the regional balance of power shifted when Sadat launched the October War (or Yom Kippur War) to push the Israelis back. Sadat's forces, tactically far superior to the Egyptian army of 1967, took the Israeli defenders on the east bank of the Suez Canal by surprise, while Syria attacked Israel from the north. Eventually, the Israeli Defence Forces turned a potentially disastrous situation around; but in revealing Israeli vulnerabilities, Sadat emerged from the war as an Arab hero.

It was from this position of renewed self-confidence that he was able to project himself, four years later, as a statesman and peacemaker. He under-stood that the Arab states would be unlikely to defeat Israel in war, especially since Israel could rely on US backing. Sadat grasped this reality and pursued its logic – that a permanent basis for peaceful coexistence needed to be found. He put out peace feelers in 1977, and in a historic move he became the first Arab leader to visit Israel. There, he addressed a special session of the Israeli parliament, the Knesset, in Jerusalem, laying out his goals.

ANWAR AL-SADAT

Born 25 December 1918 in Mit Abu al-Kum, Egypt.

He graduated from the Royal Military Academy, Cairo (1938), where he shared fellow officer Nasser's hostility to British authority and the Egyptian monarchy. He was imprisoned for alleged conspiracy with German officers (1941–2), and in 1945 joined Nasser's Free Officers grouping in Egypt's army, which toppled King Farouk in 1952. By 1970, he had risen to vice-president under Nasser, and took over the presidency on Nasser's death. He attempted to rebalance foreign relations more towards the West, and in 1972 expelled thousands of Soviet military advisers. With Syria, Egypt launched the October (Yom Kippur) War in 1973: despite later reversals, the early successes enhanced his authority. He launched his Arab–Israeli peace initiative in 1977, which resulted in a Nobel Peace Prize (1978), an Egyptian–Israeli peace treaty (1979), but expulsion from the Arab League.

Assassinated 6 October 1981 by Egyptian soldiers at a parade in Cairo.

His speech, given in Arabic, stressed the common humanity of Jews and Arabs. He peppered it with references to the Bible and the Koran, reinforcing the shared heritage of Judaism, Christianity and Islam. He scoffed at the previous inability of Arab and Israeli diplomats to communicate except through proxies. He acknowledged that his visit had earned him Arab astonishment and Israeli cynicism; but he also presented himself as representing not just Egypt but the wider 'Arab nation' in his search for a 'permanent peace based on justice'. He frankly stated that peace needed, on the Israeli side, a solution of the Palestinian problem and the return of the territories occupied in 1967. Finally, he returned to the theme of shared suffering, appealing to the ordinary citizens of the Middle East who deserved to live without fear of violence.

The road down which Sadat embarked did lead to a peace treaty, after President Jimmy Carter hosted an Egyptian–Israeli summit in 1978 at Camp David, earning Sadat (and Israeli Prime Minister Menachim Begin) a Nobel Prize. In the end though, it was a bilateral Egyptian–Israeli accord, which resulted in the return of the Sinai but not the other Occupied Territories. Nor did it resolve the future of Palestinians. Sadat paid a heavy price for his historic agreement, becoming a pariah in the wider Arab world and facing increasing dissent at home, to which he responded with repressive measures. The Sadat era ended in 1981, when he was assassinated at a military parade by disaffected army officers. The Egyptian–Israeli peace agreement, though, survived.

PEACE AND THE MERCY OF GOD ALMIGHTY be upon you and may peace be for us all, God willing . . . I come to you today on solid ground, to shape a new life, to establish peace. We all, on this land, the land of God; we all, Muslims, Christians and Jews, worship God and no one but God. God's teachings and commandments are love, sincerity, purity and peace.

I do not blame all those who received my decision – when I announced it to the entire world before the Egyptian People's Assembly – with surprise and amazement. Some, gripped by the violent surprise, believed that my decision was no more than verbal juggling to cater for world public opinion. Others, still, interpreted it as political tactics to camouflage my intention of launching a new war. I would go as far as to tell you that one of my aides at the presidential office contacted me at a late hour following my return home from the People's Assembly and sounded worried as he asked me: 'Mr. President, what would be our reaction if Israel should actually extend an invitation to you?' I replied calmly, 'I will accept it immediately . . . .' After long thinking, I was convinced that the obligation of responsibility before God, and before the people, make it incumbent on me that I should go to the farthest corner of the world, even to Jerusalem, to address Members of the Knesset, the representatives of the people of Israel, and acquaint them with all the facts surging in me.

. . . Any life lost in war is a human life, irrespective of its being that of an Israeli or an Arab. A wife who becomes a widow is a human being entitled to a happy family life, whether she be an Arab or an Israeli. Innocent children who are deprived of the care and compassion of their parents are ours, be they living on Arab or Israeli land.

. . . Let us be frank with each other as we answer this important question: How can we achieve permanent peace based on justice?

. . . The first fact: no one can build his happiness at the expense of the misery of others.

'The call for permanent and just peace'

The second fact: never have I spoken or will ever speak in two languages. Never have I adopted or will adopt two policies. I never deal with anyone except in one language, one policy, and with one face.

The third fact: direct confrontation and a straight line are the nearest and most successful methods to reach a clear objective.

The fourth fact: the call for permanent and just peace, based on respect for the UN resolutions, has now become the call of the whole world.

. . . The fifth fact: and this is probably the clearest and most prominent, is that the Arab nation, in its drive for permanent peace based on justice, does not proceed from a position of weakness or hesitation, but it has the potential of power and stability which tells of a sincere will for peace.

. . . I would also wish to warn you in all sincerity; I warn you against some thoughts that could cross your minds; frankness makes it incumbent upon me to tell you the following:

First: I have not come here for a separate agreement between Egypt and Israel. This is not part of the policy of Egypt.

. . . Second: I have not come to you to seek a partial peace, namely to terminate the state of belligerency at this stage, and put off the entire problem to a subsequent stage . . . I have come to you so that together we might build a durable peace based on justice, to avoid the shedding of one single drop of blood from an Arab or an Israeli.

. . . Here, I would go back to the answer to the big question: how can we achieve a durable peace based on justice? In my opinion . . . the answer is neither difficult nor impossible, despite long years of feud, blood vengeance, spite and hatred, and breeding generations on concepts of total rift and deep-rooted animosity.

. . . You want to live with us in this part of the world. In all sincerity, I tell you, we welcome you among us, with full security and safety. This, in itself, is a tremendous turning point; one of the landmarks of a decisive historical change. We used to reject you. We had our reasons and our claims, yes. We used to brand you as 'so-called' Israel, yes. We were together in international conferences and organizations and our representatives did not, and still do not, exchange greetings, yes. This has happened and is still happening. It is also true that we used to set, as a precondition for any negotiations with you, a mediator who would meet separately with each party. Yes, this has happened.

Yet, today I tell you, and declare it to the whole world, that we accept to live with you in permanent peace based on justice. We do not want to encircle you or be encircled ourselves by destructive missiles ready for launching, nor by the shells of grudges and hatred. I have announced on more than one occasion that Israel has become a *fait accompli*, recognized by the world, and that the two super powers have undertaken the responsibility of its security and the defence of its existence.

As we really and truly seek peace, we really and truly welcome you to live among us in peace and security.

'The Palestinian people and their rights to statehood'

. . . I have come to Jerusalem, as the City of Peace, which will always remain as a living embodiment of coexistence among believers of the three religions. It is inadmissible that anyone should conceive the special status of the City of Jerusalem within the framework of annexation or expansionism, but it should be a free and open city for all believers.

. . . Complete withdrawal from the Arab territories occupied in 1967 is a logical and undisputed fact. Nobody should plead for that. Any talk about permanent peace based on justice, and any move to ensure our coexistence in peace and security in this part of the world, would become meaningless, while you occupy Arab territories by force of arms.

. . . As for the Palestinians cause, nobody could deny that it is the crux of the entire problem. The cause of the Palestinian people and their legitimate rights are no longer ignored or denied today by anybody. Rather, nobody who has the ability of judgement can deny or ignore it . . . I hail the Israeli voices that called for the recognition of the Palestinian people's rights to achieve and safeguard peace. Here I tell you, ladies and gentlemen, that it is no use refraining from recognizing the Palestinian people and their rights to statehood and rights of return. We, the Arabs, have faced this experience before, with you and with the reality of Israeli existence. The struggle took us from war to war, from victims to more victims, until you and we have today reached the edge of a horrifying abyss and a terrifying disaster, unless, together, we seize the opportunity, today, of a durable peace based on justice . . . .

'The lady's not for turning'

MARGARET THATCHER

Conservative Party Conference, 10 October 1980

MARGARET THATCHER'S ELECTION, IN 1979, as Prime Minister of the United Kingdom, transformed that country both immediately and gradually. Immediately, as she was the first (and to date only) woman to hold that office, emerging from both a Conservative party and a wider political landscape dominated by men: and gradually, as over the course of more than a decade she extensively reframed British politics and society, hugely reducing the size and power of the state.

Undoubtedly Britain's most influential post-war Prime Minister, Thatcher also emerged as one of the most divisive as she responded to the economic troubles of the 1970s with a wave of privatisation and deregulation that led both to strong economic growth and to the weakening of British trade unions and the collapse of employment in many industrial areas. 'Thatcherism' became synonymous with free markets, tax cuts and a greater role for the private sector, just as 'Reaganomics' did in the US for Thatcher's friend and ally Ronald Reagan.

Like Reagan, Thatcher was also an firm advocate for the West's interests in the final years of the Cold War, and a proponent of assertive foreign policy around the world: she refused to negotiate in Northern Ireland and fought back against the Argentine invasion of the Falkland Islands, winning immense popularity for her leadership: popularity she eventually lost as her premiership wore on and she came to be perceived as divisive and unfeeling.

Certainly she was uncompromising, and much of the debate over Thatcher's legacy has been shaped by her own unusually direct advocacy for her political positions: her speeches and statements projected a definite, complete worldview in the face of criticism and of calls for a more conciliatory tone. For many, she

MARGARET THATCHER

Born Margaret Roberts, 13 October 1925 in Lincolnshire, England.

Daughter of a grocer, she attended Somerville College, Oxford, where she studied chemistry. She worked as an industrial chemist while unsuccessfully standing as a Conservative MP in the 1950 and 1951 elections, but was elected from the reliably Conservative seat of Finchley in the 1958 election. She emerged as a prominent Conservative politician, being appointed Education secretary in 1970. After the Conservatives were defeated in 1974 she stood successfully for leadership of the party, becoming Leader of the Opposition against the Wilson and Callaghan governments before winning the election of 1979. Re-elected in 1983 and 1987, she was eventually ousted in 1990 by her own party, with John Major succeeding her as Prime Minister. She remained active in the House of Lords as Baroness Thatcher until the early 2000s, when she began to suffer from dementia.

Died 8 April 2013 in London.

remains an object of hatred - in some parts of Britain, street parties were thrown when the news of her death broke - while to others she is the UK's greatest political figure since Churchill.

This speech, delivered to her party conference a little over a year into her first term, is a famous example, and the positions it outlined served as a template for the next decade of her premiership. 'The lady's not for turning' line in particular came not only to define the speech but her entire political persona, as someone unafraid to take controversial decisions and to see them through in the teeth of pressure to relent and to compromise: at the time, her economic reforms were widely perceived to have failed and the UK was entering a recession.

This version of the text, reflecting not the speech as written but as ultimately spoken, also showcases her wit – the response to the interruption by protesters was unplanned. The speech was greeted with a 5-minute standing ovation.

MR CHAIRMAN, LADIES AND GENTLEMEN, most of my Cabinet colleagues have started their speeches of reply by paying very well deserved tributes to their junior Ministers. At Number 10 I have no junior Ministers. There is just Denis [Thatcher] and me, and I could not do without him…

At our party conference last year I said that the task in which the Government were engaged – to change the national attitude of mind – was the most challenging to face any British Administration since the war. Challenge is exhilarating. This week we Conservatives have been taking stock, discussing the achievements, the set-backs and the work that lies ahead as we enter our second parliamentary year. As you said Mr Chairman our debates have been stimulating and our debates have been constructive. This week has demonstrated that we are a party united in purpose, strategy and resolve. And we actually like one another.

When I am asked for a detailed forecast of what will happen in the coming months or years I remember Sam Goldwyn's advice: "Never prophesy, especially about the future." [Interruption by protestors] Never mind, it is wet outside. I expect that they wanted to come in. You cannot blame them; it is always better where the Tories are. And you – and perhaps they – will be looking to me this afternoon for an indication of how the Government see the task before us and why we are tackling it the way we are…

'I expect that they wanted to come in. You cannot blame them; it is always better where the Tories are.'

There are many things to be done to set this nation on the road to recovery, and I do not mean economic recovery alone, but a new independence of spirit and zest for achievement.

It is sometimes said that because of our past we, as a people, expect too much and set our sights too high. That is not the way I see it. Rather it seems to me that throughout my life in politics our ambitions have steadily shrunk. Our response to disappointment has not been to lengthen our stride but to shorten the distance to be covered. But with confidence in ourselves and in our future what a nation we could be!

In its first seventeen months this Government have laid the foundations for recovery. We have undertaken a heavy load of legislation, a load we do not intend to repeat because we do not share the Socialist fantasy that achievement is measured by the number of laws you pass. But there was a formidable barricade of obstacles that we had to sweep aside…

'If I could press a button and genuinely solve the unemployment problem, do you think that I would not press that button this instant?'

Today our country has more than 2 million unemployed. Now you can try to soften that figure in a dozen ways. You can point out and it is quite legitimate to do so that 2 million today does not mean what it meant in the 1930s; that the percentage of unemployment is much less now than it was then. You can add that today many more married women go out to work. You can stress that, because of the high birthrate in the early 1960s, there is an unusually large number of school leavers this year looking for work and that the same will be true for the next two years. You can emphasise that about a quarter of a million people find new jobs each month and therefore go off the employment register. And you can recall that there are nearly 25 million people in jobs compared with only about 18 million in the 1930s. You can point out that the Labour party conveniently overlooks the fact that of the 2 million unemployed for which they blame us, nearly a million and a half were bequeathed by their Government.

But when all that has been said the fact remains that the level of unemployment in our country today is a human tragedy. Let me make it clear beyond doubt. I am profoundly concerned about unemployment. Human dignity and self respect are undermined when men and women are condemned to idleness. The waste of a country's most precious assets – the talent and energy of its people – makes it the bounden duty of Government to seek a real and lasting cure.

If I could press a button and genuinely solve the unemployment problem, do you think that I would not press that button this instant? Does anyone imagine that there is the smallest political gain in letting this unemployment continue, or that there is some obscure economic religion which demands this unemployment as part of its ritual? This Government are pursuing the only policy which gives any hope of bringing our people back to real and lasting employment.

Our vision and our aims go far beyond the complex arguments of economics, but unless we get the economy right we shall deny our people the opportunity to share that vision and to see beyond the narrow horizons of economic necessity. Without a healthy economy we cannot have a healthy society. Without a healthy society the economy will not stay healthy for long.

But it is not the State that creates a healthy society. When the State grows too powerful people feel that they count for less and less. The State drains society, not only of its wealth but of initiative, of energy, the will to improve and innovate as well as to preserve what is best. Our aim is to let people feel that they count for more and more. If we cannot trust the deepest instincts of our people we should not be in politics at all. Some aspects of our present society really do offend those instincts.

'Our aim is to let people feel that they count for more and more'

Decent people do want to do a proper job at work, not to be restrained or intimidated from giving value for money. They believe that honesty should be respected, not derided. They see crime and violence as a threat not just to society but to their own orderly way of life. They want to be allowed to bring up their children in these beliefs, without the fear that their efforts will be daily frustrated in the name of progress or free expression. Indeed, that is what family life is all about.

There is not a generation gap in a happy and united family. People yearn to be able to rely on some generally accepted standards. Without them you have not got a society at all, you have purposeless anarchy.
A healthy society is not created by its institutions, either. Great schools and universities do not make a great nation any more than great armies do. Only a great nation can create and involve great institutions – of learning, of healing, of scientific advance. And a great nation is the voluntary creation of its people – a people composed of men and women whose pride in themselves is founded on the knowledge of what they can give to a community of which they in turn can be proud.

If our people feel that they are part of a great nation and they are prepared to will the means to keep it great, a great nation we shall be, and shall remain. So, what can stop us from achieving this? What then stands in our way? The prospect of another winter of discontent? I suppose it might.

But I prefer to believe that certain lessons have been learnt from experience, that we are coming, slowly, painfully, to an autumn of understanding. And I hope that it will be followed by a winter of common sense. If it is not, we shall not be – diverted from our course.

To those waiting with bated breath for that favourite media catchphrase, the "U" turn, I have only one thing to say. "You turn if you want to. The lady's not for turning." I say that not only to you but to our friends overseas and also to those who are not our friends…

> 'I have only one thing to say. "You turn if you want to. The lady's not for turning."'

This afternoon I have tried to set before you some of my most deeply held convictions and beliefs. This Party, which I am privileged to serve, and this Government, which I am proud to lead, are engaged in the massive task of restoring confidence and stability to our people.

I have always known that that task was vital. Since last week it has become even more vital than ever. We close our Conference in the aftermath of that sinister Utopia unveiled at Blackpool. Let Labour's Orwellian nightmare of the Left be the spur for us to dedicate with a new urgency our every ounce of energy and moral strength to rebuild the fortunes of this free nation.

If we were to fail, that freedom could be imperilled. So let us resist the blandishments of the faint hearts; let us ignore the howls and threats of the extremists; let us stand together and do our duty, and we shall not fail.

'Our Polish freedom costs so much'

POPE JOHN PAUL II
Address to his Polish compatriots, 18 June 1983

In 1978, the Roman Catholic Church broke with a tradition lasting 455 years by electing a pope who was not Italian. The College of Cardinals chose, by a huge majority, Karol Wojtyła, who took the papal title John Paul II. He was also the first ever Polish pope, and as such his election took on layers of political significance. He came from a country with a very deep Catholic tradition, but which, since 1945, had lain behind the Cold War's iron curtain, governed by a Soviet-backed regime that was, at root, antipathetic to religious belief.

During the early 1950s, Poland's Roman Catholic primate, Cardinal Wyszyńksi, had spent some years in prison on account of his anti-communist criticisms. But, as Stalinism went into retreat and Poland's new leader, Wladysław Gomulka, began to adapt party rule to local circumstances, church–state relations evolved. For the price of avoiding overt comment on politics, the church was able to maintain its traditional role. It was an uneasy if workable compromise.

The election of Karol Wojtyła to the see of Rome changed that. Poland now had an independent voice on the world stage – one of maximum moral and spiritual integrity – who could not fail but be listened to as an alternative source of leadership and authority for Poles. Moreover, Wojtyła was not a man to compartmentalize spiritual matters from social life. He was a former university professor of ethics, and as Archbishop of Krákow since 1963 he had been at the forefront of defending the church's position.

In 1979, the new pope visited his homeland just as rising popular discontent at the country's low standards of living was reaching a critical phase. The following year, striking shipyard workers in Gdansk created an independent trade union movement, Solidarity (in Polish, *Solidarność*), to which Polish workers flooded, overawing the regime. But in 1981 a backlash swung into place: Solidarity was declared illegal, its leaders imprisoned, and nervous Poles feared military intervention from the Soviet Union and their other Warsaw Pact allies. During that year, John Paul II narrowly survived an assassination attempt, which an Italian investigation laid at the door of the Soviet leader Leonid Brezhnev – though the debate continues.

POPE JOHN PAUL II

Born Karol Wojtyła on 18 May 1920 in Wadowice, Poland.

He studied Polish literature and later theology (in which he graduated) at Jagiellonian University, Krákow, in 1938–9 and 1945–6, working in industrial jobs for much of the intervening war period while Poland was occupied. In 1946 he published the first of several volumes of poetry and was ordained a priest. He undertook graduate research in Rome, earning a Ph.D. in 1948. After service as a parish priest and further academic research, he was appointed as Professor of Social Ethics at the Catholic University, Lublin (1954). He was active in the modernizing Vatican II council's deliberations of 1962–5 (which he helped to implement), rose to the Archbishopric of Krákow in 1963 and became a cardinal in 1967. In 1978 he was elected as the 265th pope, taking the name John Paul II. As pope, he narrowly survived an assassination attempt (1981), became a figurehead for Polish national aspirations, and inaugurated a new style of international papal appearances and large-scale events. His encyclicals rejected both communism and unrestrained capitalism, while his theological and moral stance reinforced core Catholic values and practices (such as rejecting birth control or the ordination of women).

Died 2 April 2005 in Rome.

In 1983, John Paul II returned to Poland for his second visit as pope. He addressed more than a million people at the large Jasna Góra monastery, in Częstochowa. The important pilgrimage site contains an ancient artifact of huge religious-national symbolism, an icon of the Virgin Mary, and in times of crisis or thankfulness Poles have gathered there. They did the same on 18 June 1983 to hear John Paul II's words. Carefully embedded among those words were some that implicitly acknowledged the current struggle of the Polish people. On hearing references to 'solidarity' or 'workers', the crowd raised Solidarity banners, and they clapped tumultuously in appreciation as the speech ended.

A few years later, John Paul II witnessed the collapse of Poland's communist regime in 1989. His period in office subsequently saw an increasingly conservative stance on church and social matters; but in the 1980s he seemed almost a political revolutionary.

Our Lady of Jasna Góra is the teacher of true love for all. And this is particularly important for you, dear young people. In you, in fact, is decided that form of love which all of your life will have and, through you, human life on Polish soil: the matrimonial, family, social and national form – but also the priestly, religious and missionary one. Every life is determined and evaluated by the interior form of love. Tell me what you love, and I will tell you who you are.

I watch! How beautiful it is that this word is found in the call of Jasna Góra. It possesses a profound evangelical ancestry: Christ says many times 'watch'. . . Perhaps also from the Gospel it passes into the tradition of scouting. In the call of Jasna Góra it is the essential element of the reply that we wish to give to the love by which we are surrounded in the sign of the Sacred Icon.

The response to this love must be precisely the fact that I watch! What does it mean, 'I watch'?

It means that I make an effort to be a person with a conscience. I do not stifle this conscience and I do not deform it; I call good and evil by name, and I do not blur them; I develop in myself what is good, and I seek to correct what is evil, by overcoming it in myself. This is a fundamental problem, which can never be minimized or put on a secondary level. No! It is everywhere and always a matter of the first importance. Its importance is all the greater in proportion to the increase of circumstances which seem to favour our tolerance of evil and the fact that we easily excuse ourselves from this, especially if adults do so.

My dear friends! It is up to you to put up a firm barrier against immorality, a barrier – I say – to those social vices which I will not here call by name but which you yourselves are perfectly aware of. You must demand this of yourselves, even if others do not demand it of you. Historical experiences tell us how much the immorality of certain periods cost the whole nation. Today when we are fighting for the future form of our social life, remember that this form depends on what people will be like. Therefore: watch!

'I wish to give thanks for all the proofs of this solidarity'

. . . 'I watch' also means: I see another. I do not close in on myself, in a narrow search for my own interests, my own judgements. 'I watch' means: love of neighbour, it means: fundamental interhuman solidarity.

Before the Mother of Jasna Góra I wish to give thanks for all the proofs of this solidarity which have been given by my compatriots, including Polish youth, in the difficult period of not many months ago. It would be difficult for me to enumerate here all the forms of this solicitude which surrounded those who were interned, imprisoned, dismissed from work, and also their families. You know this better than I. I received only sporadic news about it.

. . . 'I watch' also means: I feel responsible for this great common inheritance whose name is Poland. This name defines us all. This name obliges us all. This name costs us all.

Perhaps at times we envy the French, the Germans or the Americans because their name is not tied to such a historical price and because they are so easily free: while our Polish freedom costs so much.

My dear ones, I will not make a comparative analysis. I will only say that it is what costs that constitutes value. It is not, in fact, possible to be truly free without an honest and profound relationship with values. We do not want a Poland that costs us nothing. We watch, instead, beside all that makes up the authentic inheritance of the generations, seeking to enrich it. A nation, then, is first of all rich in its people. Rich in man. Rich in youth. Rich in every individual who watches in the name of truth: it is truth, in fact, that gives form to love.

. . . Even if I am not among you every day, as was the case for many years in the past, nevertheless I carry in my heart a great solicitude. A great, enormous solicitude. A solicitude for you. Precisely because on you depends tomorrow.

I pray for you every day.

'**Mr Gorbachev,
tear down this wall!**'

RONALD REAGAN
Speech in West Berlin supporting democratic principles, 12 June 1987

AFEELGOOD FACTOR CHARACTERIZED the presidency of Ronald Reagan, who was inaugurated in January 1981. His sunny disposition exuded a relaxed confidence, his certainties about the world reassured, and his self-deprecating humour connected with ordinary Americans. Whereas Nixon seemed to embody the agonies of being president, and Jimmy Carter the inability to translate principles into effectiveness, Reagan made the presidency sound like a hobby. One of his best lines was 'It's true that hard work never killed anybody. But why take the chance?' Not for nothing was Reagan known as the Great Communicator, and his platform of lower taxes, smaller government, hometown values, balanced budgets and a beefed-up military made so-called 'Reagan Democrats' switch allegiance and flock to him.

Famously, Reagan's first career was as a screen and television actor, and accordingly his political speeches were invariably immaculately delivered. He would brief his speechwriter, Peggy Noonan, on what he wanted to say and she crafted his speeches to suit his unpretentious style. His critics would often cite his acting background, seeing his presidency as a triumph of image over substance. But critics and admirers do agree on one point: that while Reagan delegated much to his subordinates, he provided a quietly unshakeable set of long-held beliefs to underpin White House policy.

Nowhere was that clearer than in his attitude to the Soviet Union, which, abandoning the language of *détente*, he described as an 'evil empire'. Liberals mocked his comic-book language, but it accurately reflected his belief in the fundamental immorality of the Soviet political system.

In June 1987, Reagan appeared before the Brandenburg Gate in the emblematic Cold War city of Berlin, as US presidents had done before him, to make an address. He contrasted the prosperity, cultural richness, and freedoms West Berliners had cultivated since 1945 with the 'backwardness' of the totalitarian world behind the Berlin Wall – a world that, as he described it, 'does such violence to the spirit'. But Reagan also had an agenda,

RONALD REAGAN

Born 6 February 1911 in Tampico, Illinois.

A talented athlete and actor, he graduated (1932) in economics and sociology at Eureka College, before working as a radio sports broadcaster and, from 1937, a contract actor with Warner Brothers: he went on to make 53 films in his career. During the Second World War he served with an army film unit. He was President of the Screen Actors Guild (1947–52) and participated in Democratic Party politics. In 1949 he was a 'friendly' witness for the House Un-American Activities Committee investigating communist infiltration. On TV, he hosted General Electric Theater (1954–62). Having transferred allegiance to the Republican Party in the early 1950s, he won the governorship of California in 1966 and 1970. After two failed bids, he won the Republican presidential nomination in 1980, and then the presidency, easily beating Jimmy Carter. His presidency (1981–9) saw tax and welfare cuts, large increases in defence spending, the Strategic Defence Initiative (the 'star wars' plan for a missile defence shield), an economic slump followed by a five-year boom, and a $3 trillion budget deficit. Internationally, he negotiated arms reductions with Soviet premier Mikhail Gorbachev, bombed Libya to dissuade it from terrorism, but became embroiled in the 'Iran–Contra' scandal, whereby officials diverted funds from secret arms sales to Iran to support anti-communist Contra guerrillas in Nicaragua. He narrowly survived assassination in 1981, in Washington, D.C., and after he left office he suffered from Alzheimer's disease.

Died 5 June 2004 in Los Angeles, California.

summarized in the demand 'General Secretary Gorbachev . . . if you seek liberalization . . . tear down this wall!' On one level, this was an obvious piece of populist rhetoric. But times were rapidly changing, for now there *was* a reformist leading the Soviet Union, in the shape of Mikhail Gorbachev, a man with whom Reagan signed a missile-reduction treaty that same year.

Reagan predicted that 'this wall will fall. For it cannot withstand faith; it cannot withstand truth'. Two years later, the Berlin Wall did come down. Historians may argue the extent to which Reagan's presidency contributed to the end of the Cold War. But the relationship between the hawkish president and his urbane Communist Party opposite number formed the important prelude to those events.

The last years of Reagan's life were overshadowed by Alzheimer's disease. His speechmaking days now over, the Great Communicator still managed an eloquent farewell, albeit this time in print: 'I now begin the journey that will lead me into the sunset of my life.'

TWENTY-FOUR YEARS AGO, President John F. Kennedy visited Berlin, speaking to the people of this city and the world at the City Hall. Well, since then two other presidents have come, each in his turn, to Berlin. And today I, myself, make my second visit to your city. We come to Berlin, we American presidents, because it's our duty to speak, in this place, of freedom. But I must confess, we're drawn here by other things as well: by the feeling of history in this city, more than 500 years older than our own nation; by the beauty of the Grunewald and the Tiergarten; most of all, by your courage and determination. Perhaps the composer Paul Lincke understood something about American Presidents. You see, like so many presidents before me, I come here today because wherever I go, whatever I do, *Ich hab noch einen Koffer in Berlin*, I still have a suitcase in Berlin.

. . . Behind me stands a wall that encircles the free sectors of this city, part of a vast system of barriers that divides the entire continent of Europe. From the Baltic, south, those barriers cut across Germany in a gash of barbed wire, concrete, dog runs, and guard towers. Farther south, there may be no visible, no obvious wall. But there remain armed guards and checkpoints all the same – still a restriction on the right to travel, still an instrument to impose upon ordinary men and women the will of a totalitarian state. Yet it is here in Berlin where the wall emerges most clearly; here, cutting across your city, where the news photo and the television screen have imprinted this brutal division of a continent upon the mind of the world. Standing before the Brandenburg Gate, every man is a German, separated from his fellow men. Every man is a Berliner, forced to look upon a scar.

. . . Where four decades ago there was rubble, today in West Berlin there is the greatest industrial output of any city in Germany – busy office blocks, fine homes and apartments, proud avenues and the spreading lawns of parkland. Where a city's culture seemed to have been destroyed, today there are two great universities, orchestras and an opera, countless theatres and museums. Where there was want, today there's abundance – food, clothing, automobiles – the wonderful goods of the Ku'damm. From devastation, from utter ruin, you Berliners have, in freedom, rebuilt a city that once again ranks as one of the greatest on earth. The Soviets may have had other plans. But my friends, there were a few things the Soviets didn't count on – *Berliner Herz, Berliner Humor, ja, und Berliner Schnauze,* Berliner heart, Berliner humour, yes, and Berliner Schnauze.

'Soviets themselves may . . . be coming to understand the importance of freedom'

In the 1950s, Khrushchev predicted: 'We will bury you.' But in the West today, we see a free world that has achieved a level of prosperity and well-being unprecedented in all human history. In the communist world, we see failure, technological backwardness, declining standards of health, even want of the most basic kind – too little food. Even today, the Soviet Union still cannot feed itself. After these four decades, then, there stands before the entire world one great and inescapable conclusion: Freedom leads to prosperity. Freedom replaces the ancient hatreds among the nations with comity and peace. Freedom is the victor.

And now the Soviets themselves may, in a limited way, be coming to understand the importance of freedom. We hear much from Moscow about a new policy of reform and openness.* Some political prisoners have been released. Certain foreign news broadcasts are no longer being jammed. Some economic enterprises have been permitted to operate with greater freedom from state control. Are these the beginnings of profound changes in the Soviet state? Or are they token gestures, intended to raise false hopes in the West, or to strengthen the Soviet system without changing it? We welcome change and openness; for we believe that freedom and security go together, that the advance of human liberty can only strengthen the cause of world peace.

There is one sign the Soviets can make that would be unmistakeable, that would advance dramatically the cause of freedom and peace. General Secretary Gorbachev, if you seek peace, if you seek prosperity for the

*A reference to the Russian reformist concepts of *perestroika* and *glasnost.*

Soviet Union and Eastern Europe, if you seek liberalization: come here to this gate! Mr Gorbachev, open this gate! Mr Gorbachev, tear down this wall!

. . . Today the city thrives in spite of the challenges implicit in the very presence of this wall. What keeps you here? Certainly there's a great deal to be said for your fortitude, for your defiant courage. But I believe there's something deeper, something that involves Berlin's whole look and feel and way of life – not mere sentiment. No one could live long in Berlin without being completely disabused of illusions. Something instead that has seen the difficulties of life in Berlin but chose to accept them, that continues to build this good and proud city in contrast to a surrounding totalitarian presence . . . Something that speaks with a powerful voice of affirmation, that says 'yes' to this city, 'yes' to the future, 'yes' to freedom. In a word, I would submit that what keeps you in Berlin is love – love both profound and abiding.

'The totalitarian world finds even symbols of love and of worship an affront'

Perhaps this gets to the root of the matter, to the most fundamental distinction of all between East and West. The totalitarian world produces backwardness because it does such violence to the spirit, thwarting the human impulse to create, to enjoy, to worship. The totalitarian world finds even symbols of love and of worship an affront. Years ago, before the East Germans began rebuilding their churches, they erected a secular structure: the television tower at Alexander Platz. Virtually ever since, the authorities have been working to correct what they view as the tower's one major flaw, treating the glass sphere at the top with paints and chemicals of every kind. Yet even today when the sun strikes that sphere – that sphere that towers over all Berlin – the light makes the sign of the cross. There in Berlin, like the city itself, symbols of love, symbols of worship, cannot be suppressed.

As I looked out a moment ago from the Reichstag, that embodiment of German unity, I noticed words crudely spray-painted upon the wall, perhaps by a young Berliner: 'This wall will fall. Beliefs become reality.' Yes, across Europe, this wall will fall. For it cannot withstand faith; it cannot withstand truth. The wall cannot withstand freedom.

. . . Thank you and God bless you all.

'Freedom of choice is
a universal principle'

MIKHAIL GORBACHEV

United Nations speech about Soviet reforms, 7 December 1988

I**N THE LATER 1980s, TWO RUSSIAN WORDS** were making an impact in the West: *glasnost* ('transparency', 'openness') and *perestroika* ('restructuring'). They were the twin pillars on which Soviet leader Mikhail Gorbachev hoped to rebuild the moribund economy and politics of his country and transform its relations with satellite nations and the West. In the end, it became a revolution. By 1991, not only were the Central and Eastern European countries free of Soviet (and communist) control and Germany reunified, but the Soviet Union itself had ceased to exist, dissolving into its constituent republics. Not even the sublimely confident Ronald Reagan, demanding that Gorbachev 'tear down' the Berlin Wall in 1987, could have foreseen the rapidity of events. For setting this in motion, Gorbachev is one of the three key figures of Soviet history, along with Lenin and Stalin.

Gorbachev rose on his merits from a poor rural background to become Soviet leader in 1985, after the deaths in quick succession of two elderly leaders, Andropov and Chernenko. He outmanoeuvred a conservative old guard, brought in like-minded modernizers and quickly set out a reform agenda. The Soviet Union he inherited was mired in an unwinnable war in Afghanistan, its command economy was under strain, its satellite nations a drain on resources, and the bloated military was badly equipped and demoralized. The United States under Reagan had embarked on a massive expansion in defence, which it was clear the Soviet Union could not match in technology or resources. Furthermore, the US Strategic Defence Initiative – the plan for a space-based system to intercept missiles – posed the possibility that the entire Soviet arsenal would become useless in the event of a superpower war. In short, there were very good reasons to attempt to bring the era of superpower confrontation to a close. But beyond that, Gorbachev also believed in the essential rightness of liberalizing his society.

Gorbachev used his speech to the United Nations on 7 December 1988 to affirm his new direction. He rejected ideology as a source of conflict among nations. He described *perestroika*. Most eye-catchingly, he unveiled unilateral reductions in the Soviet military presence in the satellite nations and the adoption of an 'unambiguously

MIKHAIL GORBACHEV

Born 2 March 1931 into a peasant family in Privolnoye, Stavropol, in Russia's North Caucasus.

He studied diligently while working on the collective farm. Studied law at Moscow University (graduating 1955), where he joined the Communist Party (1952) and got involved in the Komsomol (Communist Youth Union). As an agricultural administrator in Stavropol he gained a reputation for honesty and innovation, and rose in the party hierarchy, reaching the Central Committee in 1971. In 1978 he was promoted to Moscow, and entered the governing Politburo in 1980, its youngest full member. He became general secretary and Soviet leader after the death of Konstantin Chernenko in 1985 and set about a reformist agenda: he took the army out of Afghanistan, allowed Soviet bloc countries to pursue their own paths, improved relations with the West (including a missile-reduction treaty) and China, and allowed new political parties and multiparty elections (1990), which saw power devolve to individual Soviet republics. In 1991 hardliners arrested him for three days as they attempted (unsuccessfully) a coup, after which he resigned as party leader and the Soviet Union dissolved itself. Still active politically, he created the Union of Social Democrats umbrella group in 2007 and (with the wealthy Alexander Lebedev) the Independent Democratic Party in 2008.

defensive' posture for those troops remaining. He thus signalled the Soviet Union's disinterest in launching any armoured attack on Western Europe, which had always been the West's invasion nightmare. He also indicated that military interventions of the kind that happened in Hungary in 1956 and Czechoslovakia in 1968, to ensure the passivity of their client governments, were off the agenda.

Gorbachev did not want quite the revolution that he got. Once multiparty elections were permitted in the Soviet republics, the Union could not hold, despite a brief attempt by communist hardliners to reverse the process in a hapless coup. His own reputation in Russia plummeted though; he was scorned by communists for destroying the Soviet Union and the party (from which he was expelled), and condemned by liberals for not going far enough. He remains, however, active in public affairs and in the West his reputation still remains high as the man who guided the Cold War era to a far more peaceful conclusion than most could have ever imagined.

FREEDOM OF CHOICE IS A UNIVERSAL PRINCIPLE to which there should be no exceptions. We have not come to the conclusion of the immutability of this principle simply through good motives. We have been led to it through impartial analysis of the objective processes of our time.

. . . Our country is undergoing a truly revolutionary upsurge. The process of restructuring [*perestroika*] is gaining pace . . . Under the badge of democratization, restructuring has now encompassed politics, the economy, spiritual life and ideology. We have unfolded a radical economic reform, we have accumulated experience, and from the new year we are transferring the entire national economy to new forms and work methods . . . We are more than fully confident. We have both the theory, the policy and the vanguard force of restructuring a party which is also restructuring itself in accordance with the new tasks and the radical changes throughout society.

. . . Today I can inform you of the following. The Soviet Union has made a decision on reducing its armed forces. In the next two years, their numerical strength will be reduced by 500,000 persons, and the volume of conventional arms will also be cut considerably. These reductions will be made on a unilateral basis ... By agreement with our allies in the Warsaw Pact, we have made the decision to withdraw six tank divisions from the GDR [East Germany], Czechoslovakia and Hungary, and to disband them by 1991. Assault landing formations and units, and a number of others, including assault river-crossing forces, with their armaments and combat equipment, will also be withdrawn from the groups of Soviet forces situated in those countries. The Soviet forces situated in those countries will be cut by 50,000 persons, and their arms by 5000 tanks. All remaining Soviet divisions on the territory of our allies will be reorganized. They will be given a different structure from today's which will become unambiguously defensive, after the removal of a large number of their tanks.

. . . Finally, being on US soil, but also for other, understandable reasons, I cannot but turn to the subject of our relations with this great country . . . Relations between the Soviet Union and the United States of America span five-and-a-half decades. The world has changed, and so have the nature, role and place of these relations in world politics. For too long they were built under the banner of confrontation, and sometimes of hostility, either open or concealed. But in the last few years, throughout the world people were able to heave a sigh of relief, thanks to the changes for the better in the substance and atmosphere of the relations between Moscow and Washington.

'An end to the era of wars, confrontation and regional conflicts'

No one intends to underestimate the serious nature of the disagreements, and the difficulties of the problems which have not been settled. However, we have already graduated from the primary school of instruction in mutual understanding and in searching for solutions in our and in the common interests. The USSR and the United States created the biggest nuclear missile arsenals, but after objectively recognizing their responsibility, they were able to be the first to conclude an agreement on the reduction and physical destruction of a proportion of these weapons, which threatened both themselves and everyone else. Both sides possess the biggest and the most refined military secrets. But it is they who have laid the basis for and are developing a system of mutual verification with regard to both the destruction and the limiting and banning of armaments production. It is they who are amassing experience for future bilateral and multilateral agreements. We value this.

. . . I finish my first speech at the United Nations with the same feeling with which I began it: a feeling of responsibility to my own people and to the world community. We have met at the end of a year that has been so significant for the United Nations, and on the threshold of a year from which all of us expect so much. One would like to believe that our joint efforts to put an end to the era of wars, confrontation and regional conflicts, aggression against nature, the terror of hunger and poverty, as well as political terrorism, will be comparable with our hopes. This is our common goal, and it is only by acting together that we may attain it. Thank you.

'We live in a
contaminated moral
environment'

VÁCLAV HAVEL
Broadcast reviewing the Czech communist past, 1 January 1990

I N 1939, HITLER'S ARMIES SNUFFED OUT Czechoslovakia's independence. After the Second World War, a communist coup delivered the country to effective Soviet domination, and when the reforming Alexander Dubček attempted to liberalize the system in 1968, in the so-called 'Prague Spring', he incurred the armed intervention of Warsaw Pact tanks. Czechoslovakia only truly regained its freedom in the peaceful 'Velvet Revolution' of December 1989, when the Czech communist regime collapsed, as did others in the region. The man chosen to be the new president was the country's leading playwright, leading dissident, and in many people's eyes the moral conscience of the nation: Václav Havel.

VÁCLAV HAVEL

Born 5 October 1936 in Prague, Czechoslovakia

In the 1950s he worked as a lab technician, was conscripted into the army, and attended technical college (1955–7) before working as a stagehand at the ABC Theatre, Prague. He began writing plays and magazine articles, becoming particularly associated with Prague's Theatre on the Balustrade. After the liberalizing 'Prague Spring' (1968) was crushed, his writings were banned, and he was sent to do manual labour in a brewery in 1974. He co-founded the Charter '77 human rights group (1977) and the Committee for the Defence of the Unjustly Prosecuted (1978). He was imprisoned in 1979 for subversion, until released because of illness in 1983. Through the 1980s he continued to publish abroad and in *samizdat* (underground) media at home. In 1989 he co-founded the Civic Forum opposition movement and, after that year's Velvet Revolution overturned the regime, he was chosen as the Czechoslovak president. He was re-elected in 1990, but stood down in 1992. When the country split into sovereign Czech and Slovak states, he became President of the Czech Republic (1993–2003), retiring at the end of his second elected term. His accolades have been many.

Died 18 December 2011

It is something of a truism that literature and the arts tend to be attributed a higher status in authoritarian countries, where they are scrutinized for possible criticism of the prevailing regime, and this was certainly the case in Czechoslovakia. Havel first went into the theatre after being denied a university education (on account of his wealthy background). During the 1960s he wrote plays in a broadly 'absurdist' genre, slyly and wittily criticizing the illogicalities and corruptions of the communist system. But systematic repression of intellectuals and artists followed the Prague Spring, and Havel was declared a 'class enemy', his passport confiscated and his plays banned. He was later offered the chance to leave the country several times, but he preferred to remain a thorn in the authorities' side, noting: 'The solution of this human situation does not lie in leaving it.'

In 1977 the playwright, supported by hundreds of Czech intellectuals, helped to draw up the important Charter '77 human rights document. His essay 'The Power of the Powerless' (1978) accused the regime of creating a society of morally corrupt individuals, and the next year he was given a four-and-a-half-year jail sentence. Yet his plays flourished abroad, he received numerous foreign prizes, and he was championed by the likes of playwright Tom Stoppard (also of Czech origin). It was difficult to ignore Havel, who became one of the world's most high-profile political prisoners. In 1989, the Civic Forum opposition movement, which Havel had helped found, finally managed to lever the Communist Party out of government, and in December the new Czechoslovak Parliament elected Havel as the country's president. It was an extraordinary turning of the tables.

On 1 January 1990, Havel made a broadcast to his people. It delivered, in many ways, a surprising message. It was not triumphalist; rather, it reflected on the way that a morally bankrupt regime had made its people complicit in its iniquities. He described a system that had corroded values and human feelings, creating a pervading cynicism and a sense of powerlessness. It was a powerfully crafted message, with a wider application to authoritarian regimes around the world.

After leaving office in 2003, Havel continued to work on human-rights projects while also writing, including a memoir of his presidential years. He died in 2011.

WE LIVE IN A CONTAMINATED MORAL ENVIRONMENT. We fell morally ill because we became used to saying something different from what we thought. We learned not to believe in anything, to ignore each other, to care only about ourselves. Concepts such as love, friendship, compassion, humility or forgiveness lost their depth and dimensions, and for many of us they represented only psychological peculiarities, or they resembled gone-astray greetings from ancient times, a little ridiculous in the era of computers and spaceships. Only a few of us were able to cry out loud that the powers that be should not be all-powerful, and that special farms, which produce ecologically pure and top-quality food just for them, should send their produce to schools, children's homes and hospitals if our agriculture was unable to offer them to all. The previous regime – armed with its arrogant and intolerant ideology – reduced man to a force of production and nature to a tool of production. In this it attacked both their very substance and their mutual relationship. It reduced gifted and autonomous people, skilfully working in their own country, to nuts and bolts of some monstrously huge, noisy and stinking machine, whose real meaning is not clear to anyone. It cannot do more than slowly but inexorably wear down itself and all its nuts and bolts.

'We had all become used to the totalitarian system and accepted it as an unchangeable fact'

When I talk about contaminated moral atmosphere, I am not talking just about the gentlemen who eat organic vegetables and do not look out of the plane windows. I am talking about all of us. We had all become used to the totalitarian system and accepted it as an unchangeable fact and thus helped to perpetuate it. In other words, we are all – though naturally to differing extents – responsible for the operation of the totalitarian machinery; none of us is just its victim: we are all also its co-creators.

Why do I say this? It would be very unreasonable to understand the sad legacy of the last forty years as something alien, which some distant relative bequeathed us. On the contrary, we have to accept this legacy as a sin we committed against ourselves. If we accept it as such, we will understand that it is up to us all, and up to us only, to do something about it. We cannot blame the previous rulers for everything, not only because it would be untrue but also because it could blunt the duty that each of us faces today, namely, the obligation to act independently, freely, reasonably and quickly. Let us not be mistaken: the best government in the world, the best parliament and the best president, cannot achieve much on their own. And it would also be wrong to expect a general remedy from them only. Freedom and democracy include participation and therefore responsibility from us all.

'People, your government has returned to you!'

If we realize this, then all the horrors that the new Czechoslovak democracy inherited will cease to appear so terrible. If we realize this, hope will return to our hearts.

. . . In conclusion, I would like to say that I want to be a president who will speak less and work more. To be a president who will not only look out of the windows of his aeroplane but who, first and foremost, will always be present among his fellow citizens and listen to them well.

You may ask what kind of republic I dream of. Let me reply: I dream of a republic independent, free and democratic, of a republic economically prosperous and yet socially just, in short, of a humane republic which serves the individual and which therefore holds the hope that the individual will serve it in turn. Of a republic of well-rounded people, because without such it is impossible to solve any of our problems, human, economic, ecological, social or political.

The most distinguished of my predecessors opened his first speech with a quotation from the great Czech educator Comenius. Allow me to round off my first speech with my own paraphrase of the same statement: People, your government has returned to you!

'It is not power that
corrupts, but fear'

AUNG SAN SUU KYI
*Written to mark acceptance of the Sakharov Prize for
Freedom of Thought, July 1991*

SUU KYI RAISED HER FAMILY IN THE UK before returning to Burma in 1988 to nurse her ailing mother. Her arrival coincided with an uprising against the government that was put down by the army at a cost of several thousand civilian lives. A military junta was then installed, prompting Suu Kyi to address some 500,000 pro-democracy supporters in Yangon and to establish the National League for Democracy (NLD). In 1989 she survived an assassination attempt while on the campaign trail and was then placed under house arrest, thus disqualifying her from standing in multi-party elections the following year.

Although unable to campaign freely, the NLD won over 80 per cent of parliamentary seats but the ruling junta refused to acknowledge the electoral result. Instead, it retained martial law, effectively banned Parliament from meeting, and closed many universities. It was against this backdrop that Suu Kyi made – or at least wrote – the most important speech of her life. Having been awarded the European Parliament's Sakharov Prize for Freedom of Thought in 1990, she authored the following essay which, owing to her house arrest, she was unable to deliver at the prize ceremony, held in Strasbourg on 10 July 1991. However, in that week the address was printed in numerous international publications including the *Bangkok Post*, the *Far Eastern Economic Review*, the *New York Times*, *The Times Literary Supplement* and the *Times of India*.

AUNG SAN SUU KYI

Born 19 June 1945 in Rangoon (Yangon) in Burma (Myanmar) into a family prominent in winning the nation's independence from the British.

Her father, Aung San – widely regarded as the father of the nation – was assassinated in 1947 a few months before independence was declared. Her mother, Khin Kyi, held several offices in the post-independence government. Suu Kyi was schooled in Delhi, studied at the University of Oxford and worked for the United Nations in New York. In 1972 she married a British academic, Michael Aris. In 1988 she returned to Burma, becoming the focal point of the pro-democracy movement. The ruling military junta put her under house arrest for 15 years between 1989 and 2010 and in 1990 refused to recognize the electoral victory of her political party, the National League for Democracy. Freed from house arrest in 2010, she took up a seat in Parliament two years later at a time of tentative government reform.

The lecture helped to keep the flame of Burma's pro-democracy movement alive over the years that followed, even in the face of Suu Kyi's ongoing incarceration and continued government suppression. In 1999 she turned down the chance of returning to the UK to visit her dying husband for fear of being refused entry back into her homeland. She remained in detention for all but a few short spells in the 1990s and 2000s despite intense international pressure for her to be freed. However, after further flawed elections, she was released from house arrest in November 2010 and won a seat in the nation's lower house at polls held in 2012. In the same year she made her first visit abroad since her return to Myanmar 24 years earlier.

An icon of peaceful resistance throughout the world, she received many prestigious awards in recognition of her campaigning work, including the 1991 Nobel Peace Prize. Burma seemingly made significant progress in democratic reforms after 2012 and in 2015 Suu Kyi—who was constitutionally prevented from standing for President — assumed the newly created position of State Counsellor (effectively, head of government). However, her reputation as a human rights champion subsequently took a battering as she received international condemnation for her inaction in the face of a genocide perpetrated by the military against the minority Muslim Rohingya people. Back in October 2013, however, she had addressed the European Parliament in Strasbourg, taking the opportunity to reflect on the forward steps taken since her 'Freedom from Fear' address, even as she emphasized that it was a job half done:

'We have made progress since 1990, but we have not made sufficient progress. Our people are just beginning to learn that freedom of thought is possible, but we want to make sure that the right to think freely and to live in accordance with a conscience has to be preserved . . . That is why we insist that the present constitution must be changed to be a truly democratic one.'

IT IS NOT POWER THAT CORRUPTS, BUT FEAR.

Fear of losing power corrupts those who wield it and fear of the scourge of power corrupts those who are subject to it. Most Burmese are familiar with the four *a-gati*, the four kinds of corruption. *Chanda-gati*, corruption induced by desire, is deviation from the right path in pursuit of bribes or for the sake of those one loves. *Dosa-gati* is taking the wrong path to spite those against whom one bears ill will, and *moga-gati* is aberration due to ignorance. But perhaps the worst of the four is *bhaya-gati*, for not only does *bhaya*, fear, stifle and slowly destroy all sense of right and wrong, it so often lies at the root of the other three kinds of corruption. Just as *chanda-gati*, when not the result of sheer avarice, can be caused by fear of want or fear of losing the goodwill of those one loves, so fear of being surpassed, humiliated or injured in some way can provide the impetus for ill will. And it would be difficult to dispel ignorance unless there is freedom to pursue the truth unfettered by fear. With so close a relationship between fear and corruption it is little wonder that in any society where fear is rife corruption in all forms becomes deeply entrenched.

Public dissatisfaction with economic hardships has been seen as the chief cause of the movement for democracy in Burma, sparked off by the student demonstrations 1988.

'*In any society where fear is rife corruption in all forms becomes deeply entrenched*'

. . . The students were protesting not just against the death of their comrades but against the denial of their right to life by a totalitarian regime which deprived the present of meaningfulness and held out no hope for the future. And because the students' protests articulated the frustrations of the people at large, the demonstrations quickly grew into a nationwide movement . . . The people of Burma had wearied of a precarious state of passive apprehension where they were 'as water in cupped hands' of the powers that be.

Emerald cool we may be. As water in cupped hands. But oh that we might be. As splinters of glass. In cupped hands.

Glass splinters, the smallest with its sharp, glinting power to defend itself against hands that try to crush, could be seen as a vivid symbol of the spark of courage that is an essential attribute of those who would free themselves from the grip of oppression. Bogyoke Aung San regarded himself as a revolutionary and searched tirelessly for answers to the problems that beset Burma during her times of trial. He exhorted the people to develop courage: 'Don't just depend on the courage and intrepidity of others. Each and every one of you must make sacrifices to become a hero possessed of courage and intrepidity. Then only shall we all be able to enjoy true freedom.'

. . . The Universal Declaration of Human Rights of the United Nations proclaims that 'every individual and every organ of society' should strive to promote the basic rights and freedoms to which all human beings regardless of race, nationality or religion are entitled. But as long as there are governments whose authority is founded on coercion rather than on the mandate of the people, and interest groups which place short-term profits above long-term peace and prosperity, concerted international action to protect and promote human rights will remain at best a partially realized struggle . . . The quintessential revolution is that of the spirit, born of an intellectual conviction of the need for change in those mental attitudes and values which shape the course of a nation's development. A revolution which aims merely at changing official policies and institutions with a view to an improvement in material conditions has little chance of genuine success. Without a revolution of the spirit, the forces which produced the iniquities of the old order would continue to be operative, posing a constant threat to the process of reform and regeneration.

'The quintessential revolution is that of the spirit'

. . . Saints, it has been said, are the sinners who go on trying. So free men are the oppressed who go on trying and who in the process make themselves fit to bear the responsibilities and to uphold the disciplines which will maintain a free society. Among the basic freedoms to which men aspire that their lives might be full and uncramped, freedom from fear stands out as both a means and an end. A people who would build a nation in which strong, democratic institutions are firmly established as a guarantee against state-induced power must first learn to liberate their own minds from apathy and fear.

Always one to practise what he preached, Aung San himself constantly demonstrated courage – not just the physical sort but the kind that enabled him to speak the truth, to stand by his word, to accept criticism, to admit his faults, to correct his mistakes, to respect the opposition, to parley with the enemy and to let people be the judge of his worthiness as a leader. It is for such moral courage that he will always be loved and respected in Burma – not merely as a warrior hero but as the inspiration and conscience of the nation. The words used by Jawaharlal Nehru to describe Mahatma Gandhi could well be applied to Aung San:

'The essence of his teaching was fearlessness and truth, and action allied to these, always keeping the welfare of the masses in view.'

. . . Fearlessness may be a gift but perhaps more precious is the courage acquired through endeavour, courage that comes from cultivating the habit of refusing to let fear dictate one's actions, courage that could be described as 'grace under pressure' – grace which is renewed repeatedly in the face of harsh, unremitting pressure.

'At the root of human responsibility is the concept of perfection'

. . . The wellspring of courage and endurance in the face of unbridled power is generally a firm belief in the sanctity of ethical principles combined with a historical sense that despite all setbacks the condition of man is set on an ultimate course for both spiritual and material advancement. It is his capacity for self-improvement and self-redemption which most distinguishes man from the mere brute. At the root of human responsibility is the concept of perfection, the urge to achieve it, the intelligence to find a path towards it, and the will to follow that path if not to the end at least the distance needed to rise above individual limitations and environmental impediments. It is man's vision of a world fit for rational, civilized humanity which leads him to dare and to suffer to build societies free from want and fear. Concepts such as truth, justice and compassion cannot be dismissed as trite when these are often the only bulwarks which stand against ruthless power.

'Women's rights are human rights'

HILLARY CLINTON
*Address to the United Nations Fourth World Conference on Women,
Beijing, 5 September 1995*

ONE OF THE MOST DEFINITIVE AND DIVISIVE FIGURES not just of her time but of ours, Hillary Rodham Clinton is undoubtedly the most important woman in modern American politics, and one of the most influential women in the world: all this despite so far having held elective office for only eight years, relatively late in her career.

Initially emerging as a public figure as the wife of Arkansas' youngest ever Governor, Bill Clinton, in 1978, Hillary went on to be unusually closely associated with her husband's political career, working with him on issues of policy while also retaining a career of her own and – initially – her unmarried name. This became controversial in conservative Arkansas, although it did not stop the Clintons from serving five terms in the Governor's mansion in Little Rock.

Hillary was subsequently further scrutinised when her husband ran successfully for President in 1992, with Hillary again adopting an unusually high profile: he said that America was being offered 'two for the price of one', but struggled when accusations of infidelity emerged. Hillary stood by him at this point, creating a surge of public sympathy for her: together they won election, with Hillary heading a protracted and increasingly bitter attempt at healthcare reform within the Clinton administration which ultimately led to nothing. After Bill's 1996 re-election the Monica Lewinsky scandal, providing definitive proof of his infidelities while in office, consumed much of his second term and once again led to heavy media scrutiny of Hillary.

She nevertheless used her time as First Lady to advance many causes: this speech, made in 1995, was part of her many efforts to advance women's rights and has become emblematic of her efforts in that area. Delivered to a UN conference in Beijing, the

HILLARY RODHAM CLINTON

Born Hillary Rodham, 26 October 1947 in Chicago, Illinois.

Born into a middle-class family in Chicago, Hillary Rodham became involved in progressive politics while studying political science at Wellesley College. She subsequently attended law school at Yale where she met her future husband, Bill Clinton, and became increasingly active in politics: after graduating in 1973 she worked for a time on the staff of the Watergate Inquiry before moving to Clinton's home state of Arkansas where he was elected as governor in 1978 aged only 32. He continued to serve as governor, with one short interruption, until 1990, while Hillary worked both as First Lady of Arkansas and as a successful lawyer. Bill Clinton ran for, and won, the presidency in 1992 and was re-elected in 1996: Hillary came under enormous scrutiny during the Monica Lewinsky scandal. At the end of Clinton's presidency, Hillary ran for and won a Senate seat in New York, winning re-election in 2006 and mounting a strong primary campaign for the Democratic presidential nomination in 2008, in which contest she was eventually defeated by Barack Obama. After his election, Obama selected Hillary Clinton to serve as his Secretary of State, which she did until 2013. In 2015 she announced her candidacy for President in 2016, and became the Democratic nominee and the first female nominee of a major party.

central rallying cry of 'women's rights are human's rights' became a feminist slogan and helped to define Hillary's approach to politics, focusing on grassroots issues and working to empower marginalised communities.

When she subsequently entered electoral politics herself, she continued to work on similar issues, especially while serving as Secretary of State to her erstwhile rival Barack Obama. Long considered the likely first woman president of the United States, she failed to achieve that office in 2008 but is making a renewed effort in 2016.

THIS IS TRULY A CELEBRATION, a celebration of the contributions women make in every aspect of life: in the home, on the job, in the community, as mothers, wives, sisters, daughters, learners, workers, citizens, and leaders.

It is also a coming together, much the way women come together every day in every country. We come together in fields and factories, in village markets and supermarkets, in living rooms and board rooms. Whether it is while playing with our children in the park, or washing clothes in a river, or taking a break at the office water cooler, we come together and talk about our aspirations and concern. And time and again, our talk turns to our children and our families. However different we may appear, there is far more that unites us than divides us. We share a common future, and we are here to find common ground so that we may help bring new dignity and respect to women and girls all over the world, and in so doing bring new strength and stability to families as well.

'Every woman, every man, every child, every family, and every nation on this planet does have a stake in the discussion that takes place here'

By gathering in Beijing, we are focusing world attention on issues that matter most in our lives – the lives of women and their families: access to education, health care, jobs and credit, the chance to enjoy basic legal and human rights and to participate fully in the political life of our countries.

There are some who question the reason for this conference. Let them listen to the voices of women in their homes, neighborhoods, and workplaces. There are some who wonder whether the lives of women and girls matter to economic and political progress around the globe. Let them look at the women gathered here – the homemakers and nurses, the teachers and lawyers, the policymakers and women who run their own businesses. It is conferences like this that compel governments and peoples everywhere to listen, look, and face the world's most pressing problems…

Earlier today, I participated in a World Health Organization forum. In that forum, we talked about ways that government officials, NGOs, and individual citizens are working to address the health problems of women and girls. Tomorrow, I will attend a gathering of the United Nations Development Fund for Women. There, the discussion will focus on local – and highly successful – programs that give hard-working women access to credit so they can improve their own lives and the lives of their families. What we are learning around the world is that if women are healthy and educated, their families will flourish. If women are free from violence, their families will flourish. If women have a chance to work and earn as full and equal partners in society, their families will flourish. And when families flourish, communities and nations do as well. That is why every woman, every man, every child, every family, and every nation on this planet does have a stake in the discussion that takes place here.

'Women comprise more than half the world's population, 70% of the world's poor, and two-thirds of those who are not taught to read and write'

Over the past 25 years, I have worked persistently on issues relating to women, children, and families. Over the past two and a half years, I've had the opportunity to learn more about the challenges facing women in my own country and around the world.

I have met new mothers in Indonesia, who come together regularly in their village to discuss nutrition, family planning, and baby care. I have met working parents in Denmark who talk about the comfort they feel in knowing that their children can be cared for in safe, and nurturing after-school centers. I have met women in South Africa who helped lead the struggle to end apartheid and are now helping to build a new democracy. I have met with the leading women of my own hemisphere who are working every day to promote literacy and better health care for children in their countries. I have met women in India and Bangladesh who are taking out small loans to buy milk cows, or rickshaws, or thread in order to create a livelihood for themselves and their families. I have met the doctors and nurses in Belarus and Ukraine who are trying to keep children alive in the aftermath of Chernobyl.

The great challenge of this conference is to give voice to women everywhere whose experiences go unnoticed, whose words go unheard. Women comprise more than half the world's population, 70% of the world's poor, and two-thirds of those who are not taught to read and write.

We are the primary caretakers for most of the world's children and elderly. Yet much of the work we do is not valued – not by economists, not by historians, not by popular culture, not by government leaders.

At this very moment, as we sit here, women around the world are giving birth, raising children, cooking meals, washing clothes, cleaning houses, planting crops, working on assembly lines, running companies, and running countries. Women also are dying from diseases that should have been prevented or treated. They are watching their children succumb to malnutrition caused by poverty and economic deprivation. They are being denied the right to go to school by their own fathers and brothers. They are being forced into prostitution, and they are being barred from the bank lending offices and banned from the ballot box.

'Every woman deserves the chance to realize her own God-given potential'

Those of us who have the opportunity to be here have the responsibility to speak for those who could not. As an American, I want to speak for those women in my own country, women who are raising children on the minimum wage, women who can't afford health care or child care, women whose lives are threatened by violence, including violence in their own homes.

I want to speak up for mothers who are fighting for good schools, safe neighborhoods, clean air, and clean airwaves; for older women, some of them widows, who find that, after raising their families, their skills and life experiences are not valued in the marketplace; for women who are working all night as nurses, hotel clerks, or fast food chefs so that they can be at home during the day with their children; and for women everywhere who simply don't have time to do everything they are called upon to do each and every day.

Speaking to you today, I speak for them, just as each of us speaks for women around the world who are denied the chance to go to school, or see a doctor, or own property, or have a say about the direction of their lives, simply because they are women. The truth is that most women around the world work both inside and outside the home, usually by necessity.

We need to understand there is no one formula for how women should lead our lives. That is why we must respect the choices that each woman makes for herself and her family. Every woman deserves the chance to realize her own God-given potential. But we must recognize that women will never gain full dignity until their human rights are respected and protected.

Our goals for this conference, to strengthen families and societies by empowering women to take greater control over their own destinies, cannot be fully achieved unless all governments – here and around the world – accept their responsibility to protect and promote internationally recognized human rights. The international community has long acknowledged and recently reaffirmed at Vienna that both women and men are entitled to a range of protections and personal freedoms, from the right of personal security to the right to determine freely the number and spacing of the children they bear. No one should be forced to remain silent for fear of religious or political persecution, arrest, abuse, or torture.

Tragically, women are most often the ones whose human rights are violated. Even now, in the late 20th century, the rape of women continues to be used as an instrument of armed conflict. Women and children make up a large majority of the world's refugees. And when women are excluded from the political process, they become even more vulnerable to abuse. I believe that now, on the eve of a new millennium, it is time to break the silence. It is time for us to say here in Beijing, and for the world to hear, that it is no longer acceptable to discuss women's rights as separate from human rights.

'Let it be that human rights are women's rights and women's rights are human rights once and for all'

These abuses have continued because, for too long, the history of women has been a history of silence. Even today, there are those who are trying to silence our words. But the voices of this conference must be heard loudly and clearly:

It is a violation of human rights when babies are denied food, or drowned, or suffocated, or their spines broken, simply because they are born girls.

It is a violation of human rights when women and girls are sold into the slavery of prostitution for human greed – and the kinds of reasons that are used to justify this practice should no longer be tolerated.

It is a violation of human rights when women are doused with gasoline, set on fire, and burned to death because their marriage dowries are deemed too small.

It is a violation of human rights when individual women are raped in their own communities and when thousands of women are subjected to rape as a tactic or prize of war.

It is a violation of human rights when a leading cause of death worldwide among women ages 14 to 44 is the violence they are subjected to in their own homes by their own relatives.

It is a violation of human rights when young girls are brutalized by the painful and degrading practice of genital mutilation.

It is a violation of human rights when women are denied the right to plan their own families, and that includes being forced to have abortions or being sterilized against their will.

'Freedom means the right of people to assemble, organize, and debate openly. It means respecting the views of those who may disagree with the views of their governments.'

If there is one message that echoes forth from this conference, let it be that human rights are women's rights and women's rights are human rights once and for all. Let us not forget that among those rights are the right to speak freely – and the right to be heard.

Women must enjoy the rights to participate fully in the social and political lives of their countries, if we want freedom and democracy to thrive and endure. It is indefensible that many women in nongovernmental organizations who wished to participate in this conference have not been able to attend – or have been prohibited from fully taking part.

Let me be clear. Freedom means the right of people to assemble, organize, and debate openly. It means respecting the views of those who may disagree with the views of their governments. It means not taking citizens away from their loved ones and jailing them, mistreating them, or denying them their freedom or dignity because of the peaceful expression of their ideas and opinions.

In my country, we recently celebrated the 75th anniversary of Women's Suffrage. It took 150 years after the signing of our Declaration of Independence for women to win the right to vote. It took 72 years of organized struggle, before that happened, on the part of many courageous women and men. It was one of America's most divisive philosophical wars. But it was a bloodless war. Suffrage was achieved without a shot being fired.

But we have also been reminded, in V-J Day observances last weekend, of the good that comes when men and women join together to combat the forces of tyranny and to build a better world. We have seen peace prevail in most places for a half century. We have avoided another world war. But we have not solved older, deeply-rooted problems that continue to diminish the potential of half the world's population.

Now it is the time to act on behalf of women everywhere. If we take bold steps to better the lives of women, we will be taking bold steps to better the lives of children and families too. Families rely on mothers and wives for emotional support and care. Families rely on women for labor in the home. And increasingly, everywhere, families rely on women for income needed to raise healthy children and care for other relatives.

'Now it is the time to act on behalf of women everywhere'

As long as discrimination and inequities remain so commonplace everywhere in the world, as long as girls and women are valued less, fed less, fed last, overworked, underpaid, not schooled, subjected to violence in and outside their homes – the potential of the human family to create a peaceful, prosperous world will not be realized.

Let – Let this conference be our – and the world's – call to action. Let us heed that call so we can create a world in which every woman is treated with respect and dignity, every boy and girl is loved and cared for equally, and every family has the hope of a strong and stable future. That is the work before you. That is the work before all of us who have a vision of the world we want to see – for our children and our grandchildren.

The time is now. We must move beyond rhetoric. We must move beyond recognition of problems to working together, to have the comment efforts to build that common ground we hope to see.

God's blessing on you, your work, and all who will benefit from it.

Godspeed and thank you very much.

'The most hunted person of the modern age'

EARL SPENCER

Funeral oration for Diana, Princess of Wales, 6 September 1997

F OR ALMOST HER ENTIRE ADULT LIFE, Diana, Princess of Wales, was dogged by the paparazzi. They were there when the shy young nursery-school assistant was first linked to the heir to the British throne; and they were there on motorbikes, chasing her car into the Parisian tunnel where she met her death. The extraordinary life of 'the most hunted woman of the age' said much about the nature of modern celebrity, and about its difficult relationship with royalty. In his funeral oration, on 6 September 1997, her brother Earl Spencer was faced with the task of attempting to encapsulate her phenomenon.

The outlines of her story, of a 'fairytale' marriage gone bad, are well ploughed. The young debutante married the older, more experienced Prince Charles, but was then increasingly confounded by a world of stiff royal protocol. The marriage produced princes William and Harry, but in other respects it deteriorated, particularly as a consequence of the prince's lingering affection for Mrs Camilla Parker-Bowles. While Charles was able to maintain a calm exterior through a lifetime of royal experience, an unprepared Diana floundered. With the speculation be-coming intense and the media taking sides, a separation was agreed in 1992.

Yet, Diana had also begun to carve out an alternative identity, one she dubbed the 'Princess of Hearts'. This was the Diana who showed an instinctive ability to connect with those enduring adversity – from AIDS, from leprosy, from the consequences of landmines. As Earl Spencer described it, 'it was her innermost feelings of suffering that made it possible for her to connect with her constituency of the rejected'. She did exhaustive charitable work, acquiring a new

DIANA, PRINCESS OF WALES

Born 1 July 1961 in Sandringham, Norfolk, England, the third daughter of Edward, Earl Spencer of Althorp.

Her parents divorced in 1969. She was educated to age 16 at Riddlesworth Hall, Norfolk, and West Heath School, Kent. Diana moved to London, where she began working at a nursery school. She became romantically attached to Charles, Prince of Wales, leading to massive media interest which continued throughout her life. They married in St Paul's Cathedral (1981) and had two sons: the princes William (born 1982; second in line to the throne) and Henry (called Harry; born 1984). Her marriage deteriorated, with infidelity on both sides, leading to separation (1992) and divorce (1996). She was patron of numerous charities, and particularly associated with campaigns to raise awareness of the issues of HIV/Aids and landmines.

She died on 31 August 1997 in Paris, when her French driver crashed the car in which she and her amour, Dodi al-Fayed, were escaping the attendant paparazzi.

confidence and, paradoxically, an enhanced glamour. Her frank TV interview in 1995 – admitting to the eating disorder *Bulimia nervosa* and an extramarital affair, and criticizing Charles and the royal establishment – underscored a certain sense of release, formalized by divorce the next year.

The immediate aftermath of her death generated new royal dilemmas. Struggling to find the right protocols for reacting to the death of the divorcee princess, royal officials managed to render the monarchy lead-footed. By contrast, a substantial number of the British public, throwing stereotypes of English reserve aside, took the tragedy as an almost personal one in an unprecedented outpouring of public grief.

Earl Spencer's speech was a poignant valedictory message from a younger brother to his elder sister. It deftly captured the contrary nature of Diana, rejecting those who would 'canonize' her while applauding her essential 'goodness' and the fact that she remained 'intact, true to herself'. He promised princes William and Harry to nurture the 'imaginative' upbringing of their mother's influence so that their 'souls are not simply immersed by duty and tradition but can sing'. This was not just a form of rebuke from one side of a sparring family to another; the words struck a chord with all those who regarded Diana as a victim of hidebound royal tradition. Earl Spencer's speech signalled a moment of change in the mutual expectations of a people and their monarchy for the new century that was soon to begin.

I STAND BEFORE YOU TODAY, the representative of a family in grief, in a country in mourning, before a world in shock.

We are all united, not only in our desire to pay our respects to Diana, but rather in our need to do so. For such was her extraordinary appeal that the tens of millions of people taking part in this service all over the world, via television and radio, who never actually met her, feel that they, too, lost someone close to them in the early hours of Sunday morning. It is a more remarkable tribute to Diana than I can ever hope to offer her today.

Diana was the very essence of compassion, of duty, of style, of beauty. All over the world she was a symbol of selfless humanity, a standard-bearer for the rights of the truly downtrodden, a very British girl who transcended nationality. Someone with a natural nobility who was classless and who proved in the last year that she needed no royal title to continue to generate her particular brand of magic.

Today is our chance to say 'thank you' for the way you brightened our lives, even though God granted you but half a life . . . There is a temptation to rush to canonize your memory. There is no need to do so. You stand tall enough as a human being of unique qualities not to need to be seen as a saint. Indeed, to sanctify your memory would be to miss out on the very core of your being, your wonderfully mischievous sense of humour, with a laugh that bent you double.

. . . But your greatest gift was your intuition, and it was a gift you used wisely. This is what underpinned all your other wonderful attributes, and if we look to analyse what it was about you that had such a wide appeal, we find it in your instinctive feel for what was really important in all our lives. Without your God-given sensitivity we would be immersed in greater ignorance at the anguish of Aids and HIV sufferers, the plight of the homeless, the isolation of lepers, the random destruction of landmines.

Diana explained to me once that it was her innermost feelings of suffering that made it possible for her to connect with her constituency of the rejected. And here we come to another truth about her. For all the status, the glamour, the applause, Diana remained throughout a very insecure person at heart, almost childlike in her desire to do good for others so she could release herself from deep feelings of unworthiness, of which her eating disorders were merely a symptom. The world sensed this part of her character and cherished her for her vulnerability whilst admiring her for her honesty.

. . . Fundamentally, she hadn't changed at all from the big sister who mothered me as a baby, fought with me at school and endured those long train journeys between our parents' homes with me at weekends. It is a tribute to her level-headedness and strength that despite the most bizarre life imaginable after her childhood, she remained intact, true to herself.

'We will not allow them to suffer the anguish'

. . . I don't think she ever understood why her genuinely good intentions were sneered at by the media . . . My own and only explanation is that genuine goodness is threatening to those at the opposite end of the moral spectrum. It is a point to remember that of all the ironies about Diana, perhaps the greatest was this: a girl given the name of the ancient goddess of hunting was, in the end, the most hunted person of the modern age.

She would want us today to pledge ourselves to protecting her beloved boys William and Harry from a similar fate and I do this here, Diana, on your behalf. We will not allow them to suffer the anguish that used regularly to drive you to tearful despair. And beyond that, on behalf of your mother and sisters, I pledge that we, your blood family, will do all we can to continue the imaginative and loving way in which you were steering these two exceptional young men, so that their souls are not simply immersed by duty and tradition, but can sing openly as you planned. We fully respect the heritage into which they have both been born, and will always respect and encourage them in their royal role. But we, like you, recognize the need for them to experience as many different aspects of life as possible to arm them spiritually and emotionally for the years ahead. I know you would have expected nothing less from us.

. . . I would like to end by thanking God for the small mercies he has shown us at this dreadful time, for taking Diana at her most beautiful and radiant and when she had joy in her private life. Above all, we give thanks for the life of a woman I am so proud to be able to call my sister: the unique, the complex, the extraordinary and irreplaceable Diana . . . .

'The perils of indifference'

ELIE WIESEL

Speech reviewing the 20th century's calamities,
12 April 1999

ON 12 APRIL 1999, PRESIDENT BILL CLINTON, First Lady Hillary Clinton and members of Congress gathered in the White House's East Room. As part of a Millennium Series of talks, they were there to hear a man speak about the past, the present and the future. The central theme of his speech (and its title) was 'the perils of indifference', and the speaker had more authority than most to warn about the dangers.

Elie Wiesel grew up in Sighet, Romania, 'a young Jewish boy from a small town in the Carpathian Mountains', who spoke Yiddish as a first language and studied Hebrew. After the area was transferred to Hungary in 1940, the Nazis 'cleansed' Sighet of its Jews in 1944 – as many as 20,000 – deporting them *en masse* to concentration camps. On arrival at the Auschwitz-Birkenau camp system, in Poland, Wiesel was separated from his mother and younger sister and never saw them again. He and his father were chosen to undertake slave labour at a nearby rubber-producing plant, where they were starved and beaten. As the Red Army closed in, they were moved to Buchenwald, in Germany, and there Wiesel's father perished from his maltreatment short-ly before the camp was liberated by the US Third Army in 1945.

After the war, Wiesel attempted to put these horrors behind him as he reinvented himself in Paris as a journalist, writing for French and Israeli publications. After years of silence about his war experiences, and at the prompting of the French intellectual François Mauriac, he finally put pen to paper, boiling down a long narrative into a slim 1958 memoir, *La Nuit*. It appeared in English as *Night* (1960), and grew into a global phenomenon and one of the cornerstones of Holocaust literature. Many other writings were to follow, including the novels *L'Aube* (*Dawn*) and *Le Jour* (*Day*) and further memoirs. But it was *Night* that propelled Wiesel into his role as a public voice of authority on humanitarian issues, a role that earned him the Nobel Peace Prize in 1986 and which saw the creation of an Elie Wiesel Foundation 'to combat indifference, intolerance and injustice'.

On 12 April, Hillary Clinton introduced Wiesel by saying: 'You have taught us never to forget. You have made sure that we always listen to the victims of indifference, hatred and evil.' And Wiesel's message was a simple but profound one: that indifference and lack of action become the allies of evil. As he described it, 'In the place I come from, society

ELIE WIESEL

Born Eliezer Wiesel on 30 September 1928 in Sighet, Romania, the son of a traditional Jewish family.

His family were sent to the Auschwitz-Birkenau camp system in 1944, where he endured (with his father) slave labour, starvation and beatings; he was transferred to Buchenwald camp, where he was liberated by US forces in April 1945. Afterwards, in Paris, he attended the Sorbonne, taught Hebrew and ran a choir, before becoming a journalist. He published his renowned Holocaust memoir, *Night*, in 1958 (in French) and 1960 (in English). A US citizen since 1963, he has combined professorships at City University of New York, Yale and (since 1976) Boston University with his prolific literary output and campaigning work. He was Chairman of the US Holocaust Memorial Council (1978–86). His awards and honours include the Congressional Gold Medal (1985), the Presidential Medal of Freedom and the Nobel Peace Prize (1986), the latter inspiring the creation (with his wife) of the Elie Wiesel Foundation for Humanity.

was composed of three simple categories: the killers, the victims, and the bystanders.' In this way, 'indifference is always the friend of the enemy, for it benefits the aggressor'. By contrast, he remembered the US soldiers who liberated him from Buchenwald, to whom he would 'always be grateful' for their righteous rage at what they found. And, moving from the past to the present, he welcomed the 1999 intervention by NATO in Kosovo, against Serbian forces who were attempting to cleanse the region of its ethnically Albanian population. For Wiesel, the dangers of indifference must always persist, but so do the means to avoid them. He concluded that 'we walk towards the new millennium, carried by profound fear and extraordinary hope'.

FIFTY-FOUR YEARS AGO TO THE DAY, a young Jewish boy from a small town in the Carpathian Mountains woke up, not far from Goethe's beloved Weimar, in a place of eternal infamy called Buchenwald. He was finally free, but there was no joy in his heart. He thought there never would be again. Liberated a day earlier by American soldiers, he remembers their rage at what they saw. And even if he lives to be a very old man, he will always be grateful to them for that rage, and also for their compassion. Though he did not understand their language, their eyes told him what he needed to know – that they, too, would remember, and bear witness.

. . . We are on the threshold of a new century, a new millennium. What will the legacy of this vanishing century be? How will it be remembered in the new millennium? Surely it will be judged, and judged severely, in both moral and metaphysical terms. These failures have cast a dark shadow over humanity: two world wars, countless civil wars, the senseless chain of assassinations (Gandhi, the Kennedys, Martin Luther King, Sadat, Rabin), bloodbaths in Cambodia and Nigeria, India and Pakistan, Ireland and Rwanda, Eritrea and Ethiopia, Sarajevo and Kosovo; the inhumanity in the gulag and the tragedy of Hiroshima. And, on a different level, of course, Auschwitz and Treblinka. So much violence; so much indifference.

'Indifference can be tempting – more than that, seductive'

What is indifference? Etymologically, the word means 'no difference'. A strange and unnatural state in which the lines blur between light and darkness, dusk and dawn, crime and punishment, cruelty and compassion, good and evil. What are its courses and inescapable consequences? Is it a philosophy? Is there a philosophy of indifference conceivable? Can one possibly view indifference as a virtue? Is it necessary at times to practise it simply to keep one's sanity, live normally, enjoy a fine meal and a glass of wine, as the world around us experiences harrowing upheavals?

Of course, indifference can be tempting – more than that, seductive. It is so much easier to look away from victims. It is so much easier to avoid such rude interruptions to our work, our dreams, our hopes. It is, after all, awkward, troublesome, to be involved in another person's pain and despair. Yet, for the person who is indifferent, his or her neighbours are of no consequence. And, therefore, their lives are meaningless. Their hidden or even visible anguish is of no interest. Indifference reduces the other to an abstraction.

'Better an unjust God than an indifferent one'

Over there, behind the black gates of Auschwitz, the most tragic of all prisoners were the *Muselmänner*, as they were called. Wrapped in their torn blankets, they would sit or lie on the ground, staring vacantly into space, unaware of who or where they were – strangers to their surroundings. They no longer felt pain, hunger, thirst. They feared nothing. They felt nothing. They were dead and did not know it.

Rooted in our tradition, some of us felt that to be abandoned by humanity then was not the ultimate. We felt that to be abandoned by God was worse than to be punished by Him. Better an unjust God than an indifferent one. For us to be ignored by God was a harsher punishment than to be a victim of His anger. Man can live far from God – not outside God. God is wherever we are. Even in suffering? Even in suffering.

In a way, to be indifferent to that suffering is what makes the human being inhuman. Indifference, after all, is more dangerous than anger and hatred. Anger can at times be creative. One writes a great poem, a great symphony. One does something special for the sake of humanity because one is angry at the injustice that one witnesses. But indifference is never creative. Even hatred at times may elicit a response. You fight it. You denounce it. You disarm it.

Indifference elicits no response. Indifference is not a response. Indifference is not a beginning; it is an end. And, therefore, indifference is always the friend of the enemy, for it benefits the aggressor – never his victim, whose pain is magnified when he or she feels forgotten. The political prisoner in his cell, the hungry children, the homeless refugees – not to respond to their plight, not to relieve their solitude by offering them a spark of hope is to exile them from human memory. And in denying their humanity, we betray our own.

Indifference, then, is not only a sin, it is a punishment. And this is one of the most important lessons of this outgoing century's wide-ranging experiments in good and evil.

In the place that I come from, society was composed of three simple categories: the killers, the victims, and the bystanders . . . we felt abandoned, forgotten. All of us did. And our only miserable consolation was that we believed that Auschwitz and Treblinka were closely guarded secrets; that the leaders of the free world did not know what was going on behind those black gates and barbed wire; that they had no knowledge of the war against the Jews that Hitler's armies and their accomplices waged as part of the war against the Allies. If they knew, we thought, surely those leaders would have moved heaven and earth to intervene. They would have spoken out with great outrage and conviction. They would have bombed the railways leading to Birkenau, just the railways, just once. And now we knew, we learned, we discovered that the Pentagon knew, the State Department knew.

. . . The depressing tale of the *St Louis* is a case in point.* Sixty years ago, its human cargo – nearly 1000 Jews – was turned back to Nazi Germany. And that happened after the *Kristallnacht*, after the first state sponsored pogrom, with hundreds of Jewish shops destroyed, synagogues burned, thousands of people put in concentration camps. And that ship, which was already in the shores of the United States, was sent back. I don't understand. Roosevelt was a good man, with a heart. He understood those who needed help. Why didn't he allow these refugees to disembark? A thousand people – in America, the great country, the greatest democracy, the most generous of all new nations in modern history. What happened? I don't understand. Why the indifference, on the highest level, to the suffering of the victims?

But then, there were human beings who were sensitive to our tragedy. Those non-Jews, those Christians, that we call the 'Righteous Gentiles', whose selfless acts of heroism saved the honour of their faith. Why were they so few? Why was there a greater effort to save SS murderers after the war than to save their victims during the war? Why did some of America's largest corporations continue to do business with Hitler's Germany until 1942? It has been suggested, and it was documented, that the Wehrmacht could not have conducted its invasion of France without oil obtained from American sources. How is one to explain their indifference?

---

* The German liner *St Louis*, carrying Jewish refugees from Germany in 1939, was denied entry to Cuba, and then the United States and Canada. Its passengers were eventually admitted to Britain, France, Belgium and the Netherlands, and many of them eventually fell prey to the Nazis.

And yet, my friends, good things have also happened in this traumatic century: the defeat of Nazism, the collapse of communism, the rebirth of Israel on its ancestral soil, the demise of apartheid, Israel's peace treaty with Egypt, the peace accord in Ireland. And let us remember the meeting, filled with drama and emotion, between Rabin and Arafat that you, Mr President, convened in this very place. I was here and I will never forget it.

'This time, the world was not silent'

And then, of course, the joint decision of the United States and NATO to intervene in Kosovo and save those victims, those refugees, those who were uprooted by a man, whom I believe that because of his crimes, should be charged with crimes against humanity.

But this time, the world was not silent. This time, we do respond. This time, we intervene. Does it mean that we have learned from the past? Does it mean that society has changed? Has the human being become less indifferent and more human? Have we really learned from our experiences? Are we less insensitive to the plight of victims of ethnic cleansing and other forms of injustices in places near and far? Is today's justified intervention in Kosovo, led by you, Mr President, a lasting warning that never again will the deportation, the terrorization of children and their parents, be allowed anywhere in the world? Will it discourage other dictators in other lands to do the same?

'When adults wage war, children perish'

What about the children? Oh, we see them on television, we read about them in the papers, and we do so with a broken heart. Their fate is always the most tragic, inevitably. When adults wage war, children perish. We see their faces, their eyes. Do we hear their pleas? Do we feel their pain, their agony? Every minute one of them dies of disease, violence, famine. Some of them – so many of them – could be saved.

And so, once again, I think of the young Jewish boy from the Carpathian Mountains. He has accompanied the old man I have become throughout these years of quest and struggle. And together we walk towards the new millennium, carried by profound fear and extraordinary hope.

'Today, our nation saw evil'

GEORGE W. BUSH

Address to the nation after the 9/11 terrorist attacks, 11 September 2001

As THE NEW MILLENNIUM OPENED, the world appeared less dangerous in many respects than it had done for the previous 60 years. With the end of the Cold War, the spectre of a devastating superpower conflict had faded. And while the unravelling of fragile Yugoslavia in the 1990s produced ugly wars and ethnic 'cleansing', the intervention of NATO there suggested that in the 'new world order' force of arms might be put to humanitarian purposes, rather than to serve narrow national ambitions.

The United States also chose its 43rd president, albeit indistinctly. After an extremely close and disputed election in 2000, George W. Bush succeeded to the White House. He had little time to benefit from a millennial mood of optimism, however, for his greatest challenge was just around the corner, and it would define his presidency. That event was, of course, 9/11.

The events of 11 September 2001, played out live across the world's media, are indelible for anyone who witnessed the images. The terrorist attack that was mounted by members of the al-Qaeda Islamist network against the World Trade Center and the Pentagon was alarmingly simple and sophisticated: sophisticated, in that it involved careful coordination, long planning, flight training and complete surprise. Simple, in that in the end some well-dressed men with small knives exploited other people's trust and fear to turn aircraft into flying bombs. President Bush wrote in his diary that 'The Pearl Harbor of the 21st century took place today.' The death toll and element of surprise were similar; but in 1941 the aggressors were of the traditional kind – a hostile country with expansive ambitions – and the atmosphere was already tense.

The shock of 9/11 was that the new millennium had delivered a murkier, more ill-defined and potentially more frightening foe: one that was fearless because suicidal, invisible because secretive, frightening in its embrace of mass terror, and difficult to fathom in its motivations.

GEORGE W. BUSH

Born 6 July 1946 in New Haven, Connecticut, the son of future US President George H.W. Bush.

The family moved to Texas in 1948. He studied at the elite Philips Andover Academy, Massachusetts, and then at Yale University (BA, 1968). With the Texas Air National Guard he learned to fly fighter jets and reached the rank of lieutenant. At Harvard University (1972–5) he obtained an MA in Business Administration before forming an oil and gas exploration company in Texas. In 1977 he married Laura Welch: they had twin daughters. He moved to Washington, D.C., to support his father's successful presidential campaign in 1988, and subsequently moved to Dallas, Texas, where he became joint owner of Texas Rangers baseball team. He served as Governor of Texas, 1994–9, where he adroitly mixed business-friendly reforms with bipartisan diplomacy and gained a reputation for 'compassionate conservatism'. He won the Republican presidential nomination in 1999, and beat Al Gore in the 2000 election, after a Supreme Court 5–4 majority decision prevented further recounts in Florida; his second-term victory, in 2004, was much more convincing. His presidency was bracketed by crises: first the terrorist attacks of 9/11, and then the 2008 banking and 'sub-prime' mortgage debacle. His policies included tax and Medicare reforms, the No Child Left Behind education reforms and support for 'faith-based' initiatives. His popularity waned as dissent grew about post-9/11 strategy, particularly the war in Iraq.

From that day flowed a different kind of 'new world order' in response: wars in Afghanistan (2001–2) and Iraq (2003), followed by insurgencies in both countries; serious violence in Pakistan; further terror attacks in Europe, Africa and Asia; a new US Department of Homeland Security; and a controversial prison camp at Guantánamo Bay. Military forces and security agencies around the world struggled to adapt to fighting the new threat.

On 11 September itself, though, it was President Bush's role to address the nation and attempt to interpret the scarcely believable events. He was by no means a natural orator – indeed, he was better known for malapropisms and a folksy style that seemed to suggest a suspicion of words. But in the speech, compiled by Michael Gershon, he reached for *gravitas* and gave reassurance, affirming American values – and Americans' determination to defend those values – and condemning the terrorists. There were also clues as to policies to come. Bush insisted on including a phrase that became known as the 'Bush Doctrine': 'We will make no distinction between the terrorists who committed these acts and those who harbour them.' He also used the phrase 'war on terrorism', which, as the Global War on Terror (GWOT), would come to underpin his overall strategy.

GOOD EVENING.

Today, our fellow citizens, our way of life, our very freedom came under attack in a series of deliberate and deadly terrorist acts. The victims were in airplanes or in their offices: secretaries, businessmen and women, military and federal workers, moms and dads, friends and neighbours. Thousands of lives were suddenly ended by evil, despicable acts of terror. The pictures of airplanes flying into buildings, fires burning, huge structures collapsing have filled us with disbelief, terrible sadness and a quiet, unyielding anger. These acts of mass murder were intended to frighten our nation into chaos and retreat. But they have failed. Our country is strong.

'These acts shatter steel, but they cannot dent the steel of American resolve'

A great people has been moved to defend a great nation. Terrorist attacks can shake the foundations of our biggest buildings, but they cannot touch the foundation of America. These acts shatter steel, but they cannot dent the steel of American resolve. America was targeted for attack because we're the brightest beacon for freedom and opportunity in the world. And no one will keep that light from shining. Today, our nation saw evil – the very worst of human nature – and we responded with the best of America.

With the daring of our rescue workers, with the caring for strangers and neighbours who came to give blood and help in any way they could.

Immediately following the first attack, I implemented our government's emergency response plans. Our military is powerful, and it's prepared. Our emergency teams are working in New York City and Washington, D.C., to help with local rescue efforts. Our first priority is to get help to those who have been injured, and to take every precaution to protect our citizens at home and around the world from further attacks. The functions of our government continue without interruption. Federal agencies in Washington which had to be evacuated today are reopening for essential personnel tonight and will be open for business tomorrow. Our financial institutions remain strong, and the American economy will be open for business as well.

'We stand together to win the war against terrorism'

The search is underway for those who were behind these evil acts. I have directed the full resources of our intelligence and law enforcement communities to find those responsible and to bring them to justice. We will make no distinction between the terrorists who committed these acts and those who harbour them.

I appreciate so very much the members of Congress who have joined me in strongly condemning these attacks. And on behalf of the American people, I thank the many world leaders who have called to offer their condolences and assistance. America and our friends and allies join with all those who want peace and security in the world, and we stand together to win the war against terrorism.

Tonight, I ask for your prayers for all those who grieve, for the children whose worlds have been shattered, for all whose sense of safety and security has been threatened. And I pray they will be comforted by a Power greater than any of us, spoken through the ages in Psalm 23: 'Even though I walk through the valley of the shadow of death, I fear no evil for you are with me.'

This is a day when all Americans from every walk of life unite in our resolve for justice and peace. America has stood down enemies before, and we will do so this time. None of us will ever forget this day, yet we go forward to defend freedom and all that is good and just in our world.

Thank you. Good night. And God bless America.

'The audacity of hope'

Keynote address to the Democratic National Convention, Boston, 27 July 2004

'America is a place where all things are possible'

Speech after winning the US presidential election, Chicago, 4 November 2008 t

BARACK OBAMA'S RAPID RISE TO THE TOP tier of global politics – and to the presidency of the United States, the first African-American to hold that office – was nothing short of extraordinary. To many, the young senator from Illinois appeared to have come out of nowhere, unexpectedly defeating the much better-known Hillary Clinton in the race for the 2008 Democratic presidential nomination and then besting John McCain in the subsequent general election. But in fact, his emergence can be traced to one specific moment, the night of 27 July 2004, when he laid out his life story and his ideals at the Democratic National Convention and became an overnight sensation for his biography, his oratory and his optimism.

Obama was not the 2004 convention's intended star: it was in fact the nominating convention for John Kerry, the Democratic presidential nominee that year – the 'young naval lieutenant' of the speech – and his running mate John Edwards, the 'millworker's son'. But Obama, at the time not even a senator – he was a candidate running for election to the US Senate that year – was picked to deliver the keynote address, a spot often used to showcase a rising star.

In the event his speech, delivered in a political era defined by deep partisan debate about cultural issues and the response to 9/11 – especially the Iraq War – was an appeal for cooperation and a paean to common ground, framed through Obama's own life story as the son of a white American woman from Kansas and a black Kenyan father.

Kerry lost the election to George W. Bush, but Obama's career was just beginning: he won election to the Senate that November. His speech electrified the convention and Obama's indisputably powerful rhetoric has more generally reinvigorated interest in the art of public speaking: he is generally seen as the finest orator to hold the Presidency since, at least, John F Kennedy half a century before him.

BARACK OBAMA

Born 4 August 1961 in Honolulu, Hawaii, the son of a Kenyan father and a white American mother from Kansas.

After his parents divorced, he moved to Indonesia (1967–71) with his mother and Indonesian stepfather, before returning to Hawaii and the care of his grandmother. He graduated from Columbia University in 1983 (majoring in political science) and moved to Chicago, where he ran a community organization. He attended Harvard University Law School (1988–91), and became president of the influential *Harvard Law Review*. At Chicago University, he lectured at the Law School (1992–2004). In 1995 he published a family memoir, *Dreams from My Father*, and the following year was elected to the first of his three terms as a Democratic Party state senator in Illinois. In 2004, he entered the US Senate as junior senator for Illinois, and in 2007 he announced his bid for the presidency. After a closely fought nomination battle, he went on to win the presidency against his Republican opponent John McCain in 2008. His political autobiography, expounding his ideas, was *The Audacity of Hope* (2006). In 2009 he received the Nobel Peace Prize. He was re-elected to the Presidency in 2012 for a second term, defeating Republican Mitt Romney.

His term in office, however – ironically, given the speech that first brought him to notice and the conciliatory victory speech also included here – has been marked by the most entrenched partisan politics in recent memory and widespread concern about dysfunction in American government.

TONIGHT IS A PARTICULAR HONOR FOR ME because, let's face it, my presence on this stage is pretty unlikely. My father was a foreign student, born and raised in a small village in Kenya. He grew up herding goats, went to school in a tin-roof shack. His father, my grandfather, was a cook, a domestic servant to the British.

But my grandfather had larger dreams for his son. Through hard work and perseverance my father got a scholarship to study in a magical place; America, that shone as a beacon of freedom and opportunity to so many who had come before. While studying here, my father met my mother. She was born in a town on the other side of the world, in Kansas. Her father worked on oil rigs and farms through most of the Depression. The day after Pearl Harbor my grandfather signed up for duty, joined Patton's army, marched across Europe. Back home, my grandmother raised a baby and went to work on a bomber assembly line. After the war, they studied on the GI Bill, bought a house through FHA, and later moved west – all the way to Hawaii – in search of opportunity.

'In no other country on earth is my story even possible'

And they, too, had big dreams for their daughter, a common dream, born of two continents. My parents shared not only an improbable love; they shared an abiding faith in the possibilities of this nation. They would give me an African name, Barack, or "blessed," believing that in a tolerant America your name is no barrier to success. They imagined me going to the best schools in the land, even though they weren't rich, because in a generous America you don't have to be rich to achieve your potential. They are both passed away now. And yet, I know that on this night, they look down on me with great pride.

They stand here and I stand here today, grateful for the diversity of my heritage, aware that my parents' dreams live on in my two precious daughters. I stand here knowing that my story is part of the larger American story, that I owe a debt to all of those who came before me, and that in no other country on earth is my story even possible. Tonight, we gather to affirm the greatness of our nation, not because of the height of our skyscrapers, or the power of our military, or the size of our economy. Our pride is based on a very simple premise, summed up in a declaration made over two hundred years ago, "We hold these truths to be self-evident, that all men are created equal. That they are endowed by their

Creator with certain inalienable rights. That among these are life, liberty and the pursuit of happiness."

That is the true genius of America, a faith in the simple dreams, an insistence on small miracles. That we can tuck in our children at night and know that they are fed and clothed and safe from harm. That we can say what we think, write what we think, without hearing a sudden knock on the door. That we can have an idea and start our own business without paying a bribe. That we can participate in the political process without fear of retribution, and that our votes will be counted – at least most of the time.

'If there's a child on the south side of Chicago who can't read, that matters to me, even if it's not my child'

This year, in this election, we are called to reaffirm our values and our commitments, to hold them against a hard reality and see how we are measuring up, to the legacy of our forbearers, and the promise of future generations. And fellow Americans – Democrats, Republicans, Independents – I say to you tonight: we have more work to do. More work to do for the workers I met in Galesburg, Illinois, who are losing their union jobs at the Maytag plant that's moving to Mexico, and now are having to compete with their own children for jobs that pay seven bucks an hour. More to do for the father that I met who was losing his job and choking back the tears, wondering how he would pay $4,500 a month for the drugs his son needs without the health benefits that he counted on. More to do for the young woman in East St. Louis, and thousands more like her, who has the grades, has the drive, has the will, but doesn't have the money to go to college.

Now don't get me wrong. The people I meet in small towns and big cities, in diners and office parks, they don't expect government to solve all their problems. They know they have to work hard to get ahead and they want to. Go into the collar counties around Chicago, and people will tell you they don't want their tax money wasted by a welfare agency or by the Pentagon. Go into any inner city neighborhood, and folks will tell you that government alone can't teach our kids to learn. They know that parents have to teach, that children can't achieve unless we raise their expectations and turn off the television sets and eradicate the slander that says a black youth with a book is acting white. They know those things. People don't expect government to solve all their problems. But they sense, deep in their bones, that with just a slight change in priorities, we can make sure that every child in America has a decent shot at life, and that the doors of opportunity remain open to all. They know we can do better…

If there's a child on the south side of Chicago who can't read, that matters to me, even if it's not my child. If there's a senior citizen somewhere who can't pay for their prescription drugs and having to choose between medicine and the rent, that makes my life poorer, even if it's not my grandparent. If there's an Arab American family being rounded up without benefit of an attorney or due process, that threatens my civil liberties. It is that fundamental belief – I am my brother's keeper, I am my sister's keeper – that makes this country work. It's what allows us to pursue our individual dreams, and yet still come together as one American family. "E pluribus unum." Out of many, one.

'There is not a liberal America and a conservative America – there is the United States of America'

Now even as we speak, there are those who are preparing to divide us, the spin masters, the negative ad peddlers who embrace the politics of anything goes. Well, I say to them tonight, there is not a liberal America and a conservative America – there is the United States of America. There is not a black America and white America and Latino America and Asian America; there is the United States of America. The pundits like to slice-and-dice our country into Red States and Blue States; Red States for Republicans, Blue States for Democrats. But I've got news for them, too. We worship an awesome God in the Blue States, and we don't like federal agents poking around our libraries in the Red States. We coach Little League in the Blue States, and yes we've got some gay friends in the Red States. There are patriots who opposed the war in Iraq and there are patriots who supported the war in Iraq. We are one people, all of us pledging allegiance to the stars and stripes, all of us defending the United States of America.

In the end, that's what this election is about. Do we participate in a politics of cynicism or do we participate in a politics of hope? I'm not talking about blind optimism here – the almost willful ignorance that thinks unemployment will go away if we just don't think about it, or the health care crisis will solve itself if we just ignore it. That's not what I'm talking about. I'm talking about something more substantial. It's the hope of slaves sitting around a fire singing freedom songs; the hope of immigrants setting out for distant shores; the hope of a young naval lieutenant bravely patrolling the Mekong Delta; the hope of a millworker's son who dares to defy the odds; the hope of a skinny kid with a funny name who believes that America has a place for him, too. Hope in the face of difficulty. Hope in the face of uncertainty. The audacity of hope!

In the end, that is God's greatest gift to us, the bedrock of this nation; a belief in things not seen; a belief that there are better days ahead. I believe that we can give our middle class relief and provide working families with a road to opportunity. I believe we can provide jobs to the jobless, homes to the homeless, and reclaim young people in cities across America from violence and despair. I believe that we have a righteous wind at our backs and that as we stand on the crossroads of history, we can make the right choices, and meet the challenges that face us…Thank you very much everybody. God bless you.

FOUR YEARS LATER, AFTER A METEORIC RISE and a hard-fought primary campaign against Hillary Clinton, Obama addressed a huge rally in Grant Park, Chicago, the night that news of his election broke. A victory speech of this kind must include certain stock elements, and Obama paid tribute to his opponent John McCain, thanked his aides, friends and family, and – beginning the process of moderating impossibly high expectations – referred to the major challenges ahead. Kennedy famously invited American citizens to ask what they could do for their country. Obama did not quite do that, but his metaphors of renewed effort – appropriately for a Democratic candidate – were blue-collar ones of hard manual labour, a communal project of 'remaking' the nation 'calloused hand by calloused hand'. For the wider world, Obama promised 'a new dawn of American leadership'. If the Bush presidency expressed the difficulties of the 9/11 world, then Obama sought to reclaim US idealism in the post-9/11 world, espousing strength through the soft power of 'our ideals: democracy, liberty, opportunity, and unyielding hope' rather than the hard power of arms and wealth. The debate about whether his presidency has lived up to these ideals, and if not, who is to blame, will continue for decades.

Obama returned to the historic qualities of his victory by way of a story, in its way as extraordinary as his own: that of a 106-year-old African-American voter in Atlanta, whose life span had encompassed all the modern struggles and triumphs faced by America as a nation, and by African-Americans and women in terms of civil rights. Making this connection between one humble, once-marginalized, voter and the new US president was a rhetorical *tour de force*. It encapsulated the journey from the periphery of society to the centre of power that Obama's victory represented.

IF THERE IS ANYONE OUT THERE who still doubts that America is a place where all things are possible; who still wonders if the dream of our founders is alive in our time; who still questions the power of our democracy, tonight is your answer. It's the answer told by lines that stretched around schools and churches in numbers this nation has never seen; by people who waited three hours and four hours, many for the very first time in their lives, because they believed that this time must be different; that their voice could be that difference . . . It's the answer that led those who have been told for so long by so many to be cynical, and fearful, and doubtful of what we can achieve to put their hands on the arc of history and bend it once more toward the hope of a better day. It's been a long time coming, but tonight . . . change has come to America.

'So let us summon a new spirit of patriotism'

. . . I was never the likeliest candidate for this office. We didn't start with much money or many endorsements. Our campaign was not hatched in the halls of Washington – it began in the backyards of Des Moines and the living rooms of Concord and the front porches of Charleston. It was built by working men and women who dug into what little savings they had to give five dollars and ten dollars and twenty dollars to this cause . . . the millions of Americans who volunteered, and organized, and proved that . . . a government of the people, by the people and for the people has not perished from this Earth. This is your victory. I know you didn't do this just to win an election and I know you didn't do it for me. You did it because you understand the enormity of the task that lies ahead. For even as we celebrate tonight, we know the challenges that tomorrow will bring are the greatest of our lifetime – two wars, a planet in peril, the worst financial crisis in a century . . . There is new energy to harness and new jobs to be created; new schools to build and threats to meet and alliances to repair.

The road ahead will be long . . . There will be setbacks and false starts. There are many who won't agree with every decision or policy I make as president, and we know that government can't solve every problem. But I will always be honest with you about the challenges we face. I will listen to you, especially when we disagree. And above all, I will ask you [to] join in the work of remaking this nation the only way it's been done in America for 221 years – block by block, brick by brick, calloused hand by calloused hand.

. . . So let us summon a new spirit of patriotism; of service and responsibility where each of us resolves to pitch in and work harder and look after not only ourselves, but each other. Let us remember that if this financial crisis taught us anything, it's that we cannot have a thriving Wall Street while Main Street suffers – in this country, we rise or fall as one nation; as one people.

Let us resist the temptation to fall back on the same partisanship and pettiness and immaturity that has poisoned our politics for so long . . . while the Democratic Party has won a great victory tonight, we do so with a measure of humility and determination to heal the divides that have held back our progress. As Lincoln said to a nation far more divided than ours, 'We are not enemies, but friends . . . though passion may have strained, it must not break our bonds of affection.' And to those Americans whose support I have yet to earn – I may not have won your vote, but I hear your voices, I need your help, and I will be your president too.

'To those who would tear this world down – we will defeat you'

And to all those watching tonight from beyond our shores, from parliaments and palaces to those who are huddled around radios in the forgotten corners of our world – our stories are singular, but our destiny is shared, and a new dawn of American leadership is at hand. To those who would tear this world down – we will defeat you. To those who seek peace and security – we support you. And to all those who have wondered if America's beacon still burns as bright – tonight we proved once more that the true strength of our nation comes not from the might of our arms or the scale of our wealth, but from the enduring power of our ideals: democracy, liberty, opportunity, and unyielding hope.

. . . This election had many firsts and many stories that will be told for generations. But one that's on my mind tonight is about a woman who cast her ballot in Atlanta. She's a lot like the millions of others who stood in line to make their voice heard in this election except for one thing – Ann Nixon Cooper is 106 years old. She was born just a generation past slavery; a time when there were no cars on the road or planes in the sky; when someone like her couldn't vote for two reasons – because she was a woman and because of the colour of her skin.

And tonight, I think about all that she's seen throughout her century in America – the heartache and the hope; the struggle and the progress; the times we were told that we can't, and the people who pressed on with that American creed: Yes we can.

At a time when women's voices were silenced and their hopes dismissed, she lived to see them stand up and speak out and reach for the ballot. Yes we can.

When there was despair in the dust bowl and depression across the land, she saw a nation conquer fear itself with a New Deal, new jobs and a new sense of common purpose. Yes we can.

When the bombs fell on our Harbor and tyranny threatened the world, she was there to witness a generation rise to greatness and a democracy was saved. Yes we can.

She was there for the buses in Montgomery, the hoses in Birmingham, a bridge in Selma, and a preacher from Atlanta who told a people that 'We Shall Overcome.' Yes we can.

'That timeless creed that sums up the spirit of a people: Yes We Can'

A man touched down on the moon, a wall came down in Berlin, a world was connected by our own science and imagination. And this year, in this election, she touched her finger to a screen, and cast her vote, because after 106 years in America, through the best of times and the darkest of hours, she knows how America can change. Yes we can.

America, we have come so far. We have seen so much. But there is so much more to do. So tonight, let us ask ourselves – if our children should live to see the next century; if my daughters should be so lucky to live as long as Ann Nixon Cooper, what change will they see? What progress will we have made? This is our chance to answer that call. This is our moment. This is our time – to put our people back to work and open doors of opportunity for our kids; to restore prosperity and promote the cause of peace; to reclaim the American Dream and reaffirm that fundamental truth – that out of many, we are one; that while we breathe, we hope, and where we are met with cynicism, and doubt, and those who tell us that we can't, we will respond with that timeless creed that sums up the spirit of a people: Yes We Can.

. . . God bless you, and may God bless the United States of America.

'Our struggle has reached a defining moment'

GERRY ADAMS

Speech asking the Irish Republican Army to abandon violence

N 1998, THE GOOD FRIDAY AGREEMENT appeared to offer hope for peace in Northern Ireland. In 1922, by the terms of the Anglo-Irish Treaty, the future independent Republic of Ireland was born, leaving the northern, Protestant-dominated six counties within the United Kingdom as a province. From the 1960s, civil rights protests by the province's Catholic minority provoked loyalist reactions, which in turn saw spiralling violence, the intervention of the British Army and direct rule from London. Thus were born 'The Troubles' and over 20 years violence, in which Catholic-republican paramilitaries – principally the Provisional IRA (Irish Republican Army) – battled and bombed British forces and institutions, with Protestant loyalist paramilitaries joining the fray.

By the early 1990s, some politicians of the IRA's political wing, Sinn Féin, had come to the conclusion that the military campaign needed to end in order to advance the republican cause, and feelers were put out to other parties and even to the British government, covertly. The pivotal figure was Gerry Adams, the controversial Sinn Féin president who may (commentators differ) have also been on the IRA's Army Council at one time. Eventually, the Good Friday Agreement emerged from discussions among the main republican and loyalist parties and the British and Irish governments, and it seemed to offer a road map: the creation of cross-border institutions, a devolved assembly in Northern Ireland, an early release of jailed IRA and loyalist prisoners, and a commitment to ending violence.

GERRY ADAMS

Born 6 October 1948 into a strongly republican family in (West) Belfast, Northern Ireland.

He left school at 17, joined Sinn Féin and deepened his republican activism. He was arrested and interned in 1971 and 1973, accused being an IRA leader but the evidence was deemed insufficient. In 1983 he became Sinn Féin president and was elected as Member of Parliament for West Belfast (1983–92, 1997–present), pursuing a policy of not attending Westminster sessions. He moved to professionalize Sinn Féin, began discreet negotiations with other parties and the British and Irish governments, and in 1994 the IRA declared a ceasefire: it broke down in 1996, but was resumed the next year. After the Good Friday Agreement (1998), he became a member of the Northern Ireland Assembly until its suspension during 2002–7. He was instrumental in persuading the IRA to demonstrate its commitment to the peace process in 2005–6, and remains the leading voice of Northern Irish republican politics.

Problems struck in 2002, when the new Northern Ireland Assembly was suspended amid allegations of infiltration by IRA spies. Other actions were laid at the IRA's door: the continuing imposition of violent vigilante justice in Catholic neighbourhoods, a huge £26.5 million bank raid in 2004, and the fatal stabbing of a Belfast man, Robert McCartney, in a 2005 pub fight. In February 2005, the IRA withdrew its offer to decommission its weapons. In a highly symbolic gesture during St Patrick's week in 2005, President George W. Bush invited relatives of McCartney to meet him at the White House while snubbing Gerry Adams. And longtime republican sympathizer Senator Ted Kennedy cancelled a meeting with Adams because of the IRA's 'ongoing criminal activity'.

Adams and Sinn Féin faced a loss of credibility, and statesmanship was called for. It was under these circumstances that Adams delivered a statement to the IRA leadership, which, while criticizing Unionist politicians and the two governments, had as its core an appeal for the IRA to lay down arms once and for all. On 6 April 2005 he read out to the attendant media a version of the statement. As Adams observed, he had often in the past 'defended the right of the IRA to engage in armed struggle', but the Ireland of the 21st century was 'a very different place from 15 years ago'. In plain terms, he told the IRA that its help was now vital to 'rebuild the peace process'.

The politics of Northern Ireland remain complex, and small republican splinter groups (Real IRA, Continuity IRA) still pursue violence. But in 2006 monitors announced that the mainstream IRA had decommissioned its weapons, and in 2007 the Northern Ireland Assembly was restored.

I WANT TO SPEAK DIRECTLY to the men and women of *Óglaigh na hÉireann*, the volunteer soldiers of the Irish Republican Army. In time of great peril you stepped into the *Bearna Bhaoil*, the gap of danger. When others stood idly by, you and your families gave your all, in defence of a risen people and in pursuit of Irish freedom and unity. Against mighty odds you held the line and faced down a huge military foe, the British Crown forces and their surrogates in the Unionist death squads . . . For over 30 years, the IRA showed that the British government could not rule Ireland on its own terms. You asserted the legitimacy of the right of the people of this island to freedom and independence. Many of your comrades made the ultimate sacrifice. Your determination, selflessness and courage have brought the freedom struggle towards its fulfilment. That struggle can now be taken forward by other means. I say this with the authority of my office as president of Sinn Féin.

In the past I have defended the right of the IRA to engage in armed struggle. I did so because there was no alternative for those who would not bend the knee, or turn a blind eye to oppression, or for those who wanted a national republic.

Now there is an alternative.

I have clearly set out my view of what that alternative is. The way forward is by building political support for republican and democratic objectives across Ireland and by winning support for these goals internationally.

I want to use this occasion therefore to appeal to the leadership of *Óglaigh na hÉireann* to fully embrace and accept this alternative. Can you take courageous initiatives which will achieve your aims by purely political and democratic activity? I know full well that such truly historic decisions can only be taken in the aftermath of intense internal consultation. I ask that you initiate this as quickly as possible.

I understand fully that the IRA's most recent positive contribution to the peace process was in the context of a comprehensive agreement. But I also hold the very strong view that republicans need to lead by example. There is no greater demonstration of this than the IRA cessation [of violence] in the summer of 1994.

Sinn Féin has demonstrated the ability to play a leadership role as part of a popular movement towards peace, equality and justice. We are totally committed to ending partition and to creating the conditions for unity and independence. Sinn Féin does have the potential and capacity to become the vehicle for the attainment of republican objectives.

'Your courage is now needed for the future'

The Ireland we live in today is also a very different place from 15 years ago. There is now an all-Ireland agenda with huge potential. Nationalists and republicans now have a confidence that will never again allow anyone to be treated as second-class citizens. Equality is our watchword. The catalyst for much of this change is the growing support for republicanism.

Of course, those who oppose change are not going to simply roll over. It will always be a battle a day between those who want maximum change and those who want to maintain the status quo.

But if republicans are to prevail, if the peace process is to be successfully concluded and Irish sovereignty and reunification secured, then we have to set the agenda – no one else is going to do that.

So, I also want to make a personal appeal to all of you – the women and men volunteers who have remained undefeated in the face of tremendous odds. Now is the time for you to step into the *Bearna Bhaoil* again; not as volunteers risking life and limb, but as activists in a national movement towards independence and unity.

Such decisions will be far-reaching and difficult. But you never lacked courage in the past. Your courage is now needed for the future. It won't be easy. There are many problems to be resolved by the people of Ireland in the time ahead. Your ability as republican volunteers to rise to this challenge will mean that the two governments and others cannot easily hide from their obligations and their responsibility to resolve these problems.

Our struggle has reached a defining moment.

I am asking you to join me in seizing this moment, to intensify our efforts, to rebuild the peace process and to decisively move our struggle forward.

'Political will is a
renewable resource.'

AL GORE

Address to the United Nations Bali Climate Change Conference,
14 December 2007

ESPITE CONSENSUS AMONG THE INTERNATIONAL SCIENTIFIC COMMUNITY that global warming threatens the very future of the planet, attempts at a coordinated international response were faltering as the 21st century began. Among the challenges faced was the reluctance of successive Washington governments to sign up to a defined plan of action, such as the Kyoto Agreement to reduce greenhouse gas emissions. Without the backing of the world's biggest economy, successive well-intentioned initiatives lacked teeth.

Many powerful voices within the USA argued that such commitments placed the nation's ongoing economic prosperity at unacceptable risk. Why, they demanded, should the USA potentially endanger its industrial capacity while emerging rivals like China and India carried on their rapid growth unhindered by comparable environmental obligations? Was global warning, they asked, simply the ultimate scare story?

AL GORE

Born on 31 March 1948 in Washington, D.C., USA, his father, Al Gore Sr, was a Democratic politician who represented Tennessee in the House of Representatives and the Senate.

Gore Jr followed his father into front-line politics for the Democrats. He was elected to the US House of Representatives in 1976, 1978, 1980 and 1982. He became a Senator in 1984 and served eight years as Vice-President in the administration of Bill Clinton from 1993. Narrowly losing the presidency to George W. Bush in 2000, he became active in private enterprise but is most famous for raising awareness of the dangers of global warning.

So it was something of a coup for the Climate Change-believers that a former Vice-President became one of the movement's most outspoken advocates. A campaigner on environmental issues since the 1970s, Gore has written several highly influential books, including *Earth in the Balance* and *An Inconvenient Truth* – the latter also the title of an Oscar-winning 2006 documentary about his efforts to educate the public about global warming. In the same year, he established two not-for-profit organizations: the Alliance for Climate Protection (which promoted civic action) and the educational Climate Project.

The United Nations Climate Change Conference in Bali in December 2007 brought together representatives from more than 180 nations. The aim was to lay down a road map for a successor agreement to Kyoto. Yet reaching agreement proved as hard as many had feared, with the US once again at the forefront of dissent.

Having just jointly received the Nobel Peace Prize (along with the Inter-governmental Panel on Climate Change) for 'informing the world of the dangers posed by climate change', Gore was able to command a global audience. He laid out the dangers of global warning rationally and with authority. This was, he assured those listening, 'a planetary emergency' and the clock was ticking. Crucially, he took the opportunity to speak his 'inconvenient truth'. 'My own country,' he acknowledged, 'is principally responsible for obstructing progress here in Bali.' It was a speech that won headlines around the world.

The job of dealing with global warming is not even half done, but Gore's Bali address drew an important line in the sand.

We, the human species, face a planetary emergency. That phrase still sounds shrill to some ears but it is deadly accurate as a description of the situation that we now confront, and as Dr Pachauri and his three thousand colleagues in the IPCC have freshly reminded us, the accumulation of greenhouse gases continues to trap more and more heat from the sun in our atmosphere, threatening the stable climate balance that has been an unappreciated but crucial assumption for the development of human civilization.

Just this week new evidence has been presented. I remember years ago listening to the scientists who specialize in the study of ice and snow express concern that some time towards the end of the 21st century we might even face the possibility of losing the entire North Polar ice cap. I remember only three years ago when they revised their estimates to say it could happen halfway through the 21st century, by 2050.

'This is not the time for business as usual'

I remember at the beginning of this year when I was shocked to hear them say along with others that it could happen in as little as 34 years and now, this week, they tell us it could completely disappear in as little as five to seven years.

. . . For those who believed that this climate crisis was going to affect their grandchildren, and still said nothing, and were shaken a bit to hear that it would affect their children, and still said and did nothing, it is affecting us in the present generation, and it is up to us in this generation to solve this crisis.

A sense of urgency that is appropriate for this challenge is itself a challenge to our own moral imagination. It is up to us in this generation to see clearly and vividly exactly what is going on. Twenty of the 21 hottest years ever measured in atmospheric record have come in the last 25 years – the hottest of all in 2005, this year on track to be the second hottest of all. This is not natural variation. It is far beyond the bounds of natural variation and the scientists have told us so over and over again with increasing alarm.

But because our new relationship to the earth is unprecedented we have been slow to act. And because CO_2 is invisible, it is easy for us to put the climate crisis out of sight and out of mind until we see the consequences beginning to unfold.

. . . I am not an official of the United States and I am not bound by the diplomatic niceties. So I am going to speak an inconvenient truth. My own country, the United States, is principally responsible for obstructing progress here in Bali. We all know that, but my country is not the only one that can take steps to ensure that we move forward from Bali with progress and with hope.

. . . So, we must leave here with a strong mandate. This is not the time for business as usual. Somehow we have to summon, and each of you must summon a sense of urgency here in Bali . . . I don't know how to tell you how you can find the grace to navigate around this enormous obstacle, this elephant in the room that I've just been undiplomatic enough to name, but I'm asking you to do it . . .

. . . If you decide to continue the progress that has already been made here on all of the items other than the targets and timetables for mandatory reductions; on the hope (and with the expectation) that, before this process is concluded in Copenhagen, you will be able to fill in that blank (with the help of a different position from the United States); then you can make great progress here.

For starters, that means a plan that fully funds an ambitious adaptation fund, to build an adaptive capacity in the most vulnerable countries to confront the climate crisis. It means creating truly innovative means for technology transfer, to allow for mobilizing technology and capital throughout the world.

We need a deforestation-prevention plan. Deforestation accounts for 20 per cent of global carbon emissions – the equivalent to the total emissions of the US or China. It is difficult to forge such an agreement here.

'These are not political problems. They are moral imperatives'

Believe me, if I could snap my fingers and change the position of the United States of America, and change the position of some other countries, and make it instantly much easier to move forward with targets and timetables, I would do so in an instant. But if we look realistically at the situation that confronts us, then wisdom would call for moving forward in spite of that obstacle.

I can tell you that there is a growing realization all over the world – including in my country – beyond these actions that have already been taken that I've described to you. Mothers and fathers, grandparents, community leaders, business leaders, all around the world, are beginning to look much more clearly at what is involved here.

. . . These are not political problems. They are moral imperatives. But our capacity to strip away the disguise, and see them for what they really are, and then find the basis to act together, to successfully address them, is what is missing.

. . . We are one people on one planet. We have one future, one destiny. We must pursue it together, and we can.

The great Spanish poet from Seville, Antonio Machado, wrote: 'Pathwalker, there is no path. You must make the path as you walk.'

. . . There are two paths you can choose. They lead to two different futures. Not too long from now, when our children assess what you did here in Bali, what we and our generation did here in this world, as they look backward at 2007, they will ask one of two questions. I don't know which one they will ask. I know which one I prefer that they ask, but trust me, they will ask one of these two questions.

They'll look back, and either they will ask 'What were you thinking? Didn't you hear the IPCC four times unanimously warning the world to act? Didn't you see the glaciers melting? Didn't you see the North Polar ice cap disappearing? Didn't you see the deserts growing, and the droughts deepening, and the crops drying up? Didn't you see the sea level rising? Didn't you see the floods? Didn't you pay attention to what was going on? Didn't you care? What were you thinking?'

Or they will ask a second question, one that I'd much prefer them to ask. I want them to look back on this time, and ask: 'How did you find the moral courage to successfully address a crisis that so many said was impossible to address? How were you able to start the process that unleashed the moral imagination of humankind to see ourselves as a single, global civilization?' And when they ask that question, I want you to tell them that you saw it as a privilege to be alive at a moment when a relatively small group of people could control the destiny of all generations to come.

. . . We ought to feel a sense of exhilaration that we are the people alive at a moment in history when we can make all the difference.

That's who you are. You have everything that you need. We have everything we need, save political will. But political will is a renewable resource.

'To the stolen generations . . . I am sorry'

KEVIN RUDD

Parliamentary motion apologizing for the mistreatment of Australia's Aboriginal people, 13 February 2008

WHEN THE LABOR PARTY WON Australia's 2007 general election, the result overturned a decade of Liberal Party rule and delivered the prime ministership to Kevin Rudd, the Labor leader. A diplomat turned politician, with a strong religious conviction, Rudd headed a government that was broadly to the left of his predecessor John Howard's. Among his first priorities, he was gearing up for a landmark speech on the historic maltreatment of Australia's Aboriginal peoples.

In 1997 an official report, *Bringing Them Home*, examined former federal and state policies to remove young Aboriginal children from their families and send them to institutions or white foster homes. Between 1910 and 1970, as many as 30 per cent of Aboriginal children – the 'stolen generations', numbering 50,000 people – were treated in this way, all part of an attempt to assimilate them into modern Australian culture. Campaigners and activists had claimed that the consequences of such dislocation were often disastrous for the individuals concerned, not to mention their birth families, and numerous stories began to emerge of physical and psychological maltreatment. John Howard had held the widespread view that an apology would open the floodgates to litigation (and expensive compensation) and that the present generations could not be held to account for past actions of others. But on 13 February 2008, Rudd fulfilled an electoral promise when he addressed Parliament on, as he put it, 'this unfinished business of the nation', in order to offer 'an apology without qualification'.

KEVIN RUDD

Born 21 September 1957 into a poor rural family in Nambour, Queensland, Australia.

He joined the Australian Labor Party in 1972. He graduated in Chinese history and Mandarin at the Australian National University, Canberra, and worked for the Department of Foreign Affairs in 1981–8, where he was posted to China and Sweden. Having returned to Queensland, he rose up the state government to become Director-General of the Cabinet (1992–5). He also worked as a consultant in China. Election to Australia's Parliament (as Member for Griffith) finally came in 1998; he was appointed shadow minister for foreign affairs in 2001 and (additionally) minister for trade in 2005, before gaining the leadership of the Labor Party in 2006. He became Australia's prime minister after the 2007 election.

Rudd spoke at length to a full House of Representatives and a packed public gallery, containing many prominent members of the Aboriginal community. Outside Parliament, crowds gathered, listening to the live broadcast. Rudd – a calm, measured speaker rather than a charismatic orator – gave a speech that owed much to the language and cadences of a church service, reflecting a pattern of reiteration, and statement and response: 'For the pain, suffering and hurt . . . we say sorry . . . for the indignity and degradation . . . we say sorry.' As well as making – and justifying – a formal apology on behalf of the federal government, Rudd highlighted individual cases of suffering and administrative cynicism which had emerged from the investigations. He was coruscating about the 'stony, stubborn and deafening silence for more than a decade' that he laid at the door of his predecessor's administration. On 13 February, however, he won bipartisan support for his speech and his proposals.

In practical terms, Rudd did not propose compensation for the stolen generations but rather new initiatives on 'indigenous policy' and new funds to 'close the gap that lies between us in life expectancy, educational achievement and economic opportunity'. Some among the Aboriginal community still pursue compensation claims, however, though thus far they have had little success in court.

Rudd's willingness to apologize formally has clearly resonated beyond Australia, perhaps most notably in Canadian Prime Minister Stephen Harper's apology on 11 June 2008 to Canada's equivalent of Australia's stolen generations – the children forced into Indian Residential Schools since the 1870s. And in 2009 Rudd apologized to another group of often mistreated Australians – the generations of child migrants from Britain.

I MOVE: THAT TODAY WE HONOUR the indigenous peoples of this land, the oldest continuing cultures in human history. We reflect on their past mistreatment. We reflect in particular on the mistreatment of those who were stolen generations – this blemished chapter in our nation's history.

The time has now come for the nation to turn a new page in Australia's history by righting the wrongs of the past and so moving forward with confidence to the future. We apologize for the laws and policies of successive parliaments and governments that have inflicted profound grief, suffering and loss on these our fellow Australians. We apologize especially for the removal of Aboriginal and Torres Strait Islander children from their families, their communities and their country. For the pain, suffering and hurt of these stolen generations, their descendants and for their families left behind, we say sorry. To the mothers and the fathers, the brothers and the sisters, for the breaking up of families and communities, we say sorry. And for the indignity and degradation thus inflicted on a proud people and a proud culture, we say sorry. We the parliament of Australia respectfully request that this apology be received in the spirit in which it is offered as part of the healing of the nation.

. . . There comes a time in the history of nations when their peoples must become fully reconciled to their past if they are to go forward with confidence to embrace their future. Our nation, Australia, has reached such a time. That is why the Parliament is today here assembled: to deal with this unfinished business of the nation, to remove a great stain from the nation's soul and, in a true spirit of reconciliation, to open a new chapter in the history of this great land, Australia.

. . . The hurt, the humiliation, the degradation and the sheer brutality of the act of physically separating a mother from her children is a deep assault on our senses and on our most elemental humanity. These stories cry out to be heard; they cry out for an apology. Instead, from the nation's Parliament there has been a stony, stubborn and deafening silence for more than a decade; a view that somehow we, the Parliament, should suspend our most basic instincts of what is right and what is wrong; a view that, instead, we should look for any pretext to push this great wrong to one side, to leave it languishing with the historians, the academics and the cultural warriors, as if the stolen generations are little more than an interesting sociological phenomenon. But the stolen generations are not intellectual curiosities. They are human beings, human beings . . . The uncomfortable truth for us all is that the parliaments of the nation, individually and collectively, enacted statutes and delegated authority under those statutes that made the forced removal of children on racial grounds fully lawful . . . We, the parliaments of the nation, are ultimately responsible, not those who gave effect to our laws. And the problem lay with the laws themselves. Therefore, for our nation, the course of action is clear: that is, to deal now with what has become one of the darkest chapters in Australia's history.

'We apologize for the hurt, the pain and suffering'

. . . To the stolen generations, I say the following: as Prime Minister of Australia, I am sorry. On behalf of the government of Australia, I am sorry. On behalf of the parliament of Australia, I am sorry. I offer you this apology without qualification. We apologize for the hurt, the pain and suffering that we, the Parliament, have caused you by the laws that previous parliaments have enacted. We apologize for the indignity, the degradation and the humiliation these laws embodied. We offer this apology to the mothers, the fathers, the brothers, the sisters, the families and the communities whose lives were ripped apart by the actions of successive governments under successive parliaments.

. . . My proposal is this: if the apology we extend today is accepted in the spirit of reconciliation, in which it is offered, we can today resolve together that there be a new beginning for Australia. And it is to such a new beginning that I believe the nation is now calling us.

It is for the nation to bring the first two centuries of our settled history to a close, as we begin a new chapter. We embrace with pride, admiration and awe these great and ancient cultures we are truly blessed to have among us cultures that provide a unique, uninterrupted human thread linking our Australian continent to the most ancient prehistory of our planet.

Let us turn this page together: indigenous and non-indigenous Australians, government and opposition, commonwealth and state, and write this new chapter in our nation's story together.

'This great responsibility is the responsibility to the people'

XI JINPING

The Communist Party General Secretary's speech to the Politburo Standing

BY THE TIME XI TOOK OFFICE IN 2013, China was already an economic superpower, having overtaken Japan as the world's second largest economy (behind the USA) in 2010. Average annual GDP growth in the first decade of the century regularly exceeded 10 per cent.

As the global economic slowdown of the late 2000s starkly illustrated the inherent weak points of the Western economic model that had reigned unchallenged for so long, China stood poised to end centuries of stalled progress and take its place at the international top table. With neighbouring India experiencing its own impressive boom, political commentators across the globe have spent years heralding the rise of the East and relative decline of the West.

Yet the picture is not quite so simple as that. Certainly, China's economic progress – ushered in by the market-focused reforms of Deng Xiaoping in the late 1970s – has been nothing less than awesome. The country has enormous reserves of manpower too, accounting for almost one-fifth of the global population. But after a quarter-century of rapid expansion, the government continues to strive to improve income equality. While it is estimated that some 400 million people have emerged from poverty since the early 1990s, wealth has fallen almost exclusively to those living in urban centres, leaving much of the rural population struggling to keep up.

XI JINPING

Born 15 June 1953 in Beijing, China, to a father who was among the first generation of communist leaders.

Xi joined the Chinese Communist Party (CCP) in 1974 and five years later graduated in chemical engineering from Tsinghua University. He worked his way through a series of Party administrative posts, becoming governor of Fujian Province in 2000 and receiving acclaim for overseeing an economic upturn. Regarded as an opponent of corruption, in 2007 he took a senior party position in Shanghai and joined the Politburo's standing committee. Within three years, he had been earmarked as Hu Jintao's likely successor as national president. In 2012 he was named CCP general-secretary and chairman of the Central Military Commission. He was sworn in as China's president in March 2013. Although he was little known on the international stage, there were high hopes that he would spearhead liberalizing social and political reforms. He also faced the tricky task of navigating the next stage of China's economic revolution.

Meanwhile, China's influence on the international scene has grown significantly thanks to a mixture of shrewd investment and generous aid giving, most notably in Africa. The 2008 Summer Olympic Games held in Beijing were a no-expense-spared spectacular designed to cement China's position among the global big-hitters, even if protests by pro-Tibetan activists before and during the Games were an unwelcome distraction for Beijing.

Against this backdrop, Xi's speech was an important statement of how China sees itself and its role in the world. It also marked the beginning of the road to achieving what he would term in the following months 'the Chinese dream', namely the 'great rejuvenation of the Chinese nation' – a slogan that captured the imagination of a nation hungry to resume its world-leading status after a hiatus of centuries. Xi himself embraced a refreshing brevity in his oratory, with a preference for plain speaking often missing from the addresses of his predecessors. It was a performance of some charisma.

Xi's speech did not represent a sea-change in how China operates. At one level, it merely reasserted the centrality of the CCP in Chinese life. However, it also bought into a tradition that stretches back far beyond the darkest days of Maoism, recalling a nation that has 'made an indelible contribution to the civilization and advancement of mankind'. Such a narrative is an easy sell to most Chinese. Next, to persuade the West to embrace the 'New China'.

GOOD DAY, LADIES, GENTLEMEN, AND FRIENDS.

... Yesterday, the 18th CCP National Congress victoriously concluded.

During these days, friends in the press have given lots of coverage to the Congress and conveyed China's voice in abundance to every country around the world. Everyone has been very dedicated, professional and hardworking. For this, on behalf of the Secretariat of the 18th Party Congress, I would like to express sincere gratitude to you.

... Here, on behalf of the members of the new central leadership organization, I sincerely thank all comrades of the Party for their trust in us. We will live up to the great trust placed on, and the mission assigned to, us.

The great trust of all members of the Party and the expectations of people of all ethnic groups around the country are not only a tremendous encouragement to our doing the work well, but also a heavy burden on our shoulders.

This great responsibility is the responsibility to our nation. Our nation is a great nation.

'Every bit of happiness in the world has to be created by diligent work and labour'

During the civilization and development process of more than 5,000 years, the Chinese nation has made an indelible contribution to the civilization and advancement of mankind.

In the modern era, our nation experienced constant hardship and difficulties. The Chinese nation reached its most dangerous period. Since then, countless people, with lofty ideals to realize the great revival of the

Chinese nation, rose to resist and fight, but failed one time after another.

Since the founding of the CPC, we have united and led the people to advance and struggle tenaciously, transforming the impoverished and backward Old China into the New China that has become prosperous and strong gradually. The great revival of the Chinese nation has demonstrated unprecedentedly bright prospects.

Our responsibility is to unite and lead the people of the entire Party and of all ethnic groups around the country, while accepting the baton of history and continuing to work to realize the great revival of the Chinese nation in order to let the Chinese nation stand more firmly and powerfully among all nations around the world and make a greater contribution to mankind.

'The metal itself must be hard to be turned into iron'

This great responsibility is the responsibility to the people. Our people are a great people. During the long process of history, by relying on our own diligence, courage and wisdom, Chinese people have opened up a good and beautiful home where all ethnic groups live in harmony, and fostered an excellent culture that never fades.

Our people love life and expect better education, more stable jobs, better income, more reliable social security, medical care of a higher standard, more comfortable living conditions, and a more beautiful environment.

They hope that their children can grow up better, work better and live better. People's yearning for a good and beautiful life is the goal for us to strive for.

Every bit of happiness in the world has to be created by diligent work and labour. Our responsibility is to rally and lead the whole Party and all of China's ethnic groups, and continue to emancipate our way of thinking, insist on reform and opening-up, further unleash and develop socially productive forces, work hard to resolve the difficulties faced by the masses in both production and life, and steadfastly take the road of common prosperity.

This is a major responsibility for the Party. Our party is a political party that serves the people wholeheartedly. The Party has led the people in scoring accomplishments that capture the attention of the world. We have every reason to be proud. However, we are proud but not complacent, and we will never rest on our laurels.

In the new situation, our party faces many severe challenges, and there are many pressing problems within the party that need to be resolved – especially problems such as corruption and bribe-taking by some Party members and cadres, being out of touch with the people, placing undue emphasis on formality and bureaucracy, and these must be addressed with great effort.

The whole Party must be vigilant.

'It is the people who create history'

The metal itself must be hard to be turned into iron. Our responsibility is to work with all comrades in the Party to be resolute in ensuring that the Party supervises its own conduct; enforces strict discipline; effectively deals with the prominent issues within the Party; earnestly improves the Party's work style; and maintains close ties with the people. So that our party will always be the firm leadership core for advancing the cause of socialism with Chinese characteristics.

It is the people who create history. The masses are the real heroes. Our strength comes from the people and masses. We deeply understand that the capability of any individual is limited, but as long as we unite as one, there is no difficulty that we cannot overcome. Individuals have limited time in work, but there is no limit in serving the people wholeheartedly.

Our responsibility is weightier than Mount Tai, and our journey ahead is long and arduous. We must always be of one heart and mind with the people; share weal and woe with the people; make concerted and hard effort with the people; attend to our duties day and night with diligence; and strive to deliver a satisfactory account to history and the people.

Friends from the press, China needs to learn more about the world, and the world also needs to learn more about China. I hope you will continue to make more efforts and contributions to deepening the mutual understanding between China and the countries of the world.

Thank you, everybody.

'Peace in the whole world,
still divided by greed
looking for easy gain'

POPE FRANCIS
First Easter 'Urbi et Orbi' Message, 31 March 2013

P OPE FRANCIS BECAME PONTIFF at an extraordinary and testing moment in the history of the Vatican. When his predecessor, Joseph Ratzinger (Pope Benedict XVI) stepped down as the Vicar of Christ, he was the first to do so since Gregory XII some six hundred years earlier. While the official line was that Ratzinger had come to his decision based on his waning physical and mental capacities, others suggested that it had more to do with the so-called 'Vatileaks' scandal that had riven the Vatican. Specifically, his profile had been badly wounded when his own butler was revealed as having leaked personal papers. The grim episode spoke of dark power games going on within the walls of St Peter's, politics of the type that Pope Benedict detested.

POPE FRANCIS

Born Jorge Mario Bergoglio on 17 December 1936 in Buenos Aires, Argentina, to Italian immigrant parents.

He joined the Society of Jesuits in 1958 and was ordained as a priest eleven years later. Between 1973 and 1979 he was the Jesuit Provincial Superior for Argentina and held the post of rector of the philosophical and theological faculty at San Miguel's Jesuit University from 1980 to 1986. He was made titular Bishop of Auca and Auxiliary of Buenos Aires in 1992 and became Archbishop of Buenos Aires in 1998. Pope John Paul II appointed him a cardinal in 2001. When John Paul II died in 2005, Bergoglio was considered a favourite to replace him in the Vatican but lost out to Joseph Ratzinger. When Ratzinger sensationally resigned the office in February 2013, Bergoglio was elected by the conclave after five rounds of voting to succeed him. He is the first Jesuit Pope and the first to hail from South America.

It followed on the heels of several other damaging episodes. The Church had been scarred by years of sexual abuse scandals involving priests in Europe and North America, with the Vatican repeatedly accused of orchestrating cover-ups. There was also criticism from many non-adherents for the Church's stances on contraception (especially the refusal to promote condoms in regions with high HIV/AIDS infection rates), homosexuality and the role of women within the Church. Then there was the question of the Church's role in the post-global financial crisis world.

Many hoped that Pope Francis might serve as a new broom. Renowned for his work with the poor in Buenos Aires, he chose his papal name in honour of St Francis of Assisi, a figure heralded for his humility and non-materialism. The new Pope styled himself more austerely than his immediate predecessors, for instance doing away with the Mercedes Benz favoured by Benedict in favour of a Ford Focus.

Further evidence that he believed the Church should engage with the downtrodden came in his first Easter address in 2013, in which he laid out the central tenets of his papacy – namely to improve the lot of those on society's margins. Along with the expected pleas for world peace, he attacked the dangers of unfettered capitalism and 'greed looking for easy gain'. It was an argument that resonated with millions dealing with the aftershock of the recent global financial collapse and Pope Francis seemed to have instantly given his papacy a renewed relevance to the wider world.

DEAR BROTHERS AND SISTERS IN ROME and throughout the world, Happy Easter! Happy Easter!

What a joy it is for me to announce this message: Christ is risen! I would like it to go out to every house and every family, especially where the suffering is greatest, in hospitals, in prisons . . .

Most of all, I would like it to enter every heart, for it is there that God wants to sow this Good News: Jesus is risen, there is hope for you, you are no longer in the power of sin, of evil! Love has triumphed, mercy has been victorious! The mercy of God always triumphs!

We too, like the women who were Jesus' disciples, who went to the tomb and found it empty, may wonder what this event means (cf. Luke 24, 4). What does it mean that Jesus is risen? It means that the love of God is stronger than evil and death itself; it means that the love of God can transform our lives and let those desert places in our hearts bloom. The love of God can do this.

'This passover from evil to the freedom of goodness must be accomplished in every age'

This same love for which the Son of God became man and followed the way of humility and self-giving to the very end, down to hell – to the abyss of separation from God – this same merciful love has flooded with light the dead body of Jesus, has transfigured it, has made it pass into eternal life. Jesus did not return to His former life, to earthly life, but entered into the glorious life of God and He entered there with our humanity, opening us to a future of hope.

This is what Easter is: it is the exodus, the passage of human beings from slavery to sin and evil to the freedom of love and goodness. Because God is life, life alone, and we are His glory: the living man (cf. Irenaeus, *Adversus Haereses*, 4, 20, 5–7).

Dear brothers and sisters, Christ died and rose once for all, and for everyone, but the power of the Resurrection, this passover from slavery to evil to the freedom of goodness, must be accomplished in every age, in our concrete existence, in our everyday lives. How many deserts, even today, do human beings need to cross! Above all, the desert within, when we have no love for God or neighbour, when we fail to realize that we are guardians of all that the Creator has given us and continues to give us. God's mercy can make even the driest land become a garden, can restore life to dry bones (cf. Ezekiel 37, 1–14).

So this is the invitation which I address to everyone: Let us accept the grace of Christ's Resurrection! Let us be renewed by God's mercy, let us be loved by Jesus, let us enable the power of His love to transform our lives too; and let us become agents of this mercy, channels through which God can water the earth, protect all creation and make justice and peace flourish.

And so we ask the risen Jesus, who turns death into life, to change hatred into love, vengeance into forgiveness, war into peace. Yes, Christ is our peace, and through Him we implore peace for all the world.

Peace for the Middle East, and particularly between Israelis and Palestinians, who struggle to find the road of agreement, that they may willingly and courageously resume negotiations to end a conflict that has lasted all too long. Peace in Iraq, that every act of violence may end, and above all for dear Syria, for its people torn by conflict and for the many refugees who await help and comfort. How much blood has been shed! And how much suffering must there still be before a political solution to the crisis will be found?

Peace for Africa, still the scene of violent conflicts. In Mali, may unity and stability be restored; in Nigeria, where attacks sadly continue, gravely threatening the lives of many innocent people, and where great numbers of persons, including children, are held hostage by terrorist groups. Peace in the East of the Democratic Republic of Congo, and in the Central African Republic, where many have been forced to leave their homes and continue to live in fear.

Peace in Asia, above all on the Korean peninsula: may disagreements be overcome and a renewed spirit of reconciliation grow.

Peace in the whole world, still divided by greed looking for easy gain, wounded by the selfishness which threatens human life and the family, selfishness that continues in human trafficking, the most extensive form of slavery in this 21st century; human trafficking is the most extensive form of slavery in this 21st century! Peace to the whole world, torn apart by violence linked to drug trafficking and by the iniquitous exploitation of natural resources! Peace to this, our Earth! May the risen Jesus bring comfort to the victims of natural disasters and make us responsible guardians of creation.

Dear brothers and sisters, to all of you who are listening to me, from Rome and from all over the world, I address the invitation of the Psalm: 'Give thanks to the Lord for He is good; for His steadfast love endures for ever. Let Israel say: "His steadfast love endures for ever".'

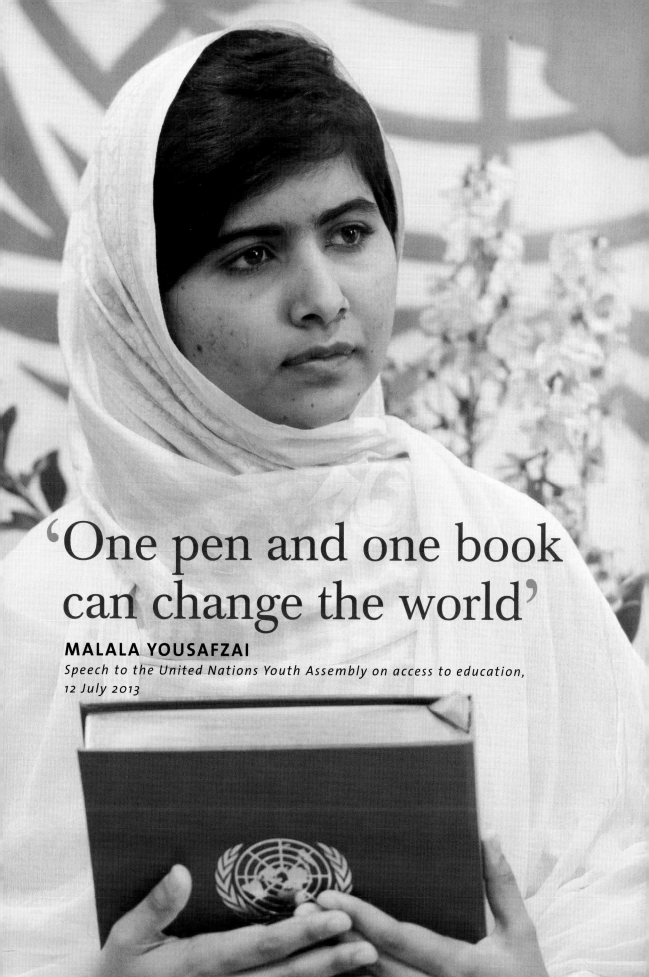

'One pen and one book can change the world'

MALALA YOUSAFZAI

Speech to the United Nations Youth Assembly on access to education, 12 July 2013

MALALA YOUSAFZAI, (now so famous that she is generally known by her first name alone) was a young educational campaigner little known outside of her native Pakistan until a merciless attack by the Taliban turned her into a global human rights icon.

After the local Islamic fundamentalist Taliban leader issued an edict (backed up with frequent violence) banning girls from attending school, Malala became a regular face in the media and took the debate to leading national figures. As she would note: 'I didn't want my future to be imprisoned in my four walls and just cooking and giving birth.'

On the evening of 9 October 2012 she boarded a bus to take her home from school. The vehicle had barely travelled 100 metres when it was stopped by a couple of young men who demanded, 'Who is Malala?' No one answered but the innocent glances of some of her schoolmates gave the game away. In a moment Malala had been shot in the head.

MALALA YOUSAFZAI

Born 12 July 1997 in Mingora in Pakistan's Swat Valley. Her father is a teacher and educational activist who inspired his daughter to campaign for girls' rights to education.

Yousafzai grew up with her parents and two brothers in a Sunni Muslim and ethnically Pashtun family. In 2009 she began writing an anonymous blog for the BBC about living in an area under heavy Taliban influence. However, it was only a matter of months before she was widely identified as the author of the blog, bringing her to the attention of the Taliban leadership. In 2011 she was nominated for the International Children's Peace Prize. The following year she became a household name after being shot by a member of the Taliban while travelling on a school bus. She narrowly survived the assault and was brought to the UK to recuperate. In 2013 she became the youngest person ever nominated for the Nobel Peace Prize.

She was airlifted to a military hospital in Peshawar where emergency surgery saved her life and she was placed into an induced coma. Later flown to Birmingham in the UK for further treatment, she made what doctors acknowledged was a remarkable recovery.

On 12 July 2013 – on her sixteenth birthday and just nine months after the attack – she was invited to address a special youth assembly of the United Nations in New York. The speech she gave on what the UN called 'Malala Day' was broadcast around the globe. The UN Secretary General, Ban Ki-moon, referred to her as 'our hero'. In an impassioned address, she called for education for all, including 'the sons and the daughters of all extremists, especially the Taliban'. She demanded compassion rather than revenge, and for peace so that education might flourish. She finished her speech with the sort of rhetorical flourish of which other more seasoned orators may only dream: 'One child, one teacher, one pen and one book can change the world. Education is the only solution. Education First.'

Some time later, a journalist asked her about the day of the attack. 'I think they may be regretting that they shot Malala,' she said. 'Now she is heard in every corner of the world.'

I<small>N THE NAME OF</small> G<small>OD</small>, The Most Beneficent, The Most Merciful.

. . . Today, it is an honour for me to be speaking again after a long time. Being here with such honourable people is a great moment in my life.

I don't know where to begin my speech. I don't know what people would be expecting me to say. But first of all, thank you to God for whom we all are equal and thank you to every person who has prayed for my fast recovery and a new life. I cannot believe how much love people have shown me.

. . . Dear brothers and sisters, do remember one thing. Malala Day is not my day. Today is the day of every woman, every boy and every girl who have raised their voice for their rights. There are hundreds of human rights activists and social workers who are not only speaking for human rights, but who are struggling to achieve their goals of education, peace and equality. Thousands of people have been killed by the terrorists and millions have been injured. I am just one of them.

So here I stand . . . one girl among many.

I speak – not for myself, but for all girls and boys.

I raise up my voice – not so that I can shout, but so that those without a voice can be heard.

Those who have fought for their rights:

Their right to live in peace.

Their right to be treated with dignity.

Their right to equality of opportunity.

Their right to be educated.

'They thought that the bullets would silence us'

Dear friends, on the 9th of October 2012, the Taliban shot me on the left side of my forehead. They shot my friends too. They thought that the bullets would silence us. But they failed. And then, out of that silence, came thousands of voices. The terrorists thought that they would change our aims and stop our ambitions but nothing changed in my life except this: weakness, fear and hopelessness died. Strength, power and courage was born. I am the same Malala. My ambitions are the same. My hopes are the same. My dreams are the same.

Dear sisters and brothers, I am not against anyone. Neither am I here to speak in terms of personal revenge against the Taliban or any other terrorist group. I am here to speak up for the right of education of every child. I want education for the sons and the daughters of all the extremists, especially the Taliban.

I do not even hate the Talib who shot me. Even if there is a gun in my hand and he stands in front of me, I would not shoot him. This is the compassion that I have learned from Muhammad the Prophet of Mercy, Jesus Christ and Lord Buddha. This is the legacy of change that I have inherited from Martin Luther King, Nelson Mandela and Muhammad Ali Jinnah. This is the philosophy of non-violence that I have learned from Gandhi Jee, Bacha Khan and Mother Teresa. And this is the forgiveness that I have learned from my mother and father. This is what my soul is telling me: be peaceful and love everyone.

Dear sisters and brothers, we realize the importance of light when we see darkness. We realize the importance of our voice when we are silenced. In the same way, when we were in Swat, in the north of Pakistan, we realized the importance of pens and books when we saw the guns.

The wise saying 'The pen is mightier than sword' was true. The extremists are afraid of books and pens. The power of education frightens them. They are afraid of women. The power of the voice of women frightens them. And that is why they killed 14 innocent medical students in the recent attack in Quetta. And that is why they killed many female teachers and polio workers in Khyber Pukhtoon Khwa and FATA. That is why they are blasting schools every day.

'Let us empower ourselves with the weapon of knowledge'

. . . Honourable Secretary General, peace is necessary for education. In many parts of the world, especially Pakistan and Afghanistan, terrorism, wars and conflicts stop children to go to their schools. We are really tired of these wars. Women and children are suffering in many parts of the world in many ways. In India, innocent and poor children are victims of child labour. Many schools have been destroyed in Nigeria. People in Afghanistan have been affected by the hurdles of extremism for decades. Young girls have to do domestic child labour and are forced to get married at an early age. Poverty, ignorance, injustice, racism and the deprivation of basic rights are the main problems faced by both men and women.

. . . Dear sisters and brothers, now it's time to speak up.

So today, we call upon the world leaders to change their strategic policies in favour of peace and prosperity.

We call upon the world leaders that all the peace deals must protect women and children's rights. A deal that goes against the dignity of women and their rights is unacceptable.

We call upon all governments to ensure free compulsory education for every child all over the world.

We call upon all governments to fight against terrorism and violence, to protect children from brutality and harm.

We call upon the developed nations to support the expansion of educational opportunities for girls in the developing world.

We call upon all communities to be tolerant – to reject prejudice based on cast, creed, sect, religion or gender. To ensure freedom and equality for women so that they can flourish. We cannot all succeed when half of us are held back.

We call upon our sisters around the world to be brave – to embrace the strength within themselves and realize their full potential.

Dear brothers and sisters, we want schools and education for every child's bright future . . . And if we want to achieve our goal, then let us empower ourselves with the weapon of knowledge and let us shield ourselves with unity and togetherness.

Dear brothers and sisters, we must not forget that millions of people are suffering from poverty, injustice and ignorance. We must not forget that millions of children are out of schools. We must not forget that our sisters and brothers are waiting for a bright peaceful future.

So let us wage a global struggle against illiteracy, poverty and terrorism, and let us pick up our books and pens. They are our most powerful weapons.

One child, one teacher, one pen and one book can change the world.

Education is the only solution. Education First.

'With Ukraine, our Western partners have crossed the line'

VLADIMIR PUTIN
Address in the Kremlin regarding the annexation of Crimea, 18 March 2014

WITH THE COLLAPSE OF THE USSR IN 1991, the ideological war between capitalism and communism seemed to have been won and the 'new world order' established. It was widely presumed that one superpower, the USA, would oversee the hegemony of Western liberal democratic ideals.

Today such arguments seem tinged with naivety. The USA remains a superpower but a faded one, diminished by years of costly interventionist foreign policy, wearied by the threat of international terrorism, and struggling to hold off the economic tiger that is China. Russia, meanwhile, continues to yield major influence over the global political balance under the steely direction of its president, Vladimir Putin.

The dominant figure in Russian politics since the turn of the century, Putin has overseen a period of domestic modernization and broad economic growth, while his handling of the war in Chechnya earned him a reputation for ruthless toughness. Accused by his critics of being an autocrat, internationally he has been unafraid to lock horns with either the USA or the European Union.

Post-Cold War tensions between East and West were never more acute than when Putin authorized the annexation of Crimea (hitherto a province of Ukraine), following the collapse of Viktor Yanukovych's regime in early 2014. In a speech to the Russian parliament in March 2014, Putin laid out what he believed to be the historical justification for the annexation. Specifically, he claimed to be protecting the region's ethnically Russian population, who had called for reunion with Moscow in a referendum earlier in the month that lacked international recognition.

Putin also used the address to attack the track record of the wider international community (and in particular, the USA) in interfering in the politics of independent nations. It was a theme he had touched on before. For instance, seven years earlier he had addressed the Munich Security Conference on what he perceived to be USA expansionism.

His 2014 speech, meanwhile, looked back ruefully on the dissolution of the Soviet Union over two decades earlier. Some commentators detected the groundwork being laid for other potential 'land grabs' where there is an ethnically Russian majority – a notion sure to strike fear into several nations that were once outposts of the

VLADIMIR PUTIN

Born in St Petersburg (then Leningrad) on 7 October 1952 to a war veteran father and mother who had survived the siege of Leningrad.

He graduated in law in 1975 before joining the Soviet security agency, the KGB. Following the collapse of the USSR, he embarked on a political career in the early 1990s. After a stint as deputy mayor of St Petersburg, he was brought into the Kremlin by President Yeltsin. He headed the FSB (Russia's successor to the KGB) and in 1999 was appointed Acting Prime Minister. When Yeltsin resigned at the end of the year, Putin became Acting President. In 2000 he was elected to the position on a permanent basis and has remained in office ever since, apart from a spell as Prime Minister between 2008 and 2012. Widely regarded as the 'hard man' of Russian politics, he has sought to give the country greater influence on the international stage.

USSR. Those who had believed Russia would retreat into itself after the collapse of communism could not possibly labour under that illusion any more.

DEAR FRIENDS,

We have have gathered here today in connection with an issue that is of vital, historic significance to all of us. A referendum was held in Crimea on 16 March in full compliance with democratic procedures and international norms.

More than 82 per cent of the electorate took part in the vote. Over 96 per cent of them spoke out in favour of reuniting with Russia. These numbers speak for themselves.

To understand the reason behind such a choice, it is enough to know the history of Crimea and what Russia and Crimea have always meant for each other.

Everything in Crimea speaks of our shared history and pride. This is the location of ancient Khersones, where Prince Vladimir was baptized. His spiritual feat of adopting Orthodoxy predetermined the overall basis of the culture, civilization and human values that unite the peoples of Russia, Ukraine and Belarus. The graves of Russian soldiers whose bravery brought Crimea into the Russian empire are also in Crimea. There is also Sevastopol – a legendary city with an outstanding history, a fortress that serves as the birthplace of Russia's Black Sea Fleet. Crimea is Balaklava and Kerch, Malakhov Kurgan and Sapun Ridge. Each one of these places is dear to our hearts, symbolizing Russian military glory and outstanding valour.

. . . Russians and Ukrainians, Crimean Tatars and people of other ethnic groups have lived side by side in Crimea, retaining their own identity, traditions, languages and faith.

Incidentally, the total population of the Crimean Peninsula today is 2.2 million people, of whom almost 1.5 million are Russians, 350,000 are Ukrainians who predominantly consider Russian their native language, and about 290,000–300,000 are Crimean Tatars, who, as the referendum has shown, also lean towards Russia.

. . . In people's hearts and minds, Crimea has always been an inseparable part of Russia. This firm conviction is based on truth and justice and was passed from generation to generation, over time, under any circumstances, despite all the dramatic changes our country went through during the entire 20th century.

After the revolution, the Bolsheviks, for a number of reasons – may God judge them – added large sections of the historical South of Russia to the Republic of Ukraine. This was done with no consideration for the ethnic make-up of the population, and today these areas form the southeast of Ukraine. Then, in 1954, a decision was made to transfer the Crimean Region to Ukraine, along with Sevastopol, despite the fact that it was a federal city.

'Everything in Crimea speaks of our shared history and pride'

. . . What matters now is that this decision was made in clear violation of the constitutional norms that were in place even then . . . Back then, it was impossible to imagine that Ukraine and Russia may split up and become two separate states. However, this has happened.

. . . And as this collapse was legalized, everyone forgot about Crimea and Sevastopol – the main base of the Black Sea Fleet. Millions of people went to bed in one country and awoke in different ones, overnight becoming ethnic minorities in former Union republics, while the Russian nation became one of the biggest, if not the biggest, ethnic group in the world to be divided by borders.

. . . Time and time again attempts were made to deprive Russians of their historical memory, even of their language, and to subject them to forced assimilation. Moreover, Russians, just as other citizens of Ukraine, are suffering from the constant political and state crisis that has been rocking the country for over twenty years.

. . . I would like to reiterate that I understand those who came out on Maidan with peaceful slogans against corruption, inefficient state management and poverty . . . However, those who stood behind the latest events in Ukraine had a different agenda: they were preparing yet another government takeover; they wanted to seize power and would stop short of nothing.

. . . It is also obvious that there is now no legitimate executive authority in Ukraine . . . Those who opposed the coup were immediately threatened with repression. Naturally, the first in line here was Crimea, the Russian-speaking Crimea. In view of this, the residents of Crimea and Sevastopol turned to Russia for help in defending their rights and lives, in preventing the events that were unfolding and are still underway in Kiev, Donetsk, Kharkov and other Ukrainian cities.

Naturally, we could not leave this plea unheeded; we could not abandon

Crimea and its residents in distress. This would have been betrayal on our part.

First, we had to help create conditions so that the residents of Crimea for the first time in history were able to peacefully express their free will regarding their own future. However, what do we hear from our colleagues in Western Europe and North America? They say we are violating norms of international law. Firstly, it's a good thing that they at least remember that there exists such a thing as international law – better late than never.

Secondly, and most importantly – what exactly are we violating? True, the President of the Russian Federation received permission from the Upper House of Parliament to use the Armed Forces in Ukraine. However, strictly speaking, nobody has acted on this permission yet. Russia's Armed Forces never entered Crimea; they were there already in line with an international agreement.

. . . Next, as it declared independence and decided to hold a referendum, the Supreme Council of Crimea referred to the United Nations Charter, which speaks of the right of nations to self-determination.

. . . Moreover, the Crimean authorities referred to the well-known Kosovo precedent – a precedent our Western colleagues created with their own hands in a very similar situation, when they agreed that the unilateral separation of Kosovo from Serbia – exactly what Crimea is doing now – was legitimate and did not require any permission from the country's central authorities.

'Isn't the desire of Crimea's residents to freely choose their fate such a value?'

. . . Like a mirror, the situation in Ukraine reflects what is going on and what has been happening in the world over the past several decades. After the dissolution of bipolarity on the planet, we no longer have stability. Key international institutions are not getting any stronger; on the contrary, in many cases, they are sadly degrading. Our Western partners, led by the United States of America, prefer not to be guided by international law in their practical policies, but by the rule of the gun. They have come to believe in their exclusivity and exceptionalism, that they can decide the destinies of the world, that only they can ever be right. They act as they please: here and there, they use force against sovereign states, building coalitions based on the principle 'If you are not with us, you are against us'.

To make this aggression look legitimate, they force the necessary resolutions from international organizations, and if for some reason this does not work, they simply ignore the UN Security Council and the UN overall.

. . . In short, we have every reason to assume that the infamous policy of containment, led in the 18th, 19th and 20th centuries, continues today. They are constantly trying to sweep us into a corner because we have an independent position, because we maintain it, and because we call things like they are and do not engage in hypocrisy. But there is a limit to everything. And with Ukraine, our Western partners have crossed the line.

. . . Today, I would like to address the people of the United States of America, the people who, since the foundation of their nation and adoption of the Declaration of Independence, have been proud to hold freedom above all else. Isn't the desire of Crimea's residents to freely choose their fate such a value?

. . . I also want to address the people of Ukraine. I sincerely want you to understand us: we do not want to harm you in any way, or to hurt your national feelings . . . We do not want to divide Ukraine; we do not need that. As for Crimea, it was and remains a Russian, Ukrainian, and Crimean-Tatar land.

. . . We want to be friends with Ukraine, and we want Ukraine to be a strong, sovereign and self-sufficient country.

. . . Russia's foreign-policy position on this matter drew its firmness from the will of millions of our people, our national unity and the support of our country's main political and public forces.

. . . Members of the Federation Council, deputies of the State Duma, citizens of Russia, residents of Crimea and Sevastopol, today, in accordance with the people's will, I submit to the Federal Assembly a request to consider a Constitutional Law on the creation of two new constituent entities within the Russian Federation: the Republic of Crimea and the city of Sevastopol, and to ratify the treaty on admitting to the Russian Federation Crimea and Sevastopol, which is already ready for signing. I stand assured of your support.

'. . . this is not just about my suffering; it is about collective suffering.'

MURAD WAS A TEENAGE STUDENT when members of the Islamic State seized her in August 2014, having attacked her Yazidi village, killing hundreds and kidnapping thousands more. Islamic State were at the time making significant advances in Iraq in their pursuit of a self-proclaimed worldwide caliphate based on its Islamist fundamentalist, jihadist doctrine.

Murad was taken to Mosul where she was kept in a house, enslaved, and physically and sexually abused. She was able to escape when her captor left his house unlocked one day, first to a nearby family and then to a refugee camp in northern Iraq. It was there, in early 2015, that her shocking experiences came to light when she was interviewed by Belgian journalists. Shortly afterwards, she was resettled in Germany.

In December that year Murad was invited to speak to the United Nations Security Council on the theme of human trafficking and conflict – the first time the Council had ever received a briefing on the subject. In 2008 the UN had adopted a resolution that recognised sexual violence as 'a tactic of war to humiliate, dominate, instil fear in, disperse and/or forcibly relocate civilian members of a community or an ethnic group'.

From Germany, Murad works as a global ambassador, listening to the testimonies of survivors of trafficking and genocide and serving as their voice. In September 2016, Murad launched 'Nadia's Initiative' in New York, an organisation dedicated to providing support for survivors of sexual violence, and the same month was appointed by the UN as its Goodwill Ambassador for the Dignity of Survivors of Human Trafficking of the United Nations.

On receiving the Nobel Peace Prize in 2018 for her work toward ending the use of sexual violence as a weapon of war, Murad noted that no award could compensate for the people who were killed solely because they were Yazidis. Instead, she pleaded for justice and protection for the rest of her community. 'Let us all unite to fight injustice and oppression,' she said. 'Let us raise our voices together and say: No to violence, yes to peace, no to slavery, yes to freedom, no to racial discrimination, yes to equality and to human rights for all.'

NADIA MURAD

Born in 1993 into a farming family in Kocho, a village in the Ninewa governorate of northern Iraq.

In 2014 Murad, an ethnic Yazidi, was kidnapped by the extremist Islamic State group (also known variously as Daesh, ISIL and ISIS) and held captive for three months. After managing to escape she eventually found her way to safety in Baden-Württemberg, Germany. There she founded Nadia's Initiative, an organization with the aim of creating 'a world where women are able to live peacefully, and where communities that have experienced trauma and suffering are supported'. In 2017 Murad published a memoir, The Last Girl: My Story of Captivity, and My Fight Against the Islamic State. The following year she was jointly awarded (along with Denis Mukwege) the Nobel Peace Prize in recognition of her 'efforts to end the use of sexual violence as a weapon of war and armed conflict'.

It is a fight to which she has been able to give extraordinary impetus, energy and vision through her courageous testimony, and never more so than with her address to the UN in 2015, made only a year after she had been held captive.

IT IS WITH GREAT SADNESS, gratitude and hope that I address the Security Council. As a Yazidi survivor, I am a descendant of one of the world's oldest religions, which is today threatened with extinction. I am here to talk about the practices against us by what is called the Islamic State/Daesh—trafficking in persons, sexual enslavement of women, recruitment of children in war, displacement and the genocide of our society. I am here to tell the Council my story, of what happened to my society, which has lost hope for life and is now moving into unknown territory. I am also here to tell the Council about the more than 3,400 women and children who have been abducted. I am here to tell the Council about this global terrorist organization, the Islamic State, which is trying to destroy our culture and take away our freedom. I am here to talk about the nightmare that, just overnight, turned the life of an entire community upside-down.

Prior to 3 August 2014, I was living with my family, my brothers and sisters in the pretty, quiet village of Kocho. But then the Islamic State attacked our region, and we found ourselves facing a true genocide.

. . . The Islamic State came with the sole aim of destroying the Yazidi identity through force, rape, recruitment of children and destruction of all of our temples, which they took control of. All of this can be interpreted only as an act of genocide against our identity, in particular against Yazidi women. Rape was used to destroy women and girls and to ensure that they could never again lead a normal life.

On 15 August, elements from the Islamic State summoned us to the village school. They separated the men from the women and children. I saw them from the second floor of the school as they took away the men and killed them. Six of my brothers were killed, while three survived the mass killing. We, the women and children, were taken by bus from the school to another area. They humiliated us along the way and touched us in a shameful way. They took me to Mosul with more than 150 other Yazidi families. There were thousands of families in a building there, including children who were given away as gifts. One of the men came up to me. He wanted to take me. I looked down at the floor. I was absolutely terrified. When I looked up, I saw a huge man. He was like a monster. I cried out that I was too young and he was huge. He kicked and beat me. A few minutes later, another man came up to me. I was still looking at the floor. I saw that he was a little smaller. I begged for him to take me. I was terribly afraid of the first man. The man who took me asked me to change my religion. I refused. One day, he came and asked me for my hand in what they called "marriage". I said that I was ill; most women were menstruating because they were so scared. A few days later, this man forced me to get dressed and put on my makeup. Then, on that terrible night, he did it.

He forced me to serve in his military company. He humiliated me daily. He forced me to wear clothes that barely covered my body. I was not able to take any more rape and torture. I decided to flee, but one of the guards stopped me. That night he beat me. He asked me to take my clothes off. He put me in a room with guards, who proceeded to commit their crime until I fainted.

I was finally able to escape three months after my abduction.

. . . But this is not just about my suffering; it is about collective suffering. Daesh gave us two options: become a Muslim or die. . . . Sixteen mass graves have been discovered so far. . . . More than 400,000 people have been displaced, and over 40 per cent of our land is still under the control of Daesh.

. . . To the Council today, I lay out our demands, and I very much hope that humanity has not yet come to an end.

First, we demand the liberation of the more than 3,400 women and children still suffering and living under the mercy of the merciless.

Secondly, we demand that the incidents that took place, including the murders, collective slavery and human trafficking, be defined as genocide.

. . . Thirdly, demand the liberation of all of our areas, including my own village of Kocho, so that we can bury our dead. We demand the establishment of international protection for the Yazidi areas and for the minorities under threat so that, one day, we can return to our regions and live in peace.

. . . Fourthly, we ask that members open up their countries to my community. We are victims and we have the right to seek a safe country that safeguards our dignity.

. . . Fifthly, and finally, we ask the Council, please, to put an end to Daesh once and for all. I suffered the pain they inflicted on me. I saw their evil. All those who commit the crimes of human trafficking and genocide must be brought to justice so that women and children can live in peace—in Iraq, Syria, Nigeria, Somalia and everywhere else in the world. These crimes against women and their freedom must be brought to an end today.

'Americanism, not globalism, will be our credo.'

DONALD J. TRUMP
Address to Republican National Convention, Ohio, 21 July 2016

WHEN DONALD J. TRUMP, the Republican Party candidate, was declared the victor of the 2016 American presidential election against Democrat Hillary Clinton, it heralded one of the most controversial presidencies in American history.

Trump's political affiliations had regularly switched over the years. He was variously aligned with the Democrats, Republicans and Reform parties, going so far as to contest several primaries for the latter ahead of the 2002 presidential election. However, after Barack Obama won the presidency for the Democrats in 2008, Trump increasingly positioned himself with the Republicans.

Trump announced his intention to seek the Republican nomination in June 2015, laying out many of his campaign priorities in a speech, delivered from his base at the Trump Tower in Manhattan. He focussed on the issues of illegal immigration, the country's burdensome debt, the threat of Islamist extremism and the loss of American jobs to other countries. He also introduced his campaign slogan: 'Make America Great Again.'

DONALD J. TRUMP

Born 14 June 1946 in the Queens borough of New York City.

A three-times-married entrepreneur and reality television star, Donald Trump took over his father Fred's real-estate business in 1971. He expanded the interests of the renamed Trump Organization from its base in Queens and Brooklyn into Manhattan and beyond. The company became known for its work on landmark projects including skyscrapers, casinos and golf courses, earning Trump a personal fortune of billions (although his financial history remains a subject of fierce debate). Trump cultivated a high-profile media image, mixing with politicians and celebrities and running the Miss Universe and Miss USA beauty pageants. From 2003 his fame grew significantly with the debut of *The Apprentice*. Initially considered an outsider in the 2016 US presidential race, he became the 45th President of the United States of America on 20 January 2017. He lost his reelection campaign in 2020 to Democratic candidate Joe Biden.

Having secured the nomination against front-runners US Senator Ted Cruz and Ohio Governor John Kasich, Trump's presidential campaign trail was characterised by often rowdy rallies in which his populist rhetoric extolling nationalist pride and protectionist economics was warmly received. Among Trump's most controversial electoral promises was a pledge to construct a border wall between the US and Mexico. Meanwhile, he espoused a tough stance on migration from Muslim-majority countries, citing the threat of terrorism. He also suggested he would undo Obama's healthcare reforms and withdraw the country from a number of its international commitments, as well as re-negotiate America's trading relationship with China.

Trump's uncompromising language made him the poster boy of the alt-right and others who felt they had been abandoned by the political establishment, while those who took issue with his claims were accused of peddling 'fake news'. Against the odds, on 8 November 2016 Trump won the presidency and was sworn in as the 45th President of the United States of America on 20 January 2017. American politics had been changed forever. But it was as Trump accepted the Republican nomination in Cleveland, Ohio, in 2016 that he delivered arguably his most complete expression of Trumpism.

FRIENDS, DELEGATES AND FELLOW AMERICANS: I humbly and gratefully accept your nomination for the presidency of the United States.

Together, we will lead our party back to the White House, and we will lead our country back to safety, prosperity, and peace. We will be a country of generosity and warmth. But we will also be a country of law and order.

. . . It is finally time for a straightforward assessment of the state of our nation. I will present the facts plainly and honestly. We cannot afford to be so politically correct anymore.

. . . Not only have our citizens endured domestic disaster, but they have lived through one international humiliation after another. We all remember the images of our sailors being forced to their knees by their Iranian captors at gunpoint.

. . . America is far less safe – and the world is far less stable – than when Obama made the decision to put Hillary Clinton in charge of America's foreign policy. I am certain it is a decision he truly regrets. Her bad instincts and her bad judgment – something pointed out by Bernie Sanders – are what caused the disasters unfolding today…

. . . But Hillary Clinton's legacy does not have to be America's legacy. The problems we face now – poverty and violence at home, war and destruction abroad – will last only as long as we continue relying on the same politicians who created them. A change in leadership is required to change these outcomes. Tonight, I will share with you my plan of action for America.

The most important difference between our plan and that of our opponents, is that our plan will put America First. Americanism, not globalism, will be our credo. As long as we are led by politicians who will not put America First, then we can be assured that other nations will not treat America with respect. This will all change in 2017.

The American People will come first once again. My plan will begin with safety at home – which means safe neighborhoods, secure borders, and protection from terrorism. There can be no prosperity without law and order. On the economy, I will outline reforms to add millions of new jobs and trillions in new wealth that can be used to rebuild America.

A number of these reforms that I will outline tonight will be opposed by some of our nation's most powerful special interests. That is because these interests have rigged our political and economic system for their exclusive benefit.

. . . I have joined the political arena so that the powerful can no longer beat up on people that cannot defend themselves. Nobody knows the system better than me, which is why I alone can fix it.

. . . The first task for our new Administration will be to liberate our citizens from the crime and terrorism and lawlessness that threatens their communities.

. . . To make life safe in America, we must also address the growing threats we face from outside America: we are going to defeat the barbarians of ISIS. . . . Instead, we must work with all of our allies who share our goal of destroying ISIS and stamping out Islamic terror. This includes working with our greatest ally in the region, the State of Israel. Lastly, we must immediately suspend immigration from any nation that has been compromised by terrorism until such time as proven vetting mechanisms have been put in place.

. . . Decades of record immigration have produced lower wages and higher unemployment for our citizens, especially for African-American and Latino workers. We are going to have an immigration system that works, but one that works for the American people.

. . . We are going to build a great border wall to stop illegal immigration, to stop the gangs and the violence, and to stop the drugs from pouring into our communities.

. . . Yet Hillary Clinton is proposing mass amnesty, mass immigration, and mass lawlessness. Her plan will overwhelm your schools and hospitals, further reduce your jobs and wages, and make it harder for recent immigrants to escape from poverty.

I have a different vision for our workers. It begins with a new, fair trade policy that protects our jobs and stands up to countries that cheat. It's been a signature message of my campaign from day one, and it will be a signature feature of my presidency from the moment I take the oath of office.

. . . America is a nation of believers, dreamers, and strivers that is being led by a group of censors, critics, and cynics.

Remember: all of the people telling you that you can't have the country you want, are the same people telling you that I wouldn't be standing here tonight. No longer can we rely on those elites in media, and politics, who will say anything to keep a rigged system in place.

. . . To all Americans tonight, in all our cities and towns, I make this promise: We Will Make America Strong Again.

We Will Make America Proud Again.

'Enough is enough.'

TARANA BURKE
TEDWomen 2018, Palm Springs,
California, 28 November 2018

IT WAS IN 1997 that Burke encountered a young teen called Heaven at a youth camp she was directing. Heaven told Burke how she had been abused by her mother's boyfriend, but Burke was unsure how to respond: 'I was horrified by her words, the emotions welling inside of me ran the gamut, and I listened until I literally could not take it anymore . . . which turned out to be less than 5 minutes.' Burke cut their conversation short and directed Heaven to another counsellor whom she believed would be better able to help. She never saw Heaven again but the expression on the girl's face haunted her. Burke became determined to find the right words for the next time she encountered a fellow abuse survivor, words that would convey her empathy and reassure the other party that they were not alone. Her solidarity, she realised, could be summed up in one short phrase: 'Me too.'

In 2006, Burke introduced the phrase to the users of MySpace, the dominant social media platform of the day. The slogan, she hoped, would both unite survivors and shine a light on the extent of abuse and harassment that women endure every day. Her campaign gained a foothold but it would be more than a decade before the 'Me Too' movement became a global phenomenon.

In October 2017, the *New York Times* and the *New Yorker* ran stories quoting numerous women's accounts that over several decades they had been sexually abused by Harvey Weinstein, one of Hollywood's heavyweight movie producers. After years of supressed rumours about Weinstein's conduct, the flood gates now opened as many more complainants came forward, including several household names. On 15 October, Alyssa Milano, best known for long-running television roles in *Who's the Boss?* and *Charmed* – and not one of Weinstein's specific accusers – wrote on Twitter: 'If all the women who have been sexually harassed or assaulted wrote "Me too" as a status, we might give people a sense of the magnitude of the problem.' The MeToo hashtag rapidly gained traction and soon had millions of users around the globe. Having been unaware of Burke's role in creating the 'Me Too' phrase, Milano duly credited her.

TARANA BURKE

Born in New York City in 1973 and grew up in a working-class Bronx housing project.

A survivor of childhood sexual abuse, Tarana Burke has worked as an activist and advocate of social, sexual and racial justice since the 1980s. After completing university studies in Alabama, she took a job with a youth development organization, 21st Century Leaders, in Selma, Alabama. There, she gained insight into the extent of sexual violence and abuse suffered by young, black females often unable to access suitable support systems. In 2006 she introduced the phrase 'Me Too' to social media in a bid to bring together victims of sexual abuse, from criminal assaults to workplace harassment, empowering them through solidarity. The following year, Burke created Just Be Inc., an organization aimed at increasing the empowerment and wellness of young women of colour. She has subsequently worked for several not-for-profit agencies. In 2017, the 'Me Too' movement gained renewed momentum when the slogan was adopted by a number of high-profile celebrities. Burke is now senior director of the Brooklyn-based Girls for Gender Equity (GGE).

Burke used her newly expanded platform to promote her message of social and sexual justice, and to shape the MeToo movement into an expression of what she has called 'empowerment through empathy'. *Time* counted her among a group of leading female activists that the magazine described as 'the silence breakers', jointly awarding them the 2017 *Time* 'Person of the Year' accolade. Burke's TEDWomen talk in 2018 provided her with the opportunity to emphasise that MeToo was nonetheless a work in progress. She spoke eloquently of the backlash the movement had received, whereby the impact of abuse accusations on perpetrators was too often prioritised over the experiences of survivors. She talked of her own sense of numbness in the face of the cultural war in which the movement was engaged, while urging supporters to remember the reason they were fighting at all and extolling the 'power of empathy'. While acknowledging that they might not win every battle, she ended with an appeal to continue the struggle with hope: 'We owe future generations a world free of sexual violence. I believe we can build that world. Do you?'

I'VE BEEN TRYING TO FIGURE OUT what I was going to say here for months. Because there's no bigger stage than TED, it felt like getting my message right in this moment was more important than anything. And so I searched and searched for days on end, trying to find the right configuration of words. And although intellectually, I could bullet point the big ideas that I wanted to share about Me Too and this movement that I founded, I kept finding myself falling short of finding the heart. I wanted to pour myself into this moment and tell you why even the possibility of healing or interrupting sexual violence was worth standing and fighting for. I wanted to rally you to your feet with an uplifting speech about the important work of fighting for the dignity and humanity of survivors. But I don't know if I have it.

The reality is, after soldiering through the Supreme Court nomination process and attacks from the White House, gross mischaracterizations, internet trolls and the rallies and marches and heart-wrenching testimonies, I'm faced with my own hard truth. I'm numb. And I'm not surprised. I've traveled all across the world giving talks, and like clockwork, after every event, more than one person approaches me so that they can say their piece in private. And I always tried to reassure them. You know, I'd give them local resources and a soft reassurance that they're not alone and this is their movement, too. I'd tell them that we're stronger together and that this is a movement of survivors and advocates doing things big and small every day.

And more and more people are joining this movement every single day. That part is clear. People are putting their bodies on the line and raising their voices to say, "Enough is enough."

So why do I feel this way? Well . . . Someone with credible accusations of sexual violence against him was confirmed to the Supreme Court of the United States of America, again. The US President, who was caught on tape talking about how he can grab women's body parts wherever he wants, however he wants, can call a survivor a liar at one of his rallies, and the crowds will roar. And all across the world, where Me Too has taken off, Australia and France, Sweden, China and now India, survivors of sexual violence are all at once being heard and then vilified. And I've read article after article bemoaning . . . wealthy white men who have landed softly with their golden parachutes, following the disclosure of their terrible behavior. And we're asked to consider their futures.

But what of survivors? This movement is constantly being called a watershed moment, or even a reckoning, but I wake up some days feeling like all evidence points to the contrary.

It's hard not to feel numb. I suspect some of you may feel numb, too. But let me tell you what else I know. Sometimes when you hear the word "numb," you think of a void, an absence of feelings, or even the inability to feel. But that's not always true. Numbness can come from those memories that creep up in your mind that you can't fight off in the middle of the night. They can come from the tears that are locked behind your eyes that you won't give yourself permission to cry. For me, numbness comes from looking in the face of survivors and knowing everything to say but having nothing left to give. It's measuring the magnitude of this task ahead of you versus your own wavering fortitude. Numbness is not always the absence of feeling. Sometimes it's an accumulation of feelings. And as survivors, we often have to hold the truth of what we experience. But now, we're all holding something, whether we want to or not. Our colleagues are speaking up and speaking out, industries across the board are re-examining workplace culture, and families and friends are having hard conversations about closely held truths. Everybody is impacted.

And then, there's the backlash. We've all heard it. "The Me Too Movement is a witch hunt." Right? "Me Too is dismantling due process." Or, "Me Too has created a gender war." The media has been consistent with headline after headline that frames this movement in ways that make it difficult to move our work forward, and right-wing pundits and other critics have these talking points that shift the focus away from survivors. So suddenly, a movement that was started to support all survivors of sexual violence is being talked about like it's a vindictive plot against men. And I'm like, "Huh?"

How did we get here?

We have moved so far away from the origins of this movement that started a decade ago, or even the intentions of the hashtag that started just a year ago, that sometimes, the Me Too movement that I hear some people talk about is unrecognizable to me.

But be clear: This is a movement about the one in four girls and the one in six boys who are sexually assaulted every year and carry those wounds into adulthood. It's about the 84 percent of trans women who will be sexually assaulted this year and the indigenous women who are three-and-a-half times more likely to be sexually assaulted than any other group. Or people with disabilities, who are seven times more likely to be sexually abused. It's about the 60 percent of black girls like me who will be experiencing sexual violence before they turn 18, and the thousands and thousands of low-wage workers who are being sexually harassed right now on jobs that they can't afford to quit.

This is a movement about the far-reaching power of empathy. And so it's about the millions and millions of people who, one year ago, raised their hands to say, "Me too," and their hands are still raised while the media that they consume erases them and politicians who they elected to represent them pivot away from solutions . . .

My vision for the Me Too Movement is a part of a collective vision to see a world free of sexual violence, and I believe we can build that world. Full stop. But in order to get there, we have to dramatically shift a culture that propagates the idea that vulnerability is synonymous with permission and that bodily autonomy is not a basic human right. In other words, we have to dismantle the building blocks of sexual violence: power and privilege. So much of what we hear about the Me Too Movement is about individual bad actors or depraved, isolated behavior, and it fails to recognize that anybody in a position of power comes with privilege, and it renders those without that power more vulnerable. Teachers and students, coaches and athletes, law enforcement and citizen, parent and child: these are all relationships that can have an incredible imbalance of power. But we reshape that imbalance by speaking out against it in unison and by creating spaces to speak truth to power…

Part of the work of the Me Too Movement is about the restoration of that humanity for survivors, because the violence doesn't end with the act. The violence is also the trauma that we hold after the act. Remember, trauma halts possibility. It serves to impede, stagnate, confuse and kill. So our work rethinks how we deal with trauma. For instance, we don't believe that survivors should tell the details of their stories all the time. We shouldn't have to perform our pain over and over again for the sake of your awareness…

I have been propelled by possibility for most of my life. I am here because somebody, starting with my ancestors, believed I was possible.

In 2006, 12 years ago, I laid across a mattress on my floor in my one-bedroom apartment, frustrated with all the sexual violence that I saw in my community. I pulled out a piece of paper, and I wrote "Me Too" on the top of it, and I proceeded to write out an action plan for building a movement based on empathy between survivors that would help us feel like we can heal, that we weren't the sum total of the things that happened to us. Possibility is a gift, y'all. It births new worlds, and it births visions.

I know some of y'all are tired, because I'm tired. I'm exhausted, and I'm numb. Those who came before us didn't win every fight, but they didn't let it kill their vision. It fueled it. So I can't stop, and I'm asking you not to stop either.

We owe future generations a world free of sexual violence. I believe we can build that world. Do you?

Thank you.

'... change is coming,
whether you like it
or not'

GRETA THUNBERG
United Nations Climate Action Summit, New York, 23 September 2019

OVER THE COURSE OF A YEAR OR SO, Greta Thunberg was transformed from an unknown high school student, deeply concerned by the threat of climate change, into the leader of a global youth movement intent on staving off environmental disaster.

Thunberg came to national attention as increasing numbers of fellow student protestors joined her regular Friday 'school strike days' (known as 'Fridays for Future') throughout 2018. The young activist was then invited to address that year's United Nations Climate Change Conference where she observed that world leaders were 'not mature enough to tell it like is'. It became clear that she regarded it as her mission to step up where world leaders were falling short and to speak out on what she described as 'the greatest crisis in human history'. In a TEDx Talk she gave in November 2018 she explained: 'I was diagnosed with Asperger's syndrome, OCD and selective mutism. That basically means I only speak when I think it's necessary. Now is one of those moments.'

During the summer of 2019, Thunberg made a high-profile Atlantic crossing aboard a racing yacht, in line with her refusal to fly. On 23 September she arrived at the UN Climate Action Summit in New York City where she gave a withering address that made headlines around the world as it critiqued the inaction of world leaders. She accused them of complacency in the face of 30 years of scientific evidence, prioritising their generations' economic prosperity over preserving the planet's ecosystems for those generations still to come. Her power to inspire popular action had been demonstrated three days earlier, when an estimated four-million people participated in co-ordinated climate strikes across 4,500 locations in 150 countries. Millions more took part in Thunberg-inspired protests in what was known as the Global Week for Future, of which her speech emerged as the centrepiece. By the end of the year, *Time* magazine would name her their 'Person of the Year'—the youngest ever recipient of the accolade—for 'transforming millions of vague, middle-of-the-night anxieties into a worldwide movement calling for urgent change'.

Thunberg's message throughout her activism has been potently simple. In November 2019, she summed it up as she prepared for her return voyage to Europe: 'My

GRETA THUNBERG

Born 3 January 2003 in Stockholm, Sweden, the daughter of an actor and an opera singer.

Greta Thunberg first learned about climate change around 2011 and consequently urged her family to reduce their carbon footprint by adopting veganism and giving up flying. In 2018, she refused to attend school for days and weeks at a time, instead picketing the Swedish parliament to demand stronger action on climate change. Her activism soon gained media attention as well as attracting other young people to boycott school on specific days in favour of protest. Thunberg found herself the figurehead of an international movement, extolled by some and vilified by others. In 2019 she became the youngest person in history to be named Time magazine's person of the year and was nominated for the Nobel Peace Prize in both 2019 and 2020.

message to the Americans is the same as to everyone – that is to unite behind the science and to act on the science.' The science does, indeed, support her claim that action is now a matter of urgency. In 2014 the Intergovernmental Panel on Climate Change (IPCC) had concluded: 'It is extremely likely that human influence has been the dominant cause of the observed warming since the mid-20th century.' By 2018 the organisation, which brings together the research of the world's leading climate scientists, was warning that the world had only until 2030 to implement the necessary, ambitious yet feasible, reforms that would restrict global warming to 1.5 Celsius (namely, a cut in global carbon emissions of 45 per cent on 2010 levels). Above that level, the scientific consensus agrees, the chances of extreme heat, flooding, droughts and related poverty are significantly raised for hundreds of millions of people.

Yet while Thunberg has achieved hero status to many, others regard her variously as a crank or the puppet of malevolent forces. Russia's Vladimir Putin and US President Donald Trump have been foremost among her critics. The latter responded to her New York address with the sarcastic Tweet: 'She seems like a very happy young girl looking forward to a bright and wonderful future. So nice to see!' Thunberg responded by changing her Twitter biography to match his description, and pondered why 'grown-ups would choose to mock children and teenagers for just communicating and acting on the science when they could do something good instead'. As she had put it during her address to the UN: 'Right here, right now is where we draw the line.'

MY MESSAGE IS THAT we'll be watching you.

This is all wrong. I shouldn't be up here. I should be back in school on the other side of the ocean. Yet you all come to us young people for hope. How dare you!

You have stolen my dreams and my childhood with your empty words. And yet I'm one of the lucky ones. People are suffering. People are dying. Entire ecosystems are collapsing. We are in the beginning of a mass extinction, and all you can talk about is money and fairy tales of eternal economic growth. How dare you!

For more than 30 years, the science has been crystal clear. How dare you continue to look away and come here saying that you're doing enough, when the politics and solutions needed are still nowhere in sight.

You say you hear us and that you understand the urgency. But no matter how sad and angry I am, I do not want to believe that. Because if you really understood the situation and still kept on failing to act, then you would be evil. And that I refuse to believe.

The popular idea of cutting our emissions in half in 10 years only gives us a 50% chance of staying below 1.5 degrees [Celsius], and the risk of setting off irreversible chain reactions beyond human control.

Fifty percent may be acceptable to you. But those numbers do not include tipping points, most feedback loops, additional warming hidden by toxic air pollution or the aspects of equity and climate justice. They also rely on my generation sucking hundreds of billions of tons of your CO_2 out of the air with technologies that barely exist.

So a 50% risk is simply not acceptable to us – we who have to live with the consequences.

To have a 67% chance of staying below a 1.5 degrees global temperature rise – the best odds given by the [Intergovernmental Panel on Climate Change] – the world had 420 gigatons of CO_2 left to emit back on Jan. 1st, 2018. Today that figure is already down to less than 350 gigatons.

How dare you pretend that this can be solved with just 'business as usual' and some technical solutions? With today's emissions levels, that remaining CO_2 budget will be entirely gone within less than 8½ years.

There will not be any solutions or plans presented in line with these figures here today, because these numbers are too uncomfortable. And you are still not mature enough to tell it like it is.

You are failing us. But the young people are starting to understand your betrayal. The eyes of all future generations are upon you. And if you choose to fail us, I say: We will never forgive you.

We will not let you get away with this. Right here, right now is where we draw the line. The world is waking up. And change is coming, whether you like it or not.

Thank you.

Quercus Editions Ltd
Carmelite House
50 Victoria Embankment
London EC4Y 0DZ

An Hachette UK company

First published in 2005
This revised edition published 2021
Copyright © 2005, 2010, 2014, 2016, 2021
    Quercus Editions Ltd

A catalogue record of this book is available from
the British Library

Hardback ISBN:
    978 1 52941 605 3

Printed and bound in China

10 9 8 7 6 5 4 3 2 1

Original edition compiled and edited by the
    Cambridge Editorial Partnership

Design: Patrick Nugent

2021 revised edition:
New text: Daniel Smith
Design: Ginny Zeal

Acknowledgements

The publishers would like to thank those sources (including in the public
domain) that have recorded or transcribed these historic speeches. Particular
mention should be made of the following, for source material and permission
to reproduce copyright material:

For the speeches of: Adolph Hitler: *The Speeches of Adolph Hitler* 1922–1939
(Oxford University Press, 1942); Winston Churchill: reproduced by kind
permission of the Crown Copyright; J. Robert Oppenheimer: University of
Chicago; Nelson Mandela: archive of the African National Congress; Martin
Luther King, Jr: The Estate of Dr Martin Luther King, Jr; Malcolm X: *Speeches
and Statements* (Grove Press); Pierre Trudeau: www.collectionscanada.ca;
Ronald Reagan: The Reagan Foundation; Aung San Suu Kyi: from *Freedom
From Fear* (Penguin Books, Revised Edition, 1995), reproduced by permission
of Penguin Books Ltd and Penguin Group (USA); Pope Francis: © Libreria
Editrice Vaticana, reproduced by permission of Libreria Editrice Vaticana;
Malala Yousafzai: reproduced with permission of Curtis Brown Group Ltd,
London on behalf of Malala Yousafzai, copyright © Malala Yousafzai, 2014;
Margaret Thatcher: © Estate of Lady Thatcher, reprinted from the text at
www.margaretthatcher.org. Nadia Murad: Security Council Report, public
domain; Tarana Burke: Tarana Burke, Me too is a movement, not a moment,
TEDWomen 2018. To watch the full talk, visit TED.com; Greta Thunberg:
From No One is Too Small to Make a Difference by Copyright ©Greta
Thunberg 2018-2019 published by Penguin Books Ltd. ©2019.

Every effort has been made to contact copyright holders.
However, the publishers will be glad to rectify in future editions any
inadvertent omissions brought to their attention.

Picture Credits:
Jesus, © Photo RMN/A Berlin; Mohammed, © Altaf Qadri/epa/Corbis;
Elizabeth I, © Bettmann/Corbis; Charles I, © Towneley Hall Art Gallery &
Museum, Burnley, Lancashire/The Bridgeman Art Library; Oliver Cromwell,
© Montclair Art Museum, New Jersey/Bridgeman; George Washington,
© Corbis; Thomas Jefferson, © Bettmann/Corbis; Napoleon Bonaparte,
© Archivo Iconografico, S.A./Corbis; Abraham Lincoln, © Bettmann/Corbis;
Susan B. Anthony, © CSU Archives/Everett Collection/Rex Features;
Emmeline Pankhurst, © Hulton-Deutsch Collection/Corbis; Patrick Pearse,
© Corbis; Woodrow Wilson, © Corbis; Vladimir Lenin, © Mrs Valerie Anne
Giscard d'Estaing/Alamy; Clarence Darrow, © Bettmann/Corbis; Mahatma
Gandhi, © Press Association Images; Franklin D. Roosevelt, © Underwood &
Underwood/Corbis; Adolf Hitler, © Bettmann/Corbis; Neville Chamberlain,
© Hulton-Deutsch Collection/Corbis; Joseph Stalin, © Popperfoto/Alamy;
Winston Churchill, © Hulton-Deutsch Collection/Corbis; Charles de Gaulle,
© Bettmann/Corbis; Vyacheslav Molotov, © Time & Life Pictures/Getty
Images; George S. Patton, © Bettmann/Corbis; Emperor Hirohito,
© Bettmann/Corbis; J. Robert Oppenheimer, © Bettmann/Corbis; Jawaharlal
Nehru, © Bettmann/Corbis; Douglas MacArthur, © Bettmann/Corbis; Nikita
Khrushchev, © Photo12.com – Keystone Pressedienst; John F. Kennedy,
© Bettmann/Corbis; Martin Luther King Jr, © Flip Schulke/Corbis; Nelson
Mandela, © Alexander Caminada/Alamy; Malcolm X, © Bettmann/Corbis;
Pierre Trudeau, © Bettmann/Corbis; Richard M. Nixon, © Bettmann/Corbis;
Indira Gandhi, © Sipa Press/Rex Features; Chaim Herzog, © Bettmann/Corbis;
Anwar al-Sadat, © Hulton Archive/Getty Images; Margaret Thatcher,
© Bettmann/Getty Images; Pope John Paul II, © Bettmann/Corbis; Ronald
Reagan, © Bettmann/Corbis; Mikhail Gorbachev, © Jacques Langevin/Corbis
Sygma; Václav Havel, © J A Giordano/Corbis Saba; Aung San Suu Kyi, © epa
european pressphoto agency b.v./Alamy; Hillary Clinton © Andrew Burton/
Getty Images; Earl Spencer, © Press Association Images; Elie Wiesel, © Robert
Maass/Corbis; George W. Bush, © Reuters/Corbis; Barack Obama, © Shawn
Thew/epa/Corbis; Gerry Adams, © Micah Walter/Reuters/Corbis; Al Gore,
© AFP/Getty Images; Kevin Rudd, © Alan Porritt/epa/Corbis; Xi Jinping,
© KeystoneUSA-ZUMA/REX; Pope Francis, © Alessia Paradisi/ABACA USA/
Empics Entertainment; Malala Yousafzai, © Sipa USA/REX; Vladimir Putin,
© Alexander Zemlianichenko/AP/Press Association Images; Nadia Murad,
© Tasos Katopodis/Getty Images; Donald Trump, © White House Photo/
Alamy; Tarana Burke, © Lev Radin/Shutterstock; Greta Thunberg, © Pacific
Press/Getty Images.